Praise for
The Customer-Funded Business

"This is THE cornerstone idea for entrepreneurs—to shun all other avenues first and pursue customers to fund their venture. This provides a critical forcing function business leaders need, in order to guarantee they are creating something truly valuable. After learning this lesson the hard way (raising angel funds and failing), my two latest ventures have followed Mullins' sage advice and flourished."

—Verne Harnish,
CEO Gazelles;
Author of *Scaling Up* and *Mastering the Rockefeller Habits*

"The customer is not just king, he can be your VC too! John Mullins' brilliance has inspired my own success for many years and his ideas can drive yours as well."

—Bernard Auyang
Entrepreneur and investor;
International Chairman 2014–15, Young Presidents' Organization

"Mullins has connected the dots. His clarity of insight blazes through in the five crisp models of the customer-funded business. He sharpens our understanding of how to use the power of market innovations and customer traction to fund emerging businesses. A great set of tools for the new and experienced entrepreneur."

—Jerry Engel
General Partner, Monitor Venture Partners;
Adjunct Professor Emeritus,
Haas School of Business, University of California Berkeley

"John Mullins' sage advice for entrepreneurs and the investors who back them is just as important for established companies that are trying to unlock innovation and growth. Customer funding is a powerful approach that too many businesses have simply forgotten, or never understood. If you don't read this book, you'll lose out to competitors who do."

—Mike Harris
Founding CEO of First Direct and Egg Banking;
Author of *Find Your Lightbulb*

"Hits the nail on the head. Customer funding isn't just another source of capital for starting or growing your business. It is—by far—the most intriguing source available. Mullins shows why, and he shows five ways to obtain it, too."

—Tom Byers
Professor and Director, Stanford Technology Ventures Program,
Stanford University;
Coauthor, *Technology Ventures*

"A timely reminder not to see your customers only as a source of credibility when you are starting out but as a valuable source of funding—particularly in the early days. Packed with good anecdotes and inspirational tales of entrepreneurial success (and failure), John Mullins nails it again!"

—Richard Gourlay
Managing Director, Sussex Place Ventures

"Happiness is a positive cash flow. I remind my students that venture capitalists (and most angels) don't typically fund new businesses, they fund businesses that are poised to grow rapidly. The five models that John highlights can help entrepreneurs launch and validate their businesses when other sources of capital are scarce and expensive."

—Andrew Zacharakis
The John H. Muller, Jr. Chair in Entrepreneurship, Babson College

"There are many books aimed at helping you develop the perfect pitch to ensure you get investment. But entrepreneurs start businesses, not investment vehicles. This book is a grand journey through many ways that we can build these businesses using other people's money or shifting our business model. And importantly—keeping the valuable equity to ourselves. Do not raise equity investment until you have read this book and considered every other option."

—Dale Murray
Cofounder Omega Logic, British Angel Investor of the Year 2011

"Worth the price of the book for Chapter 8 alone. Most startups will never have a chance to secure an institutional investment. Some may never need one. John Mullins shows entrepreneurs another path employing proven *Customer-Funded Business* alternatives. Even if you plan on eventually scaling with venture capital, customer funding can be a smart path to experiment and prove your business in advance."

—Randy Komisar
Partner, Kleiner Perkins Caufield & Byers;
Lecturer, Stanford University;
Author of *The Monk and the Riddle*

"Very accessible, thorough, and will no doubt be useful to aspiring (or struggling) entrepreneurs. The models are a great analytical tool which the case studies bring to life."

—Amar Bhidé
Schmidheiny Professor, The Fletcher School, Tufts University;
Author of *The Venturesome Economy* and *A Call for Judgment*

"With *The Customer-Funded Business,* John once again provides us with a fantastic book. If someone is looking for inspiration on how to keep their cash requirements to a minimum and de-risk their investment—this is the first book they should pick up and read."

—James King
Founder and Chairman, Find Invest Grow (FIG)

"Truly engaging. 'Ring the cash register and sit on the float—and avoid running out of money and going out of business.' John Mullins convincingly guides entrepreneurs to dump their PowerPoint slides and look to their paying customers as their 'first ports of call.' Early stage investors might want to think in similar fashion!"

—M.S. Rao
Professor, S P Jain Institute of Management and Research

"Essential reading for any budding entrepreneur—a revolutionary approach to funding a new venture. A fresh perspective on funding and scaling ambitions."

—Jim Hall
Executive Director, Entrepreneurship Centre,
Saïd Business School, University of Oxford

"Professor Mullins breaks down the myth that the key to a successful business is to raise venture capital first. His prescriptions for finding the right customers and getting them to fund your business are a great step-by-step guide to raising venture capital—build the business first and the investments will follow!"

—**Bill Earner**
Partner, Connect Ventures

"Practical and pithy, and a must read for an entrepreneur, full of pragmatic insights relevant to any entrepreneur or business executive."

—**Sunita Singh**
Cofounder and Senior Director, National Entrepreneurship Network, India

"A truly fascinating book, long overdue. John Mullins has brought out a completely new paradigm in financing businesses. A lot of business failure will be avoided if entrepreneurs really understand the message and practice it."

—**Kavil Ramachandran**
Thomas Schmidheiny Professor of Family Business
and Wealth Management, Indian School of Business

"John Mullins has done it for the third time. After *The New Business Road Test* and *Getting to Plan B*, he has produced yet another book for entrepreneurs, investors and educators that is based on rigorous research and at the same time engaging and practical. He shows how entrepreneurs can postpone raising costly venture funding by obtaining funding from customers in the early stages of their businesses."

—**Rama Velamuri**
Professor of Entrepreneurship,
China Europe International Business School, Shanghai

"A timely and healthy antidote to the almost universal focus on financing issues in starting new ventures. Mullins argues very convincingly that for most non-tech start-ups, seeking external financing not only is extremely time consuming and only rarely works, but often is counterproductive to developing sustainable businesses serving real customers' needs. Mullins builds on his evidence-based approach to entrepreneurship successfully demonstrated in his previous best-sellers *The New Business Road Test* and *Getting to Plan B* and provides would-be entrepreneurs with well-thought-through tool kits and real-life case stories."

—**Søren P. Hovgaard**
Head of Entrepreneurial Development Unit;
External Associate Professor, Department of Economics,
University of Copenhagen

"A paradigm-shift in the way we think about startup funding. While 'lean startup,' 'bootstrapping,' and other methodologies have had their day in the startup spotlight, reading this book makes me realize that the next decade belongs to customer-funded businesses. And this book shows the way. Starting up, as well as angel investing, has more madness than method. But the five customer-funded models, as well as the 'John's Business Angel Checklists' at the end of each chapter, distill the process down to its essentials."

—**Ajeet Khurana**
Top-15 Angel Investor, India, 2013

"*The Customer-Funded Business* gets it. Great practical advice for those seeking to crowdfund their ventures. I recommend John's book to those wanting a grounding in customer-funded business that is also deeply entrepreneurial in spirit. I can't wait to put this book into action!"

—**Norris Krueger**
Entrepreneurship Northwest;
Fellow, Max Planck Institute

"Spot on for the entrepreneur as well as the angel investor . . . and even the business professor. Mullins' wisdom, experience and knowledge of entrepreneurs come through on every page. Particularly insightful to me were the 'John's Business Angel Checklists' at the end of Chapters 2–7. This book should be one that every entrepreneur takes time to read so that they build their business on solid and sustainable ground."

—**Keith Williams**
Senior Vice President Member Experience;
Entrepreneurs' Organization (EO)

"John and I came to very similar insights from over a decade of very different kinds of research into what successful entrepreneurs have learned to do well. This book captures beautifully what an expert entrepreneur I studied told me, 'Treat your first customers as your partners—they are your earliest investors and your best salespeople.' The compelling stories in this book invite you and inspire you to learn how to do that."

—**Saras Sarasvathy**
Isidore Horween Research Associate Professor,
The Darden School, University of Virginia

"Two of the most critical tasks that you as a startup CEO/Founder have to do are hire the right people and keep your company appropriately financed. While venture finance can accelerate the growth of businesses where appropriate, many times a company can benefit from other, more independent forms of funding their growth, particularly in the very early stages. Applying the concepts and tools in this book will likely make your company that much more attractive to an investor, for the investment capital they give you will be used to accelerate growth, rather than just provide financial subsistence."

—Carlos Eduardo Espinal
Partner, Seedcamp

"A very timely book. Investors are thin on the ground and entrepreneurs have to turn to alternative and even better sources of investment. Entrepreneurs are asked to prove the merits of their ventures and what better way than through customers. John's gift for writing makes this an easy read and reminds us that 'cash is king.'"

—Dr Shai Vyakarnam
Director Centre for Entrepreneurial Learning,
University of Cambridge, Judge Business School

"Whether you are starting up a business in a garage or doing as I did, building one overseas on behalf of a large North American firm, this book is a relevant and compelling read. You are left in no doubt that Cash is clearly still King! John gives you the tools as well as his practical 'business angel checklists' coupled with captivating anecdotes to challenge and ultimately help you choose the right funding model for your business."

—Peter Moores
CEO and Country Manager UK, Raymond James

"Another great book that gets to the heart of building companies. I wish more entrepreneurs understood the significance and freedom that cash generation can bring to young, fledgling businesses. It puts an entrepreneur in the driver's seat. As a venture capitalist, I dream of entrepreneurs that are able to independently validate their product or service with the market, lay down early traction and are constrained only by capital to take their companies to the next level. John's book provides a comprehensive framework for thinking about how to generate cash and become self-sufficient as an entrepreneur."

—Hussein Kanji
Founding Partner, Hoxton Ventures

"Throughout my 30 years in business, finding quality books which get to the heart of key issues for both entrepreneurs and investors has been a rarity. *The Customer-Funded Business* does exactly this, providing excellent, straightforward advice along with real life examples. John has been there and done it in the business world. His knowledge and experience are clear to see."

—James Caan
Author of *Start Your Business in Seven Days* and *The Real Deal*

"John provides a vital sanity check for inexperienced founders. Time chasing investors is often better spent creating (and realising) customer value."

—Dave Chapman
Vice-Dean for Enterprise, University College London

"John Mullins' expertise is giving us forehead-slappingly new insights into taken-for-granted ideas. In this age of Kickstarter, we all *think* we know all about customer funding, but in this book John shows us Kickstarter is only one of five ways to get customers to fund our businesses. With great stories and great style, John takes what we all know and makes it fit together in new and powerful ways."

—Jerome Katz
Coleman Professor of Entrepreneurship, Saint Louis University

THE
CUSTOMER-
FUNDED
BUSINESS

THE CUSTOMER-FUNDED BUSINESS

START, FINANCE, OR GROW YOUR COMPANY WITH YOUR CUSTOMERS' CASH

JOHN MULLINS, PhD

WILEY

Library of Congress Cataloging-in-Publication Data:

Mullins, John W. (John Walker)
   The Customer-Funded Business: Start, Finance, or Grow Your Company with Your Customers' Cash/John Mullins, PhD
      pages cm.
   ISBN: 978-1-118-87885-9 (cloth); ISBN: 978-1-118-87913-9 (ebk);
   ISBN: 978-1-118-87904-7 (ebk)
 1. New business enterprises—Finance. 2. Venture capital. 3. Customer relations.
4. Entrepreneurship. I. Title.
   HG4027.6.M65 2014
   658.15'224—dc23   2013050602

Printed in the United States of America

10 9 8 7 6 5 4 3 2 1

Contents

Why This Book?

Becoming—and being!—an entrepreneur is difficult. Raising capital to fund one's entrepreneurial journey is *even more* difficult. Each year—in the good years—only about 1,500 U.S. startups get funded by venture capitalists, alongside another 50,000 or so by angel investors, a paltry number against the 5 million ventures that seek startup funding.[1] According to research from Statista, the numbers these days are worse: only 843 seed-stage deals were done by U.S. venture capital firms in 2013, though that figure is the best in years, more than double the number in 2010.[2] Difficult, indeed!

The numbers elsewhere, including in the UK, where I spend most of my time, are even more daunting. In Europe and Asia, they're tougher still. I know firsthand how difficult it is, because I've been in startup and capital-raising mode multiple times during the first half of my career. In the second half, as a professor at one of the world's leading business schools, and as a board member and investor, I've helped hundreds of individuals surmount—or circumvent!—the fundraising and other challenges to become thriving entrepreneurs. Some, you may be surprised to hear, did it inside large companies. Others, the more typical, got their start in their kitchens or garages, or over a couple of beers at the local pub.

The vast majority of them, however, *didn't* follow the proto-typical path that the conventional wisdom holds as gospel today:

- *Step 1:* Come up with an idea for a new venture.
- *Step 2:* Write a business plan.
- *Step 3:* Raise some venture capital.
- *Step 4:* Get rich!

In fact, most of the companies whose names populate the lists of the world's fastest-growing companies—the *Inc.* 5000 in the USA, the *Fast Track 100* in the UK, and similar lists everywhere—didn't follow the conventional script, either.

Do You Really Need Venture Capital?

What did they do? The vast majority of them *never* took a pound or dollar or rupee of venture capital, and they didn't mortgage or pledge their houses, either. Instead, they managed to find ways to get their businesses up and running, and then growing, *without* pandering to VCs or groveling to their company's CFO. By solving pressing customer problems, or by developing delightful customer experiences that transformed the previously mundane—think Peet's or the UK's Coffee Republic in coffee bars or Banana Republic in casual apparel—most of these entrepreneurs built vibrant, growing businesses *without* raising troves of venture capital. "So where did their funding come from?" you ask. The lion's share of them got most of their money—initially, at least, and sometimes for the entire journey—from a much more hospitable and agreeable source: their customers.

> **❝they didn't mortgage or pledge their houses, either. ❞**

The Problem: Limelight Stolen

"Why, then," you might ask, "have the business plan and the raising of venture capital become seen as the centerpiece of entrepreneurial endeavor?" Two reasons, in my view.

First, the venture capital community—VCs, business angels, incubators, and much of the rest of today's entrepreneurial ecosystem—has stolen the entrepreneurial finance limelight over the past two generations or so, first in California and Boston, and more recently practically everywhere else. They've done so for good reasons: the sometimes astonishing returns they've delivered to themselves and their investors, and the astonishingly large and valuable companies that this ecosystem has created. The valuations of companies like Apple, Amazon, and Twitter do make good headlines! If all the companies backed by the venture capital industry were thought of as a country, it would stand as one of the world's largest economies today.

> **The valuations of companies like Apple, Amazon, and Twitter do make good headlines!**

There's nothing inherently wrong with venture capital. I've both raised it and provided it myself. But as we'll see in Chapter 1, VC has some drawbacks worth understanding, especially when it's raised too early in the life of one's venture.

Second, we in the academic community have learned that we can teach people to write business plans—which can be submitted as a pile of paper with a staple in the corner—and students will flock to us in droves! Never mind that one cannot really plan very well for a highly uncertain entrepreneurial venture, and that new-venture success most often arrives in the shape of Plan B or Plan Z, not the Plan A that has been so lovingly articulated in the business plan. We can teach them to plan (and we can teach them to pitch, too), so plan (and pitch) they will!

But the vast majority of fast-growing companies don't get their money this way. As we'll see in Chapter 1, there are compelling reasons why getting the funding you need from your customers is often a much better way to go.

> **the vast majority of fast-growing companies don't get their money this way**

The Solution: The Customer-Funded Business—An Idea Whose Time Has Come

In early 2012, I embarked on a research journey to develop a deeper understanding of the plucky entrepreneurs who build great companies—sometimes small ones to fit their lifestyles, other times large ones that have become household names—and the methods (five of them, each different from the other) they've used to start and grow their businesses with their customers' cash. The book you are now holding in your hand or viewing on your screen delivers the fruits of my journey.

But the book delivers much more than just my own insights and the evidence I've gleaned. It's filled with the captivating stories of companies—Airbnb, Dell, Banana Republic, and many more—that have been built and financed this way (at least at the outset, though often not forever) and is brimming over with early-stage investors' perspectives. As a result, the book makes what I believe is a compelling case for customer funding as the *first* approach that entrepreneurs—whether in garages or around kitchen tables or in well-established companies—should consider when funding their nascent businesses. And I'm not alone in this view. Some of today's savviest investors share it, too!

Indeed, venture capital investor Fred Wilson of Union Square Ventures puts the folly of raising too much venture capital too early in stark terms. "The fact is that the amount of money startups raise in their seed and Series A rounds is inversely correlated with success. Yes, I mean that. Less money raised leads to more success. That is the data I stare at all the time."[3] Two-time entrepreneur turned venture capitalist Mark Suster of Upfront Ventures is of a like mind. "I say ring the freaking cash register," he says. "I have said so for years."[4]

> **The fact is that the amount of money startups raise in their seed and Series A rounds is inversely correlated with success.**

That's what customer funding is all about at the end of the day, through any of the five ingenious ways I've uncovered to do it. Ring the cash register early enough and often enough and you'll have the magic of customer traction—hence the funding—you need to get your fledgling business off the ground. Are Wilson, Suster, and I merely foolish or naïve? Or might we be onto something, even a customer-funded revolution, perhaps?

Who Should Read This Book?

Given the global diversity of the entrepreneurs and their companies—from Europe, Asia, and North America—whose often inspiring stories bring this book to life, there are six key practitioner audiences worldwide for whom I have written this book:

- Aspiring entrepreneurs who lack startup capital but yearn for the freedom and joy that running one's own business provides.
- Early stage entrepreneurs trying to figure out how to get their nascent but cash-starved ventures into takeoff mode.
- Angel investors, who are often an entrepreneur's first port of call when seeking capital. *You* are this book's most important audience, perhaps, for you are the ones with the power to set the entrepreneurial vessel on a more sensible course. In fact, you're so important an audience that you'll find at the end of each chapter a checklist—John's Business Angel Checklist—of due diligence questions that *you* should ask entrepreneurs seeking your capital. If you can set straight some of each year's 5 million and more who seek your capital—and that's the number in the United States alone—you'll have a made a really important contribution to tomorrow's entrepreneurial ecosystem. Better yet, I believe that in so doing, you'll win your entrepreneurs' thanks as well as preferential access to deals that have been de-risked through proven customer demand. I don't have to tell you what this can do for your investment returns!

  > **"you'll win your entrepreneurs' thanks as well as preferential access to deals that have been de-risked through proven customer demand."**

- Those running the growing number of business incubators and accelerators, another set of early ports of call for aspiring entrepreneurs. Stop talking about how many of your startups successfully raise a Series A round, *please*, and start talking about how many of them achieve early customer traction and are growing while still owning and controlling the majority of their businesses! Who kept a greater portion of the value his company created: Michael Dell or Steve Jobs? It was Dell, hands down, whose customer-funded story is told in Chapter 2.

- The fabled three Fs: the family, friends, and fools who back so many entrepreneurial ventures. I suggest you do your loved ones a favor and ask them to come back to see you when they've secured their first paying customers (yes, even before they've produced their first product!).

- Finally, let's not forget the potential innovators at the top of—or hidden in the nooks and crannies of—today's growth-starved companies. Though it is through stories of entrepreneurs and their companies that I deliver most of this book's lessons (sadly, according to venture capital investor Bill Joy, "Big companies almost never innovate. It's not that innovation itself is rare—it's occurring everywhere. Which means, mostly, elsewhere."[5]), the principles articulated in this book are for you and your company, too!

There's one other important audience I have in mind as well. I've also written this book for my fellow faculty who are teaching entrepreneurship or venture capital in the world's growing number of business schools and other academic institutions offering vibrant entrepreneurship programs. Together we are creating

> **❝I've also written this book for my fellow faculty who are teaching entrepreneurship and venture capital❞**

and empowering a new generation of entrepreneurs who are charged with creating virtually all of what will be our communities' net new jobs in the future. It's a crucially important role that we and our graduates must play in today's volatile and uncertain economic environment.

I suggest that we faculty all add a session to our business plan and entrepreneurial finance courses that offers customer funding as an alternative approach—in my mind, the *preferred* approach—to getting a young company underway. In doing so for your students yearning to start their own businesses, whether now or later, you will join me in getting them focused on customers, instead of investors. Once they have enough customers, the investors—if needed at all—will surely follow.

> **❝Once they have enough customers, the investors will surely follow❞**

Why John Mullins? Why Now?

My two earlier books, the first (*The New Business Road Test*) on how to rigorously and systematically assess an entrepreneurial opportunity *before* you get started,[6] and the second (*Getting to Plan B*) on how to get to a business model that will actually work—and might just revolutionize your industry[7]—have prepared me well and set the stage for the unanswered question that this book addresses: "How can I best start, finance or grow my company with my customers' cash, instead of that of investors?" But that's not all.

Having started two entrepreneurial companies and worked at a third, and having served on the boards of numerous others, including successes and failures, I've accumulated the scars and bruises that are always the surest sign of learning. More than that, though, for more than two decades in this, my second career, as a business school professor, I've been fortunate enough to have had the time and resources to dig deeply into the "whys" and "hows" that underlie entrepreneurial success and failure. Simply put, I'm in the right place at the right time to have researched and written this book.

In 60 Seconds or Less: The Elevator Pitch

My purpose in putting *The Customer-Funded Business* into your hands is to get entrepreneurs of nearly every kind to see that their top priority in the early going—and often later, too!—is to find a customer who will pay you on good terms (often in advance), *not* to raise venture capital. To address this purpose, the book brings to life five customer-funded models and the key questions that should be asked in considering (Chapters 2 through 7) and pursuing (Chapter 8) each of them. It also addresses the key implementation questions that will surely arise:

- when to use which model
- how best to apply them
- what to watch out for—the pitfalls that lie along the way

Whether you're an aspiring entrepreneur lacking the startup capital you need, an early-stage entrepreneur trying to get your cash-starved venture into takeoff mode, a corporate leader seeking funding to grow an established company, or an angel investor or mentor who supports high-potential entrepreneurial ventures, this book offers the most sure-footed path to starting, financing, or growing *your* business or one you support. Are you intrigued? Ready to be inspired? If so, turn the page!

❝this book offers the most sure-footed path to starting, financing, or growing *your* business.❞

1

Craving Crowdfunding? Pandering to VCs? Groveling to Your CFO?: The Magic of Traction and the Customer-Funded Revolution

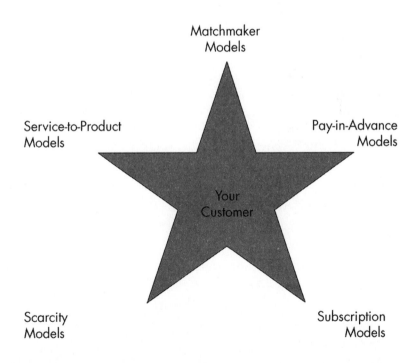

Matchmaker
Models

Service-to-Product
Models

Pay-in-Advance
Models

Your
Customer

Scarcity
Models

Subscription
Models

I magine this. It was 1995, and the Coca-Cola Company had just reentered India after an aborted earlier effort, this time by acquiring the maker of Thums Up, India's leading cola. Along with the deal came a thick book describing each of the Thums Up bottlers' territories in plenty of legal jargon, but without a single map. Coke needed a way to find and understand its newly acquired territories.

Alas, no one had maps that could show Coke where its bottlers were located. Until the mid-1960s, maps had been largely unavailable in India, at least for anyone not in the military. Even 30 years later, a mapping culture and map-reading ethos simply did not exist, perhaps in part because there were very few accurate Indian maps.

Into the breach stepped Rakesh and Rashmi Verma, who had started a small IT training business in India, CE Info Systems, serving blue-chip clients like IBM. Their company also licensed American digital mapping software to aid India's nascent map-making industry.[1] Saying to Coke, "We can give you the maps you need" (even though they had not actually ever produced a single map!), the Vermas began to build a digital mapping business. First, they bought an ordinary office scanner and took out the kitchen scissors. Next, using their native Indian ingenuity, they began cutting what rudimentary paper maps they could find into A4 size and scanning them to make them "digital." Using Rashmi's software and programming skills together with the American software they had been licensing to others, they then overlaid demographic and other data to enable Coke—and soon other commercial customers—to do in India what they took for granted in other parts of the world.

" We can give you the maps you need. "

CellularOne, entering India in a joint venture with Essar as the Indian telecommunications industry was liberalized, was their next client. "Where should we put our mobile phone towers?" CellularOne asked, from both a technical perspective (Where is the high ground? How do we achieve uncluttered line-of-sight coverage in Bombay, a city of high rises?) and from a marketing perspective (Where are there sufficiently dense concentrations of customers with the right demographics whom we can economically serve?). Once again, the Vermas delivered.

A Customer-Funded Model

So, did the Vermas need venture capital to start, finance, and grow their business? No. Instead, they identified customer after customer—even the Indian Navy—who could benefit from digital maps, charging the customers fees to cover most of the development costs of creating additional maps or applying additional demographic or other information to maps they had already created. Over the next 10 years, their mapping business grew slowly but steadily, funded by one customer assignment after another, and they became the dominant digital mapmaker in India. And they did so without raising a single rupee of venture capital.

The Vermas weren't doing anything radically new in shunning venture capital. To be realistic, such capital probably would

> **"The Vermas weren't doing anything radically new in shunning venture capital."**

not even have been available in India in the mid-1990s. But by funding the early growth of their business with their customers' cash, they were simply doing what most entrepreneurs did before business angels and venture capital investors grabbed the entrepreneurial finance spotlight more than a generation ago in the West, and today nearly everywhere else.

Customer Funding: The Vermas Are Not Alone

What the Vermas accomplished with customer funding is neither unique to India nor to the 1990s. Anyone who has booked a hotel room on Expedia.com, for example, might be surprised at the role they were playing in funding Expedia's operations and growth. Not only didn't Expedia pay the hotel for your stay until after you arrived—despite the fact that you probably paid Expedia when you booked the room—but in many cases they paid the hotel as many as six weeks *after* your stay. What is Expedia doing with your money—their customers' money—for all those weeks, or sometimes months? Running and growing their business, of course! "Sitting on the float" with the customer's money is a time-honored principle that runs throughout this book.

As we'll see in Chapter 2, starting, financing, or growing your business with your customers' cash isn't novel. It's a fundamental principle—a mind-set, really—by which many entrepreneurs live. It's how Michael Dell created one of the twentieth century's most prominent success stories and how Mel and Patricia Ziegler created Banana Republic, another customer-funded phenomenon. In the five chapters that then follow, equally remarkable are the stories, all customer funded, of Airbnb (Chapter 3), Threadless (Chapter 4), India's TutorVista (Chapter 5), Gilt Group (Chapter 6), Denmark's GoViral (Chapter 7), and nearly a dozen other inspiring companies—plus some failures as well—and the entrepreneurs who created and drove them. Whether you're an entrepreneur or a leader in an established business that wants to grow faster, you get the drift: The customer-funded business has been a widely practiced phenomenon, but has been underobserved and underdiscussed. But not any more!

A Problem: Financing Your Startup

Later in this chapter, I'll explore in some depth why I believe raising equity at the outset of a new venture's journey is, at least most of the time, an exceedingly bad idea—for both entrepreneurs and investors alike. For now, though, think of it this way:

- Most of the time, the Plan A that you have so lovingly conceived is unlikely to work, as most any experienced early-stage investor, whether a VC or a business angel, will tell you. Do you look forward to explaining to your investors why your Plan A didn't work, as you ask them for more money for your newer, brighter, and inevitably still-optimistic Plan B? I don't think so! As Peter Drucker, arguably the leading management thinker of the twentieth century, observed, "If a new venture does succeed, more often than not it is

  ❝Do you look forward to explaining to your investors why your Plan A didn't work?❞

  - in a market other than the one it was originally intended to serve
  - with products and services not quite those with which it had set out
  - bought in large part by customers it did not even think of when it started
  - and used for a host of purposes besides the ones for which the products were first designed."[2]

- There are material drawbacks to raising capital too early. Among the most daunting of them is that raising capital—whether by pandering to VCs or groveling to your CFO, if you're seeking to start something inside an established company—is a full-time job. Getting your venture underway is a full-time job, too. If you try to do both, one of them will inevitably suffer.

- As you'll see later in this chapter, the evidence is compelling that the odds of success for VC-backed companies are far worse than most entrepreneurs realize. Is joining tomorrow's failure statistics what you had in mind in pursuing your venture? Definitely not!

A Solution: The Magic of Traction

Fortunately, with the cost of technology declining ever more rapidly, it's easier and cheaper to get into a customer-funded business than ever before. As this book will make clear through the companies whose stories it tells, there are numerous benefits that all five customer-funded models provide, to entrepreneurs and their backers alike.

- First, waiting to raise capital forces the entrepreneur's attention toward his or her customers, where it should be in the first place. Customers matter, and as Peter Drucker also noted, if there's no paying customer—at least eventually—there's no business, either (the protestations of some dot-com entrepreneurs to the contrary).

  ❝if there's no paying customer—at least eventually—there's no business, either❞

- Second, winning customer orders often gives your customer a vested interest in your success. If they are happy to buy from you, they'll want you to stick around, either so they can buy again later, or so you will service what you've sold. For an entrepreneur, having your customers on your side is a good place to be. For angels, having customers rave about the company in which you are thinking of investing is a very good sign!
- Third, making do with the probably modest amounts of cash your customers will give you enforces frugality, rather than waste. Having too much money can make you stupid and lets you ignore your customer! Having less money will make you smarter, and will force you to run your business better, too.

- Fourth, when venture capital is raised later, once customer traction is proven, the investor's risk is lower, meaning the terms and valuation are better, and making the founder's stake—and perhaps control—more substantial, too. For angels, investing later reduces the number of eventual "lemons" in the portfolio and is likely to improve returns.

- Fifth, focusing your efforts to raise cash from customers who are willing and eager to buy from your yet-unproven company is likely to mercifully put to rest a half-baked or not-quite-right idea that requires more development—a pivot, in today's entrepreneurial lexicon—in order to hit the mark.

- Finally, there's freedom! Gaining one's freedom is high on every entrepreneur's priority list, and the best source of freedom—even better than cash in the bank—is positive cash flow! And with the magic of customer traction and the cash flow it brings, you'll sleep better, too!

> **The best source of freedom—even better than cash in the bank—is positive cash flow!**

These benefits accrue largely to startups or early-stage ventures, along with their possible investors, of course. "But what about me?" you may ask, if you're in a well-established company with customers—perhaps slow-paying customers—already in hand. Ryzex, a purveyor of mobile computing devices (like the handheld gadgets your gas utility uses to read your meter, your FedEx driver brings with your parcel to your door, or a supermarket clerk uses to order more of what's running low), faced a difficult challenge as the global financial crisis landed on its doorstep with a thud in the fourth quarter of 2007. Says Ryzex founder Rud Browne about oncoming recessions, "The canary in a coal mine is computer hardware sales. It's the first thing a business can stop spending money on. A huge percentage of the new capital equipment (machinery, vehicles, computers) bought by businesses each year is purchased to replace equipment they already have and typically replace on a three- to seven-year cycle. The easiest way to conserve money in a crisis is to extend the replacement cycle of stuff you already have. When this happens, suppliers like Ryzex immediately experience a significant drop in revenues."[3] For the Ryzex story and how customer funding built a thriving company and then got it through a daunting downturn more or less unscathed, see Sidebar 1.1.

Sidebar 1.1: Customer Funding Helps Ryzex Thrive, Then Survive

In its early days, Ryzex bought decommissioned mobile-computing equipment that was sitting in warehouses gathering dust and sold it to business users who needed to expand their existing fleets. When users added another few trucks or new stores, they generally wanted to buy exactly the kind of mobile devices they already were using, around which their systems had been built. Often, however, the exact such devices were no longer being made. Ryzex would find them used and—because they were gathering dust anyway—buy them, generally on 90-day terms. Ryzex then refurbished and sold them, with the customer paying in advance, or worst case, in cash on delivery.

Thanks to the 90 days or more of customer cash these buying and selling practices provided and its attractive gross margins (from buying used equipment for a song and selling it dear to customers who sorely needed it), Ryzex grew from a standing start in a tiny apartment in Vancouver, British Columbia in 1989 to $75 million in sales in 2007, with 360 people in offices spread across five countries. The arrival of the Internet was putting pressure on margins, however, and migration to larger corporate customers and the sale of new equipment, too, had put pressure on Ryzex's pay-in-advance terms. So in early 2008, Ryzex found itself with plummeting sales, declining margins, and $3 million in debt. The global financial crisis was, for Ryzex, a crisis indeed.

Ryzex founder and CEO Rud Browne went into high gear. Personally training each and every one of his 360 employees on the importance of cash flow, Ryzex made managing cash everybody's job, whether that meant getting longer payment terms from its vendors or faster payment from its customers. "On the customer side, there was no single bullet," recalls Browne. But there were several customer funding strategies that dramatically improved his company's cash flow:

- When customers wanted extra discounts (which they almost always did), granting discounts was tied to pay-in-advance or seven-day terms. "We would have had to go to the lower price anyway," Browne recalls. "So we made sure we got something for it—better terms."

- Ryzex ramped up its sales of one-year service and maintenance contracts paid in advance, instead of monthly in arrears. It also ramped up sales of vendor-provided service contracts, for which Ryzex needed no investment in parts—inventory that may take 12 months to turn, thereby further conserving precious cash.

- While everyone in the industry felt tremendous pressure to accept every purchase order, Ryzex remained disciplined and simply refused to extend credit to customers it deemed financially risky. "We'd rather take a hit to our sales than have them go belly-up," says Browne. Internal resistance to this policy evaporated when, after having insisted on prepayment, Ryzex avoided losing $1.5 million when one customer went bankrupt a week after the goods were delivered.

(*continued*)

Sidebar 1.1: Customer Funding Helps Ryzex Thrive, Then Survive (*continued*)

- Ryzex encouraged its customers, many of which were also cash starved, to use equipment leasing to finance large purchases. The leasing companies would pay Ryzex in 72 hours. Ryzex would pay its vendors (within agreed terms) 45 to 60 days later.

  Ryzex even began printing its invoices on garish, bright-green paper. "It's the ugly green one," its accounts receivables clerks would say to their customers when they claimed they couldn't find the Ryzex invoice.

  Despite a 25 percent drop in sales and a 50 percent drop in margin dollars as the recession deepened, by applying these strategies as well as others in the cost and procurement arenas, Ryzex went from having $3 million in debt to a $6.5 million cash surplus in just 17 months.

  Do customer funding principles such as these apply to companies like yours? Just ask Rud Browne. Indeed, they do!

  Source: Rud Browne, interview with the author, December 2, 2013.

Customer-Funded Models: The Five Types

In an effort to better understand customer-funded models, the circumstances and ways in which today's entrepreneurs can best put them to use, and the challenges entailed in implementing them, my research uncovered five different types of models—each surprisingly familiar when you think about them carefully—through which founders have convinced their customers to fund their companies, particularly at startup (see Table 1.1 and the appendix, "About the Research").

TABLE 1.1 Customer-Funded Models – The Five Types

Type	Category-Defining Examples	Twenty-First-Century Examples
Matchmaker models	Real estate brokers, eBay, Expedia.com	Airbnb, DogVacay, ProFounder
Pay-in-advance models	Consultants, architects, Dell, Banana Republic	Via.com, Threadless, The Loot
Subscription models	*Wall Street Journal, Financial Times,* Showtime, Netflix	TutorVista, H.Bloom
Scarcity-based models	Zara	vente-privee, Gilt Groupe, Lot18
Service-to-product models	Microsoft	MapmyIndia, Rock Solid Technologies, GoViral

What is most striking about these models is that each of them gives the company what accountants call negative—or very nearly negative—working capital: that is, the company has the customer's cash in hand before having to produce or pay for the good (or service) it sells. In exploring these models, I found that most of them—perhaps surprisingly—work for selling both goods and services. Let's define the five models.

Matchmaker Models

Some companies are in the business of matching up buyers and sellers, such as your local real estate broker, eBay, or Expedia. Because they simply take the order, but never own the goods (somebody's home or junk from your attic) or services (airline tickets or hotel rooms) that are sold, there's no need to tie up cash in inventory. The fees or commissions they earn from customers—whether from buyers, or more typically, sellers—

provide most or all of the cash required to launch the business and grow it enough to prove the concept, and sometimes take it much further. Thus, matchmaker models are those in which the business, with no or limited investment up front, brings together buyers and sellers—*without* actually owning what is bought and sold—and completes the transaction, earning fees or commissions for doing so.

> **matchmaker models are those in which the business, with no or limited investment up front, brings together buyers and sellers—*without* actually owning what is bought and sold.**

We examine matchmaker models in Chapter 3. Perhaps the most inspiring of our case histories that bring matchmaker models to life is that of Airbnb, which has grown from its 2007 start—on a couple of airbeds on the floor of founders Joe Gebbia and Brian Chesky's San Francisco apartment[4]—to a global booking system that monetizes people's extra space. As I write in late 2013, Airbnb offers more than half a million properties in 34,000 towns and cities in 192 countries.[5]

Pay-in-Advance Models

In some industries, customers traditionally pay the supplier in advance for at least part of the price of goods or services *before* receiving anything. Consultants, architects, and many kinds of other services firms are good examples. Thus pay-in-advance models are those in which the business asks (and convinces!) the customer to pay something up front—perhaps a deposit, perhaps something structured in another way, perhaps the full price—as a requirement to get started on building or procuring whatever it is that the customer has agreed to buy.

> **pay-in-advance models are those in which the business asks (and convinces!) the customer to pay something up front**

We examine pay-in-advance models in Chapter 4. The amazing story of little-known Via.com, the "Intel Inside" of the Indian travel industry, shows how a plucky entrepreneur named Vinay Gupta started a business using his customers' deposits and grew it from scratch in 2006 into India's largest travel business by 2013, with more than half a billion dollars in sales.[6] Its pay-in-advance model has served Via, and its travel agent customers, very well!

Subscription Models

There's nothing new about subscription models, of course, wherein a subscriber pays for something—the *New York Times* or Showtime, for example—and the goods or services are then delivered over an ensuing period of weeks, months, or years. Sometimes the subscription fee is paid entirely up front, as I do with my subscriptions to various periodicals and journals, and sometimes they are paid on a recurring basis—typically the case with cable TV. Thus subscription models are those in which the customer agrees to buy something that is delivered repeatedly over an extended period of time—perhaps a product, like newspapers or a box of organic veggies delivered weekly straight to your door—or

> **subscription models are those in which the customer agrees to buy something that is delivered repeatedly over an extended period of time**

a service like a cable TV subscription or your monthly Netflix fix. Or, as we saw in the Ryzex story, even a maintenance contract to make sure Ryzex customers' mobile devices—or our laptops or fridges—will be fixed at no cost if they fail.

We examine subscription models in Chapter 5. Perhaps the closest to home (literally!) of the case histories in the book is that of India's TutorVista, which helps more than 10,000 students per month around the world with their homework in their own homes. Starting with three Indian tutors and an online erasable whiteboard over a VoIP connection in 2005, Krishnan Ganesh built a company that was sold to Pearson PLC, the world's largest education company, at a $213 million valuation in 2011.[7] From zero to $200-plus million in six years: a testament to the remarkable value creation potential of companies built on customer-funded foundations.

Scarcity Models

These days, innovative specialty retailers of various kinds are using scarcity models to achieve rapid inventory turnover that gives them negative working capital: that is, the customers buy the goods before the retailers' vendors are paid. In effect, the retailer finances its business using your and my money. Thus scarcity models are those in which what's for sale is severely restricted by the seller to a limited quantity for a limited time period, with the seller's supplier being paid *after* the sale is made. When the goods are gone, they're gone, and there will be no more! In scarcity models, the scarcity is typically reflected in both the paucity of units offered for sale, typically with no reorders, and in the brief time period during which those units are available.

We examine scarcity models in Chapter 6. Imagine selling high-fashion but overstocked Parisian apparel that people didn't want and turning the business into one of France's best-known brands. That's exactly what Jacques-Anton Granjon and his founding team did with vente-privee, the originator of the flash sales concept for moving surplus fashion merchandise. Connecting the dots in 2001 between the founders' prior experience of discreetly moving unwanted inventory for high-profile brands, and the Internet's ability to create a virtual store that could move volumes of discounted merchandise without disrupting the brands' carefully honed images, Granjon and his team pioneered a new industry—flash sales—and grew vente-privee into a business selling more than 200,000 items each day to its more than 18 million members across eight European countries by 2013.[8] Alas, as we shall see in Chapter 6, not all of vente-privee's flash sales imitators have fared very well.

Service-to-Product Models

At the dawn of the personal-computing age, Bill Gates and Paul Allen won a contract from IBM to provide an operating system for its new personal computer. Their company, Microsoft, also won similar contracts to develop and deliver operating systems for other PC makers as that market exploded in the 1980s. Eventually, Microsoft began delivering software-in-a-box—the now ubiquitous Word, Excel, and other Microsoft products—thereby transforming its services business into one that shipped "products" that were ready to use. Thus service-to-product models are those in which businesses begin their lives by providing customized services and eventually draw on their accumulated expertise to deliver packaged solutions that stand on their own.

> ❝ service-to-product models are those in which businesses begin their lives by providing customized services and eventually draw on their accumulated expertise to deliver packaged solutions that stand on their own ❞

Sometimes the products are delivered in physical containers, sometimes as software-as-a-service (SaaS) digitally downloaded to our PCs, iPads, or mobile phones—ready to be used or consumed by the customer largely without seller support.

We examine service-to-product models in Chapter 7. The story of how Danish entrepreneurs Claus Moseholm and Jimmy Maymann built GoViral into the world's largest distributor of branded video content without *ever* taking a krone of external capital—and then sold the company in 2011 for 500 million Danish kroner (about $97 million),[9] a feat that took less than eight years—makes Moseholm and Maymann the most inspiring poster children and role models for the potential of customer-funded businesses.

What Customer-Funded Models Have in Common

Regardless of their type or the eventual size to which they have grown—some incredibly large, some not so large; some successful, others not—our examples of companies using customer-funded models share three attributes:

- They required little or no external capital to get started.
- At founding, most were what in today's entrepreneurial parlance would be called lean startups. For more on how today's lean startup movement and customer funding go hand in hand, see Sidebar 1.2.
- Most of them raised institutional capital eventually, and did so once the concept had been proven.

Sidebar 1.2: Lean Startups—Raising the Bar

In today's lean startup world, testing one's initial idea in an experimental fashion is the name of the game. Many such early tests involve figuring out whether what is being offered—the search for a minimum viable product (MVP), in lean startup lingo—is what the customer will buy. Applying any of the five customer-funded models raises the lean startup bar. How? It sets the standard not as what the customer *says* he or she or the business will buy, but what they *actually buy and pay for*, typically in advance! Thus, adopting any one of the five customer-funded models from the get-go should be the first option for getting any lean startup underway. When your target customer writes you a check for your MVP or a refinement thereof, you know you are on to something good!

On the flip side, putting entrepreneurial ideas to rest, or altering them earlier—thus failing early, and failing small—and moving on to better ideas, is a defining characteristic of many of today's most successful entrepreneurs. If you can't get a customer to pay for your MVP, maybe it's time for a pivot. When a customer drives the pivot, and subsequently pays for what you come back with—in advance, through one of the five customer-funded models—that pivot will have been proven to have made good sense.

Further, we observed that, in almost every case, there was at some point a queue of VCs lined up, eager to invest. Contrast that with the length of the typical queue that early-stage entrepreneurs find at their door: nil. Or, if they're really lucky and some investor shares their vision, one. Unfortunately for the entrepreneur, when there's a queue of one, it's the investor who calls the shots on the deal. Since the *successful* application of any of the five customer-funded models *always* results in customer traction, there's a far higher likelihood of eventually having a queue of

> **the *successful* application of any of the five customer-funded models *always* results in customer traction**

VCs at your door if, at some point, you decide to raise capital to grow your then-proven venture faster.

Craving Crowdfunding? What This Book Is—and What It's Not

First, this book isn't about how to "bootstrap" your business, a topic on which much has been written.[10] Bootstrapping generally connotes making do with less—sales and marketing on a shoestring, being thrifty, borrowing or sharing instead of buying, and the like, though some bootstrapping proponents also emphasize the sorts of customer-funded financing strategies that are much more fully developed in this book.[11] Bootstrapping principles, when they coexist alongside the use of customer-funded models, can be important contributors to enabling an entrepreneurial venture to proceed a long way down the road before raising capital. But, as bootstrapping is well covered elsewhere, you won't find these principles addressed here.

Second, there's Kickstarter, plus Indiegogo and the rest of the 138 crowdfunding websites up and running, in the United States alone, in 2012, not to mention their imitators springing up all over the world.[12] This book isn't about crowdfunding, either, though that phenomenon is an example—the tip of a much larger iceberg, if you like—of one kind of customer-funded model that this book explores, including that of the now-defunct Pro-Founder, whose unfortunate case history is told in Chapter 3. If you are craving crowdfunding, there's no shortage of books on that topic, too.

"Why doesn't this book address crowdfunding?" you may ask. After all, by mid-2012, more than 50,000 projects had been listed on Kickstarter alone, of which something like half had reached their (typically very modest) fundraising goals, and by early 2014 Kickstarter passed the $1 billion milestone in amounts pledged.[13] One Kickstarter-funded project, the film *Inocente*, won

> ❝ **Why doesn't this book address crowdfunding?** ❞

an Academy Award in 2013.[14] Even crowdfunding failures deliver value to their proponents, argues Ben Redford of the London-based design agency Mint Digital. If a project fails to reach its funding goal, that's "brilliant," he says, "because I (or he or she) didn't make something that nobody wants."[15]

On average, though, crowdfunding projects, many of which have more to do with artistic or cultural projects than for-profit businesses with growth potential, have raised very modest sums. On Kickstarter only 30 had raised more than $1 million as of mid-2012. Says Kickstarter co-founder Yancey Strickler, "The typical project raises five grand and is supported by 85 people." [16] Evidence from research firm Massolution provides additional and wider evidence of the very modest sums typically raised: more than 1 million campaigns have generated some $2.7 billion in funding to date, an average of less than $2,700 per campaign.[17]

Generating these modest outcomes takes lots of work. Crowdfunding projects that do well often have prototypes already developed, typically use professionally produced videos, and usually bring their own "crowds"—the proverbial friends, family and fools (or followers)—who, perhaps with their extended networks, actually contribute most of the funds. According to crowdfunding author Dan Marom, "The entrepreneur herself attracts most of the investment by mobilizing her own social network. That is, the pool of backers is not predominantly provided by the platform."[18] Indeed, data from Kickstarter suggest that, of those who invest in Kickstarter projects, some 85 percent do so only once.[19] Of course, launching a crowdfunding campaign is only the beginning. Savvy proponents then update their backers regularly with progress reports. For an example of an equity-based crowdfunding project that worked, at the time setting a European record for a crowdfunding campaign for a pure startup, see Sidebar 1.3.

Sidebar 1.3: Pizza Rossa—A Crowdfunding Campaign That Worked

Corrado Accardi was tired: tired of angel investors asking for too much of his company and tired of too many onerous terms. "First they say they love you. Then they tell you the terms," he recalls. His banker also wanted onerous terms: the Accardis' home as collateral, not exactly what Accardi's wife, Tiziana, not to mention Accardi himself, had in mind.

Fortunately, Accardi had already secured commitments of £200,000 from a varied collection of family and friends for his proposed London takeaway pizza concept, Pizza Rossa, but he needed £280,000 to get started. Ideally, he hoped to raise £430,000 to enable him to roll out the first two of a dozen planned outlets—plus a commercial kitchen to support them—across central London. He wondered whether crowdfunding might be the answer to raising the rest of the funds he required.

By studying the campaigns of other businesses that had met their crowdfunding targets, he observed some patterns from which he thought he could learn:

- Nearly every campaign that reached at least 35 percent of its target was eventually successful in reaching the 100 percent mark. "I'm already past 40 percent of my £430K goal," he figured. "I can bring my own crowd!"
- There was more activity on weekends than on weekdays.
- Every campaign was marked by spurts of activity, followed by lulls. "Momentum seems to matter," he observed. "Can I use my existing commitments judiciously to ensure that my momentum picks up whenever it starts to die away?"

Accardi launched his campaign on London's Crowd-cube with a professionally produced video on a Friday, inviting *some* of his friends and family—but not all, holding back others for managing momentum as his campaign settled in—to give his campaign a good start. By the end of the first weekend, his campaign had logged 27 investors and £152,000 in commitments. When things then went quiet early in the week, he called a few of his pre-committed investors, saying, "It would be great if you could invest NOW!"

After 18 days Accardi had reached his minimum figure of £280,000, but he wanted more. An overseas investor wanting to invest over £100,000 approached him, seeking better terms, plus franchise rights to Brazil. After a tasting session in London, the deal was sealed, with the better terms (but not the rights to Brazil!) then offered retroactively to all the earlier investors. At £380,000, Accardi was nearly there. As the campaign approached its target, he contacted everyone who had inquired: "You'd better invest now, or we'll be sold out!" In the final four hours of the campaign on day 19, he raised £150,000. His campaign—raising the most money ever in the UK for a crowdfunded startup—attracted some 12,000 views, from which 122 individuals invested, including Accardi's original investors. When crowdfunding is managed adroitly, it can be a good way to go!

Source: Corrado Accardi, interview with the author, November 20, 2013.

So why does this book give only modest attention to this fast-growing and possibly lucrative phenomenon? "While Kickstarter has helped people make things, everything else still needs to be figured out," observes Yves Behar, founder of the design consultancy Fuseproject in San Francisco.[20] Indeed, adds Brady Forrest, who runs a startup accelerator in San Francisco, "There is a big difference between being a product and being a company."[21] There's the rub.

This book is concerned with creating and building fast-growing companies through the use of customer-funded models. While a successful crowdfunding campaign—like Corrado Accardi's Crowdcube campaign in the UK—can mitigate some of the drawbacks of raising capital too early, customer traction from the crowd lacks both the credibility and repeatability of customer traction from those whose problems your business will actually solve going forward. Crowdfunded money from your family and friends—and, if you are lucky, their networks—is often provided for quite a different reason than the fundamentals of the idea: They love you, but real customers may not! As I write in late 2013, Accardi does not yet really know whether Londoners will buy the pizza that Pizza Rossa eventually offers, so consumer response to his business, though not his fund-raising prowess, remains an open question. As we'll see in the captivating case histories that comprise the heart of this book, developing and systematically applying customer-funded models involves much more than raising funds, and brings benefits that far exceed what crowdfunded money typically brings.

Thus the jury on crowdfunding is still out. It remains to be seen whether the phenomenon will evolve into an enduring way to raise startup equity or debt, in addition to its role in raising donations or other money in return for in-kind benefits—a T-shirt, a beta version of the proposed product, or whatever—given to contributors. Such offers are where most of the crowdfunding activity has focused to date. Despite supportive legislation in the United States—President Barack Obama's JOBS Act—in 2012, and Accardi's UK success notwithstanding, regulators in most countries have yet to figure out how to make equity-based crowdfunding a reality on a large scale.[22]

❝ We think that you shouldn't start with the assumption that you need to raise money. ❞

So if *The Customer-Funded Business* isn't about bootstrapping or crowdfunding, what is its purpose? As TechStars co-founders and authors David Cohen and

Brad Feld observe, "We think that you shouldn't start with the assumption that you need to raise money . . . Huge companies have been created with little or no outside investment."[23] "Okay, that's easy for Brad Feld or David Cohen to say, or for Bill Gates or Michael Dell to do," you might be muttering to yourself. "But how might I do it for *my* company?" This book's purpose is to provide the answer: five customer-funded models that inventive, creative, and motivated entrepreneurs in raw startups or executives in established companies can put to use to start, finance, or grow their companies and thereby satisfy their dreams.

Raising Capital Too Early: The Drawbacks Explained

In the first portion of this chapter, I touched on some of the reasons why raising capital too early is, in my view, an exceedingly bad idea.

> **"raising capital too early is, in my view, an exceedingly bad idea"**

Here I'd like to dig deeper into the drawbacks of doing so, just to be certain the point is driven home. It's an important issue for the entrepreneur *and* for prospective investors because these days, people starting new ventures, whether inside large companies or in their garages, often assume that the first thing they must do is raise capital to fund their startup. "A great idea plus some capital and, voilà! We (and our investors) will soon be rich!" Or so they believe. But there's something wrong with this picture that the Vermas and Ryzex's Rud Browne intuitively understood.

As you can see in Table 1.2, there are significant drawbacks to raising capital too early (or ever, for some!).

- Raising capital demands a lot of time and energy, distracting entrepreneurs from building the actual business.
- Raising capital too early means pitching the merit of the business idea to potential investors, rather than proving its merit among customers in the marketplace.

TABLE 1.2   Some Drawbacks of Attempting to Raise Capital Too Early

A distraction	Raising capital often requires full-time concentration, but so does starting an entrepreneurial business. One or the other will suffer when investment capital is sought. Why not raise money later when the business is less fragile?
Pitching vs. proving merit	Nascent entrepreneurial ideas, however promising, always raise numerous questions. *Proving* the merit of your idea (to yourself and to others), based on accumulated evidence and customer traction, is much more convincing than using your own wisdom and charm to *pitch* its merit.
Risk	The further you progress in developing your business, the lower the risk, as early uncertainties become more certain. Less risk translates into a higher valuation and a higher stake for the founding team.
Baggage	The terms and conditions attached to institutional capital are (for good reason) onerous, as investors seek to protect themselves from downside risk. The further along the path, the less onerous the baggage.
Difficulty	Raising capital, even in the best of times for the best of ventures, is a difficult task! Why make it even harder by trying to do it too early?

- Raising capital early leaves the founder with a lower ownership stake, since most risks and unknowns are still unresolved. In return for their capital, investors require significant stakes in businesses whose future is highly uncertain.
- Raising capital early brings lots of baggage: tough terms and conditions that investors rightly require to offset the risks they take by backing the venture.

- Raising capital is almost always very difficult, and may not even be possible, particularly under difficult economic conditions!

An Even Bigger Drawback: Bad Odds!

There's another reason—a more dramatic one—why raising venture capital for a startup is not such a good idea. It is graphically shown in Figure 1.1. Angel investors, please note!

Lerner's graph shows the returns generated from virtually *all* American venture capital funds from the beginning of time through 2011. He's plotted the return of each fund in order, from best to worst. Those delivering the best returns are at the upper left-hand end of the graph (north of 700% return on the funds invested!), and those delivering the worst returns are at the lower right-hand end (the worst of them lost 100%—yes, *all*—of their investors' funds!). This graph tells us some things

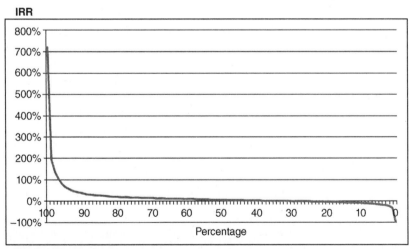

Returns from inception to 12/31/11

FIGURE 1.1   Historical U.S. Venture Fund Returns

Source: Josh Lerner analysis of Thomson/Reuters VentureXpert data.

that should be of considerable interest to those considering venture capital to fund their business:

> **This graph tells us some things that should be of considerable interest to those considering venture capital to fund their business.**

- Do most VCs deliver good returns? No! About three-quarters of VC funds (the left and center portions of the curve, where the line sits above the zero return line) deliver *at least some* return, but more than half (those in the midsection of the curve) deliver no better than low single-digit returns; many others (those at the far-right end of the curve) lose some or all of their investors' money.

- What portion of VC funds deliver decent returns? It depends on what one thinks of as "decent," of course, but let's say an annual return (internal rate of return, or IRR) in excess of 30 percent on the investors' capital is decent, given the risky nature of VC investing and the typical 10-year period for which investors' funds are committed. Only 10 percent of all funds deliver returns that are that good or better (the far-left portion of the curve). The other 90 percent don't. Lower the bar to a 20 percent IRR threshold, and only about 20 percent of all funds deliver. Lower the threshold to a 10 percent return, and still, fewer than half of all funds meet the test. Why not? There are many reasons why most VC funds deliver poor returns, but among them are these:

  - Many VCs have never themselves built an entrepreneurial business or learned to deal with the entrepreneur's inevitable challenges. Despite their best intentions, they don't really know how to help an entrepreneurial venture succeed.

  - Some lack the depth and breadth of networks that can be genuinely helpful in building a business.

  - Some tend to pour too much money into a still unproven Plan A, in a race to "get big fast" (as we'll see in Chapter 6).

- Some are like lemmings, following one another into the latest investment fad (as we'll see in Chapter 5). The latecomers often get burned.
- More fundamentally, it's really difficult to generate attractive returns by investing in entrepreneurial companies. Lest we forget, most entrepreneurs don't do so, either!

What do you get from VCs alongside their money? "Advice," of course. How good do you expect that advice will be from those managing the funds occupying the middle and right-hand end of Lerner's curve? Given their not-very-good performance at managing their funds—which derives directly from the performance of the portfolio companies in which those funds were invested—you would be forgiven if you wondered just how good their advice is likely to be. Unfortunately, the terms under which they'll invest in your company means you likely will have to follow their "advice."

There's one more fact that Lerner's graph does not show, and it's important, too. In the typical *successful* fund, the ones at the upper-left end of the curve, only 1 or 2 in 10 of the portfolio companies—the Googles and Facebooks and Twitters of the world—will actually have delivered attractive, sometimes stunning, returns. A few more portfolio companies may have paid back some or all of their invested capital, but the rest—as many as half of the companies, in a typical successful fund, and perhaps all of them in the funds toward the right end of Lerner's curve—are wipeouts. In the VC game, the few winners pay for the losses of the rest. Facebook alone accounted for more than 35 percent of the total VC exit value in the United States in 2012.[24] Thus, of the promising entrepreneurial *companies* that successfully raise venture capital, only a precious few actually deliver successful performance. Are these the kind of odds with which you'd like to play? Maybe there's a better game that has better odds: the customer-funded rather than the VC-funded game.

If you are a business angel reading this chapter, Lerner's graph should give you reason to pause. "Are angels' returns equally skewed?" you may wonder. There's been no comprehensive analysis to answer this question, unfortunately. But I expect the answer is a resounding "Yes," and perhaps even more so. Your task, then, as an investor, is simple, in concept. Just find your way to the upper-left end of the curve. Easy to say, but difficult to do!

> **If you are a business angel reading this chapter, Lerner's graph should give you reason to pause.**

I believe one way to do so, though, is to focus your investment activities on businesses with customer-funded models or to convince those who seek your capital (and your advice!) to employ such models. After all, investing your money in companies with demonstrated customer traction is much less risky than investing in the bearer of a 40-page business plan and some slick PowerPoint slides! The magic of traction is no secret, of course. But you and your fellow business angels, together with the growing number of incubators and accelerators, can be among the most important actors in driving change—away from investors as the entrepreneur's first port of call, and toward the customer and the funding he or she provides.

So, Why Now? Is a Customer-Funded Revolution at Hand?

Let's be candid. Raising capital, even in the best of times, isn't easy, and recent years have not been the best of times for entrepreneurs to raise capital. Venture capital funds have been shutting their doors right and left, which should come as no surprise to those at the far right-hand end of Josh Lerner's curve (see Figure 1.1). In 2011, U.S. venture capital investments into portfolio companies were off by more than 70 percent from their 2000 peak, just before the dot-com bubble burst.[25]

Capital flows *into* VC are off sharply, too, having fallen practically everywhere, with the underlying investors, the VCs' limited partners, having cut their allocations to the VC asset class by half during the global financial crisis of 2008–2009.[26] Sadly, for VCs and for entrepreneurs seeking capital, things have not changed. As London-based Dawn Capital's managing partner Haakon Overli noted in mid-2013, "There is simply less money around as some funds are coming to the end of their investment periods, and fewer managers are closing fresh funds."[27] The number of active VC firms in the United States has fallen from nearly 1,000 in 2000 to about 450 in 2007 and fewer than 300 in 2013.[28]

Governments, too, are broke, so in many places government funds to support startups are scarce and getting scarcer. Even the proverbial 3Fs—family, friends, and fools—have less money to invest in their loved ones' startups, because they, too, have been broke or overleveraged since the global financial crisis came calling.

Last, according to Dealogic, just one in six initial public offerings (IPOs) in 2013 were technology companies, making it the tech industry's second-worst showing in 20 years. In 1999, at the height of the 1990s technology boom, some 69 percent of IPOs were tech or Internet companies.[29] VCs are hoping that Twitter's successful IPO in 2013 will lead to a turnaround. Time will tell.

So if you need cash for your next venture—whether within an established company or for a venture you are hatching in your garage—I suggest you spend your time on your customers and your business, rather than on raising capital. Once you get customer traction, more capital is likely to follow, if you want it and need it. As we'll see in Chapters 3 through 7, many of our exemplar companies eventually raised significant institutional capital. But that's the point. **❝many of our exemplar companies eventually raised significant institutional capital.❞** Counterintuitively, by waiting to raise capital until proof points had been achieved—the magic of customer traction—raising capital, and more of it, became dramatically easier. Will we soon see a revolution in which entrepreneurs dump their PowerPoint slides and look to their customers as their first ports of call? Will tomorrow's entrepreneurs—and leaders of growth-starved established companies, too—see customers as the most sure-footed basis for starting, financing, and growing their companies? Will business angels and incubators play the role I hope they will play in driving this change, and perhaps dramatically improve their returns in the process? We'll know very soon.

Is Customer Funding the Right Approach for Every Venture?

Should every entrepreneur and executive jump onto the customer-funded bandwagon? No. Customer-funded models don't suit every business. If your idea is to build a dam with a hydroelectric power plant to meet today's voracious thirst for energy, for example, conventional project finance is a more sensible source of the funding you'll need. Users are probably unlikely to pay you for tomorrow's power today. But if one of the five customer-funded models suits your circumstances, perhaps it's a better way forward for you.

When Customer Funding Goes Wrong

A customer-funded approach can offer your business numerous benefits, as will become abundantly clear as this book unfolds. But it's no panacea, it doesn't guarantee your profitability, and it won't replace getting the rest of the fundamentals right, either.[30] As longtime venture capitalist Bill Egan famously remarked, "You may have capital and a talented management team, but if you are fundamentally in a lousy business, you won't get the kind of results you would in a good business. All businesses aren't created equal."[31] Even customer-funded ones! So does customer funding sometimes go wrong?

❝You may have capital and a talented management team, but if you are fundamentally in a lousy business, you won't get the kind of results you would in a good business.❞

Consider Groupon, the daily-deals high flyer that has experienced nothing but turmoil since its eagerly awaited IPO at the tender age of three years in November 2011, when it raised $700 million in what was the largest IPO by an American Internet company since Google's in 2004.[32] Groupon, as almost everyone on Planet Earth knows, offers its members discounted "daily deals" at a plethora of local restaurants, day spas, helicopter tour operators—you name it. Its ingenious customer-funded model—which is both a scarcity model (the deals are only open for a very short time) and a pay-in-advance model (customers pay for the deal on the day it's offered, then visit the restaurant or take the helicopter tour later, or perhaps never)—puts enormous amounts of cash into Groupon's coffers, a portion of which it then (eventually!) pays out to its merchants in installments over an extended period, often as long as 60 days. Would you like to have this kind of float in your business?

This tsunami of cash, along with subsequent VC funding, enabled Groupon to make acquisitions of 17 mostly copycat companies in a little more than a year, expand into 45 countries, grow its merchant roster to 78,466, and grow its employee base from 37 to 9,625 in only two years.[33] "Can businesses having customer-funded models grow quickly," you ask? You bet they can!

But is Groupon really a viable business? That's a very different question. Groupon was forced

❝But is Groupon really a viable business?❞

to restate its financials twice before its IPO, cutting its reported 2010 revenue by more than half, and again afterwards, increasing its quarterly loss for the fourth quarter of 2012 from $42.3 million to $64.9 million.[34] It seems that the company hadn't set aside enough money to cover customer refunds, particularly for more expensive services like laser eye surgery, where refunds were running higher than expected.[35] Why is this a problem? Some customers will change their minds ("Maybe I don't want LASIK surgery, after all."), and some merchants will go bust, leaving Groupon holding the bag for unredeemed services. Thus, because Groupon cannot be sure how much money to set aside for future refunds, which it guarantees to its customers, its revenue figures after expected returns are iffy at best.

Okay, so what about the expenses that operating Groupon's business entails? Groupon's tsunami of cash makes it easy to *pay* the expenses, but covering them with enough gross margin dollars to actually book any *profit* is quite another story. Groupon has been unprofitable every quarter, before and since its IPO, in part due to its aggressive spending to grow its user base. The losses, the financial reporting issues, the fall in Groupon's stock price to around $4.00 (one-quarter of its IPO price), the fact that Groupon's model is easily copied (thereby making its business ferociously competitive), and a decline in its international revenues all eventually took their toll, leading to the firing of founder and CEO Andrew Mason in February 2013.[36]

Groupon remains awash in cash, as I write in late 2013, but its stock price, despite its recovery from around $4.00 to $9.00, remains at around half of its IPO price.[37] Will Groupon be able to recover its mojo, or change its

❛❛Will Groupon be able to recover its mojo? ❜❜

strategy and business model to something that can generate profits as well as cash? It's anybody's guess. But the good news for Groupon is that its customer-funded model at least gives it a war chest with which to try.

The Groupon story is one example of how customer funding can go wrong, though it's fair to say that having plenty of your customers' cash—despite no profits—is a nice problem to have! Perhaps a more sinister downside of customer funding is when companies with lots of market power (e.g., large supermarket or other retail chains) use that power to demand onerous terms from their sometimes much smaller and less powerful suppliers. Supermarkets get their customer's cash on the day the customer buys, or perhaps a day or so later when the customer's credit card payment clears. That's a wonderful source of customer funding to the supermarket, which hasn't yet paid its suppliers for what the customer just bought. But if the supermarket demands 60- or 90-day terms from its suppliers, as some do, that puts stress—as well as additional cost—on the ability of its suppliers to finance their own businesses, while they wait for—or find a way to finance—the supermarket's slow payment. It's not really a downside of the supermarket's customer funding, per se, as the problem lies on the supply side, not on the customer side. But it is the customer and supplier sides of the working capital equation, working together, that deliver the necessary cash to operate the business. Abusive behavior toward suppliers is not what this book advocates.

The Vermas: The Rest of the Story[38]

At the outset of this first chapter, you read how Rakesh and Rashmi Verma built a growing services business that had grown by 2004 into what many regarded as India's premier source of navigable, accurate, detailed digital maps of all kinds. What next? On a visit to the United States that year, the Vermas observed that MapQuest had built a product wherein consumers or others could obtain exactly the maps they needed, anytime, anywhere, simply by going online. "Could we do a MapQuest for India?" they wondered, and MapmyIndia was born.

> **Could we do a MapQuest for India?**

Not content with developing a new customized mapping solution for each of its customers, as the Vermas had done in the past, MapmyIndia would "productize" its mapping data, and let its customers and users—from retailers seeking to inform consumers where stores were located, to consumers seeking location information of all kinds—do the work: zooming in for more detail, zooming out for the big picture, and more. A heretofore not very scalable services business would, if all went well, become a highly scalable product business.

Developing such a business would take capital, though, for algorithms, software development, GPS technology, and much more. No longer was it realistic for customers to fund the growth of the business. MapmyIndia's first small round of venture capital was raised from California-based investors Kleiner Perkins Caufield & Byers and Sherpalo Ventures in 2006, valuing the still-small company—whose revenue in the prior year was barely $1 million—at about $7 million.

Three further rounds of capital at higher valuations followed in 2007, 2008, and 2011, as MapmyIndia grew its product offering: consumer navigation devices for the auto aftermarket à la TomTom; fleet tracking solutions for the taxi and logistics industries in India; licensed content for automobile manufacturers' in-dash infotainment systems; locator content via the Web; and even a $50 app to turn anyone's iPhone into a navigation device for India. And the original services business kept humming along, too. One might think of the company today as MapQuest and TomTom or Garmin, for India, rolled into one.

What Angel Investors Will Want to Know—and Will Ask

I've argued that successful application of any of the customer-funded models is likely to make it possible, even relatively easy, for an aspiring entrepreneur to raise capital later from business angels or institutional VC investors. The case histories in Chapters 3 through 7 will bear me out. But that doesn't mean these investors won't ask any tough questions! Indeed, experienced investors in early-stage companies know the risks are acute, and that many if not most of their investments will not pan out.

Hence, three critical issues are always at the top of their minds as they contemplate investing in a young company:

- Does the product or technology actually work?
- Is there sufficient customer traction to indicate that market demand is genuine?
- Is the business model sufficiently capital efficient that significant further progress can be made without my writing more checks? While most venture capital investors expect to "follow their money" with additional rounds of capital as needed, most angels have learned— the hard way—that writing additional checks often amounts to throwing good money after bad.

> **most angels have learned—the hard way— that writing additional checks often amounts to throwing good money after bad.**

Let's consider an early-stage business that's off to a good start using any of the five customer-funded models, and subsequently seeks funding to ramp up its growth rate or serve new target markets. Does the technology work, and is there customer traction? It does and there is! If the business is ready to ramp up, that means both of these things are already true. Is the business capital efficient? If the business has been getting along on customer funding, this suggests that additional capital can be used to support faster growth, rather than the everyday basics, which the customer funding already covers.

But these three questions, crucial as they are, represent only the tip of the iceberg for the questions an experienced business angel will (or should!) ask. For each of the five models, there are additional, more model-specific questions that will or should arise, like these:

- What are the settings in which each of the five models is best applied? To services businesses or products? For consumables or durables? To business-to-business, business-to-consumer, or consumer-to-consumer marketing strategies?

- What are the "how-to" lessons to heed in putting each model to work? Experienced investors know that while planning is important, effective implementation is what actually delivers the results.
- What common pitfalls must the entrepreneur and his or her backer watch out for?

Thus, at the end of each of Chapters 3 through 7, I'll draw on the body of research that underlies this book to highlight the key lessons that pertain to each of the five customer-funded models. These end-of-chapter sections—and the "John's Business Angel Checklists" that summarize them—are intended to do four things for business angels, entrepreneurs, and leaders in established companies who see the potential of customer funding in growing their businesses:

- Equip you, my readers, with the tools and insights you will need to figure out which of the five models might work in *your* business or one you are considering backing.
- Draw on the experience of others who've already been down the track with each model, both entrepreneurs and their backers, to head off some of the likely mistakes *before* you make them.
- Provide business angels, other early-stage investors, and even corporate investors with a set of due diligence questions they can ask when contemplating an investment in a customer-funded business—or one that could be! My hope is that angels will nudge aspiring entrepreneurs with promising ideas into thinking about pursuing their dreams via one of the five customer-funded models, rather than seeking capital before anything is really proven. "Here are some ideas about how better to fund the launch of your

business," such an angel might say. "Come back and see me when you've put them to work and customer traction is evident, and I'll then help you ramp up."

- Assist business angels in contributing to the effective management of their customer-funded investee companies. The most important things investors bring to their investees aren't their dollars, euros, pounds, or rupees. The really important things are the sage counsel they bring when crucial decisions are faced. This book's lessons, based on the journeys of other entrepreneurs who have applied these models and the investors who backed them, can add useful perspective in facing such decisions.

> **❝The most important things investors bring to their investees aren't their dollars, euros, pounds, or rupees.❞**

Though these lessons have been gleaned largely from entrepreneurial journeys, rather than those of a more corporate kind, there's a good reason why. Out of necessity, entrepreneurs, more than their corporate brethren, have been forced by their lack of resources to find customer-funded paths. As we saw in the Ryzex story earlier in this chapter, though, the lessons apply equally to established business settings.

The Road Ahead

In Chapter 1, I've provided a brief overview of what the five customer-funded models are all about, why they might be relevant to your business or one in which you may at some point invest, and what you're in for in reading the rest of the book. Other than the story of the Vermas' journey from a small IT training company to becoming the dominant digital mapping company in India, however, I've not yet brought any of them to life in any depth. In Chapter 2, I'll address two important questions about customer-funded models: "Are these models a mirage or a mind-set?" and "Is there anything really new here?" At the end of the chapter, I'll begin posing some of the questions that angel investors will (and should!) ask, as illustrated in the case histories of the early origins of Banana Republic and Dell. These questions should help you begin thinking about whether taking a customer-funded approach might actually work to build what could turn out to be a customer-funded business for *you*.

In Chapters 3 through 7, the heart of the book, I'll bring each of the five customer-funded models to life through the case histories of more than a dozen incredibly innovative—and often inspiring—twenty-first-century entrepreneurs who have created and applied them in building their fast-growing companies. Not all of them, however, have been successful!

Then, to close the book in Chapter 8, I'll recap and bring together the key lessons—for entrepreneurs and business angels, too—that transcend the five models. I'll also pull together a number of crucial lessons about implementing each model, so you're ready to hit the ground running as you start to apply one or more of them. So, are you ready to be inspired? To take your entrepreneurial game to a new level? To improve your angel investment returns? To embark

> **So, are you ready to be inspired? To take your entrepreneurial game to a new level?**

on a customer-funded—and customer focused—journey in *your* business or one you may back? Turn the page and read on!

2

Customer-Funded Models: Mirage or Mind-Set? Old or New?

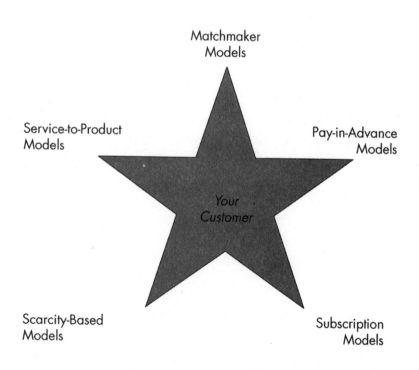

Matchmaker
Models

Service-to-Product
Models

Pay-in-Advance
Models

Your
Customer

Scarcity-Based
Models

Subscription
Models

In 1492, Queen Isabella of Castile had a problem. The Spanish court of Queen Isabella and King Ferdinand had been fighting the Moorish Kingdom in Granada, and had recently been excluded from West Africa by treaty.[1] This meant that important sources of tribute to the royal coffers had been lost. Waging a war has always been expensive, even in the late Middle Ages, and Isabella, a powerful and strikingly beautiful lover of jewelry and elegant gowns,[2] needed to replace the lost tribute with another source. Christopher Columbus, who needed capital to set off to find a new trade route to India, offered a possible solution.

Columbus, like many entrepreneurs today, had an entrepreneurial dream: to gain fame, fortune, and (not least) aristocratic status by establishing a direct trade route to India. Though it took him more than five years of dogged pursuit to convince Queen Isabella, his tenacity finally paid off. On April 17, 1492, Columbus was finally granted the funding he needed, in return for 10 percent of the profits, noble status, and hereditary governorship—to him and his descendants—of whatever new territories he might find along the way. His investor, the royal court of Spain, was at last on board! Three months later, on August 3, his expedition set sail into the vast unknown on three now-famous ships, the *Niña*, the *Pinta*, and the *Santa Maria*. Everyone knows the rest of the story of how he discovered the Americas—the New World.

> **❝Columbus, like many entrepreneurs today, had an entrepreneurial dream❞**

Financing Entrepreneurial Ventures: Nothing New

As the story of Christopher Columbus and Queen Isabella demonstrates, entrepreneurs have been getting funding from investors for a very long time. Columbus had a somewhat audacious purpose in mind—to discover a western trade route to India and its riches—and he had to convince an investor to provide the funding he needed. Fast-forwarding nearly 500 years, the venture capital industry came into being to more efficiently solve the same time-honored problem of entrepreneurs gaining funding for their often similarly audacious dreams. In return for the presence of an efficient market for capital[3] and for not having to spend months or years identifying and chasing high-net-worth individuals who might provide the backing they needed—like Queen Isabella (or later, the Rockefellers, Vanderbilts, or Rothschilds)—entrepreneurs proved willing to "pay" their backers with shares in their firms.

This more efficient way of accessing venture capital developed first in California and around Boston's Route 128 corridor in the 1950s and 60s, subsequently took off in the 1980s, and was then exported around the world.[4] Unfortunately, it has grabbed the entrepreneurial financing limelight to such a degree that winning funding from VCs and business angels has become a goal unto itself for many entrepreneurs. Indeed, many incubators and accelerators boast of their graduates' success in raising such capital.[5]

Surprisingly, however, there's been little attention given to the perhaps more prosaic but far more common practice of finding ways to get *customers* to fund your venture. Until now! So, before setting out on our journey to bring to life the five customer-funded models in Chapters 3 through 7, in this chapter I want to examine the case histories of two well-known companies that have their twentieth-century roots in customer-funded, pay-in-advance models, a fact not widely known about either of them.

> **"Surprisingly, however, there's been little attention given to the perhaps more prosaic but far more common practice of finding ways to get *customers* to fund your venture."**

First, the case history of Dell demonstrates the most widely understood, most familiar setting in which customer-funded models are pursued, that of asking business-to-business customers to pay in advance to solve a business problem or need they have.

The case history of Banana Republic and its scrappy and inventive founders, Mel and Patricia Ziegler, then goes on to show that pay-in-advance models are not confined to B2B settings, and that consumers, too, will sometimes give entrepreneurs enough money to keep them afloat and at least one step ahead of the vendors they must pay.

From Dormitory Room to Dominance: The Customer-Funded Origins of Dell[6]

Michael Dell could be said to have had an early bent toward entrepreneurship. At the ripe old age of eight he applied to take the high school equivalency exam so he could get on with his life. He also showed early interest in computers, pulling apart an early Apple II model to understand how it worked from the inside out. One summer, at age 16, Dell got a job selling newspaper subscriptions to *The Houston Post*. His job was to take the list of newly issued telephone numbers his supervisor gave him and cold-call them to offer them subscriptions.

Dell's summer job proved so lucrative that he kept it going once school resumed, doing most of the work after school and on weekends, and outsourcing some of the work to his friends. Later that school year, he was asked to do a school project that involved filing his tax return. After having sold thousands of newspaper subscriptions, his prior-year income came to about $18,000. His teacher corrected his paper, assuming he had misplaced a decimal point. When she learned he had the figure right, she was dismayed, for the ambitious 16-year-old had earned more that year than she had!

Dell's Mother Should Have Known

Soon thereafter, bending to his parents' wishes, Dell enrolled as a pre-med major at the University of Texas at Austin. But Dell's real interests were already becoming clear. "On the day I left for college, I drove off in the white BMW that I had bought with my earnings from selling newspaper subscriptions, with three computers in the backseat of the car. My mother should have been very suspicious."[7]

As Dell's first semester at college unfolded, Dell discovered that at a large institution like Texas, nobody really knew what students were doing—or not doing, in Dell's case. "So," Dell recalled, "you can drift off and do something else. Like start a business."[8] Unfortunately,

> **❝ You can drift off and do something else. Like start a business. ❞**

Dell's parents soon figured out that Dell was spending more time working on his business than attending classes, and his grades were suffering. In November 1983, they flew to Austin for a surprise visit, calling from the Austin airport to say they would see him momentarily. Dell barely had time to clear his dorm room of computers and parts and stash them behind the shower curtain in his roommate's bathroom before his parents arrived.

It should have been no surprise to his family, then, when in January 1984 as his second semester got underway, Dell formally established a company, PC's Limited, selling PC-compatible computers from his dorm room. Dell had already discovered that he could buy the parts from which a PC was made for far less than the price at which newfangled computer stores were selling PCs. Even better, computer stores, worrying about being short-shipped by IBM in the face of overwhelming demand, sometimes would order more PCs than they really wanted. If they were then sent more than they expected, as occasionally would happen, Dell would take the extra units off their hands, modify them, and sell them as souped-up PCs in the same way a lover of hot-rod automobiles would customize a car.

Customer Funding Gets Dell Off Campus

Dell's unique—and winning—approach had two key elements: He could better meet customers' needs by assembling customized configurations not otherwise available on the market, and his customers would be asked to pay up front to get what Dell would build. This approach had important benefits:

- *Lower costs:* The direct sales channel to his mostly small business and government customers eliminated costs associated with the retail outlets the other computer manufacturers used to distribute their products. Dell chose to pass these savings on to his customers, undercutting most existing sellers.
- *No investment:* The most significant implication of this business model was the investment required, or the lack thereof in this case—none! Dell didn't need to buy any components before an order was received, and didn't risk holding unsold inventory, either.

His happy pay-in-advance customers, ordering exactly the PCs they wanted, were soon funding a rapidly growing business, and Dell quickly assembled enough cash—his customers' cash—to move out of his dorm room to an off-campus two-bedroom condominium apartment, and then to a 1,000-square-foot space in North Austin, where "manufacturing" consisted of three of Dell's buddies sitting at 6-foot tables assembling or upgrading machines. Dell's homegrown operation was generating between $50,000 and $80,000 a month in sales. After three more moves in rapid succession, Dell's company made the leap into a 30,000-square-foot building, almost as big as a football field. It was still only 1985, and he'd raised not a dollar of capital! All of his growth had been funded by his customers' cash.

Customer Funding: A Lesson Often Overlooked

Today, every student of business sees Dell's direct made-to-order model as the central element in the company's success. The model delivered vastly better gross margins compared to the rest of the

PC industry by cutting out the retailer and eliminating waste. But few think about or understand the importance of the customer-funded, pay-in-advance nature of the Dell model, and the opportu-

❝few think about or understand the importance of the customer-funded, pay-in-advance nature of the Dell model❞

nity this element gave Michael Dell, particularly in his company's early years, to courageously, even outrageously, grow his business at rocket-ship speed. We'll return at the end of this chapter to the Dell story and recap its lessons learned. Before doing so, however, let's examine the story of another fast-growing business that managed a similar feat in a consumer setting.

Banana Republic: From the Short-Armed Spanish Paratrooper Shirt to Trend-Setting Fashion Retailer[9]

It was 1978, and Mel Ziegler had just stepped out of the glass doors of customs at San Francisco International Airport, returning from a trip to Australia with a group of fellow travel journalists. Greeting his wife, Patricia, whom he'd not seen for two weeks—the longest they'd been apart since meeting two years earlier at the *San Francisco Chronicle*, where they both worked—their embrace knocked his authentic Australian Army bush hat to the floor. But it wasn't the hat that caught Patricia's eye. It was the four-pocket British Burma jacket. "How perfect the color, the raised lines of twill, the slightly worn collar and cuffs. This four-pocket jacket screamed 'authentic' and 'adventure,'" she recalled.[10]

After a few subtle improvements crafted at Patricia's sewing machine—new wooden buttons, suede elbow patches, and leather trim on the cuffs and collar—the jacket became Mel's proudest passion. "I felt roguish and buoyant. I seemed to walk taller, with a worldly gait. Everywhere I went, people stopped me with a comment or question. 'What a great jacket!' or 'Excuse me, do you mind if I ask you where you bought your jacket?' Here was the business we'd been looking for."[11] The Zieglers would start a company that would sell jackets like the British Burma jacket and anything else like it they could find. Banana Republic was born, in concept at least. There was just one problem: They had virtually no money to do so, a mere $1,500 to be exact.

Using his well-honed skills as a reporter accustomed to tracking down information for a breaking story, Mel discovered several phone calls later that one of the top surplus jobbers in the country was right across San Francisco Bay in Oakland. Surely they'd find something there they could sell. The Zieglers knew they needed a credible plan for meeting with the proprietor, Zimmerman, a crusty three-hundred-pound

> **The Zieglers knew they needed a credible plan. We would pose as rich dilettantes**

veteran of the jobbing trade, whose cavernous warehouse was filled with military surplus piled floor to ceiling. Patricia quickly devised one. As Mel tells the story, "We would pose as rich dilettantes. She would wear a rich-looking dress and her highest heels to convey the impression that she was a trust fund heiress looking for some 'interesting pieces' to supplement a boutique she was about to open. I would be the indulgent husband."[12]

Strolling around the warehouse with Zimm in tow, the couple came upon a huge stack of khaki shirts, "Spanish Army shirts," in Zimm's words. After a bit of haggling, the Zieglers drove home to Mill Valley with 500 khaki shirts in their beat-up Datsun, $750 poorer. Now that they were officially in business, their first operational challenge was to wash the shirts, one washing-machine load at a time. It quickly became clear to the Zieglers why the Spaniards had declared them surplus: The sleeves were too short—*way* too short! Thinking quickly, Patricia went into entrepreneurial mode. "Nobody would think of keeping the sleeves on a shirt like this rolled down," she said, rolling them right up to the elbows.[13]

The Marin City Flea Market: The Zieglers' First Customer Cash

Every Sunday, a dusty parking lot six miles north of San Francisco was transformed into a thriving collection of merchants and customers out for a Sunday drive. The Zieglers ironed and folded every one of the 500 shirts and set off for the flea market with a sign: "Short-Armed Spanish Paratrooper Shirts $6.50." At the end of the day, though, they'd sold barely enough to pay the $30 fee for their booth. "We need to double the price," said Patricia to Mel at the end of the day. "The shirts are too cheap. People can't appreciate the value."[14]

> **We need to double the price," said Patricia. "People can't appreciate the value.**

The next Sunday, same booth, same table, same shirts, but a different sign: "Short-Armed Spanish Paratrooper Shirts $12.95." Patricia, now decked out in one of the shirts belted at the waist, wearing tight jeans and heels, dressed Mel in another, with the collar raised and the sleeves rolled up. By the end of the day, they'd sold 102 shirts, more than $1,300 worth, and $500 more than they had paid for the entire lot. With more than $1,000 in the bank, half of it provided by their flea market customers, the intrepid entrepreneurs decided that their fledgling startup, Banana Republic, needed a store!

Getting a Loan: Not!

The couple quickly realized they needed more money—at least another $1,500, they figured. Printing a business card for the occasion, the Zieglers paid a call on the manager of the bank where they had deposited their *San Francisco Chronicle* paychecks back in their salaried days. The banker, a jovial type named Fred, started by asking a few questions:

- "Did they own a home? *No.*
- Did they have a business plan? *Working on it.*

- Did they have a regular source of income? *Not since they'd left the Chronicle.*"[15]

Fred gently explained, "To make a loan, we look at your three C's: Capital, which is your collateral. Capacity, which is your income. And Character. You have no collateral. You have no income. But I'll hand you this: you two *are* characters. Look," he said, trying to help, "you don't qualify for a loan, but have you thought about asking for terms from your suppliers?"[16]

The germ of a customer-funded model—though such a concept was probably the furthest thing from their minds—danced in their heads. Thirty days' credit would give them a chance to open the store and mail the catalog they had planned.

> **All they'd have to do was talk Zimm into giving them terms.**

All they'd have to do was talk Zimm into giving them terms. Mel decided that, since they'd paid cash for the first lot of Zimm's shirts, there was no reason why he would give them terms the next time around. They would have to convince somebody else to give them terms first. They headed across town, where another jobber was located. "Let me give you a piece of advice," Zimm had said on their first visit. "Don't buy any merchandise from that swindler . . . I don't trust that son of a bitch as far as I can throw him. I haven't talked to him in ten years."[17]

The Zieglers found a few items they thought they could sell. "How are you paying?" asked the proprietor.

"We usually pay net thirty," replied Mel with a straight face.

"So who else you buy from?"

"Zimm," they replied.

"That stingy bastard gives you credit? Well, okay, thirty days, sign here."[18]

Mission accomplished—it was time to go see Zimm. They found some more items they thought they could sell, or at least cut apart and make into something else. "So thirty days? Mel said to Zimm when he added things up.

"Your husband's got a sense of humor," replied Zimm, turning to Patricia. Her reply that Zimm's competitor was giving them thirty days resulted in a stream of obscenities about his competitor, after which Zimm calmed down and replied, "Alright already, thirty days. And I don't mean thirty-one."[19]

Sacks of Customer Cash

The new store opened the day after Thanksgiving in November 1978, historically the busiest shopping day of the year in the United States. But a small strip shopping center in Mill Valley, California, wasn't at the top of people's lists of shopping destinations that day. Total sales for day one? $6.50 for one Swedish Gas Mask bag. Business didn't get much better in the days that followed, either, but finally the first order for a Short-Armed Paratrooper Shirt arrived from the catalogs they had printed—on three letter-sized pieces of paper, folded in half to make a 12-page catalog—and mailed the day before Thanksgiving. They'd sent a catalog to everyone in their Rolodexes and to others they could find in the media or on mastheads, some 400 in all.

Sales remained slow, and the typically gloomy Bay Area December weather didn't help. But one morning the phone rang, from *The John Gambling Show* on WOR Radio in New York. Patricia was, to her considerable surprise, on the air! Gambling wanted to know where they got the unusual items, why there were no hoods on the Italian camouflage jackets, and much more. Drawing on Mel's creative catalog copy, and embellishing it further, Patricia sang and danced her way through a 20-minute interview, which ended with Gambling asking how his listeners in New York, New Jersey, and Connecticut could get their hands on a copy of Banana Republic catalog number one. "All they need to do is send a dollar to post office box seven seventy four in Mill Valley California, nine four nine four two," she replied.[20] Four

"Four days later, the mailman showed up with two large sacks of mail"

days later, the mailman showed up with two large sacks of mail from the post office across the street—it wouldn't fit into the mailbox, so he had to bring it over. There were nearly a thousand envelopes, each one containing a catalog request and a dollar bill.

Mail order wisdom indicated that it was impossible to make money on one's early mailings, but the Zieglers had broken the rule: They were more than covering the cost of the catalog and its postage with the dollar they charged. Banana Republic's catalog business was on its way, with customers paying for the catalog in advance—never mind the merchandise, for which pay-in-advance orders soon followed, too. Give your customers something inventive and compelling enough, and they will pay—in advance!—to get it.

Another stroke of media good fortune arrived the next spring, when Mary Lou Luther's fashion column in the *Los Angeles Times* praised Banana Republic's 1949 Gurkha Shorts, "IN SIZE 32 ONLY," as the single most chic shorts of the summer. Luther told her readers where to send their checks to get their hands on a pair, and soon more envelopes were arriving, this time containing checks for $15, far more than the paltry sum the Zieglers had paid for the shorts! Of course, they included a catalog with the shorts they shipped, resulting in even more orders.

Funding Store Number Two

The Mill Valley store was coming around, and happily, the mail-order business was growing, too. Though there were growing pains, the Zieglers quickly learned that managing the customers' cash to stay a few days ahead of what was owed to Zimm and Banana Republic's growing roster of surplus suppliers was the key to keeping their young business afloat. But none of it was easy, and the Zieglers soon reached a breaking point. In Mel's words, "We'd been doing virtually everything on the fly, without really 'knowing' how to do any of it except as we had taught ourselves . . . But we were reaching a point where what had worked for us in getting into business was now beginning to work against us. As much as we were empowered by and loved the idea of being professional amateurs, it was wearing us ragged."[21]

Mel decided the only way out of their predicament was to grow faster: to create their best catalog ever, and mail five times as many copies, nearly a million. If the response rates held up at 6 percent—more than three times what they'd been told to expect in the mail-order catalog business—they would generate enough cash to open a second store. The only out-of-pocket expense would be postage. Everyone else was now giving them terms, a lesson well learned.

> **Mel decided the only way out of their predicament was to grow faster**

Opening Store Number Two

Two months later, they had enough customer cash to open their second store, this time in the heart of San Francisco, midway between two upscale neighborhoods—Russian Hill and Pacific Heights—that had been producing the highest responses to the catalog. They painted the new location with two-story-high zebra stripes and opened for business, supplementing their traditional surplus merchandise with new items they found at trade shows: tropical-weight wool pants, cotton safari shirts, fatigues and—imagine!—all in a full range of sizes. No more size 32 only! Sales soon doubled, then tripled, those of the Mill Valley store.

But there was an impending problem, as Patricia pointed out one day. Banana Republic had pretty well "picked the domestic surplus stockpiles clean of anything worthwhile."[22] They were filling some gaps with other wholesale merchandise, but any other retailer had access to those styles, too, and already designers were visiting the new store and grabbing one piece of everything. In retailing, a successful new concept is notoriously easy to copy. Patricia was worried, but Mel was already on the case.

The former reporter had made some calls to find foreign sources of surplus merchandise. Europe was his target. After all, Europe was a conglomeration of countries of all sizes, all of which had military organizations of one kind or another. There must be surplus there, too! And there was—at Coble's, in a decaying four-story building in the far reaches of East London. "If there was a

> **If there was a Nirvana of Surplus, we had found it.**

Nirvana of Surplus," Mel recalled, "we had found it. Sack upon sack, bale upon bale, box upon box."[23]

The quantities seemed plentiful. "We are the purveyors of the finest tailored garments for Her Majesty's Royal Navy, Army, and Air Force, and the British Empire, such as it was," said the senior Mr. Coble with pride and a wily twinkle in his eye.[24] The best news was that the prices were as good as or better than what Banana Republic had been paying for American surplus in the United States. And the terms? Coble agreed to sixty days *after* clearance at U.S. Customs. "The goods will be on the water by the end of the week," offered Coble.

Selling the Business

One of the Zieglers' favorite customers, a shopping center developer named Merritt Sher, wanted Banana Republic to put a store in his next project, across the bay in Oakland. He offered to build out the store for them and give them six months' free rent. Mel wasn't convinced. "Merritt, we'd love to do something with you someday. But Oakland's not for us, not at this time. We can't even find enough merchandise for the business we already have. What we really need to do is concentrate on manufacturing our own line."[25]

"Would you consider selling the company?" Sher replied.

> **We take his check, and he takes the headaches? Really?**

"Wow. Did he just say that? Never occurred to me," thought Mel. "Who'd want to buy it? What we do is quirky; the business depends on us. But is he serious? We take his check, and he takes the headaches? Really?"

"If you're thinking of selling, you need to talk to Don Fisher," Sher said.

"Who's he?" Mel asked.

"He owns The Gap," Sher said. "I'll give him a call."[26]

The Gap had grown from its own entrepreneurial origins to more than 500 stores across the United States in late 1982, when the Zieglers met Fisher. Four months later, on February 1, 1983, following a series of exhausting negotiations, the Zieglers signed a 50-page contract to sell the business, which had done $2.5 million worth of business in 1982, to The Gap, alongside a five-year employment contact. Banana Republic wasn't even five years old. Mel and Patricia would stay on board, equipped with the autonomy they would need to continue to build the business, total creative control, and as much money as would be needed to grow, as long as the business remained profitable. They would get paid in dribbles, based on the performance they delivered. Mel found himself wondering how soon he'd be able to remove his name from the burglar alarm company so somebody at The Gap could be the one to meet the 24-hour board-up service at the store, when somebody threw yet another brick through the storefront window in the early hours of the morning.

Oh, and one more detail. The Zieglers stayed with The Gap for just over the mandated five years, turning their quirky business into a trendsetting fashion leader with more than 100 stores and $250 million in revenue.[27] Needless to say, the "dribbles" they were paid for doing so turned into a *very* sizeable sum!

Customer Funding: Mirage or Mind-Set?

"Okay, customer funding worked for Dell and the Zieglers," you may be thinking. "But surely this is fantasy, maybe even a mirage. It can't really be that easy to do in *my* business, can it?" If you're working to bring a new venture to life in an established organization, it's probably even harder, as aversion to risk is alive and

❝Surely this is fantasy, maybe even a mirage.❞

well in most such settings. "We don't do it that way around here," as they say.

No, it's not easy, but it's not all that difficult, either, as shown by the Zieglers' crafty scheme to get Zimm to provide supplier credit—the key ingredient in letting them use their customers' cash to grow their business. Thus, there are two sides to the customer-funded coin. One side is getting the customer to pay as early as possible—up front at the time of the order for a Dell PC; at the time of purchase for a Short-Armed Spanish Paratrooper Shirt at a Banana Republic store; or with the order, if by mail. The other side of the coin is to get your suppliers to let you pay them as late as possible.

These two sides of the customer-funded coin are the fundamental principles underlying each of the five customer-funded models explored in this book. Call the result "sitting on the float" if you like. Get paid up front, or as early as you can, and pay your suppliers as late as you can. It's a mind-set, more than anything, a conviction that you can do two things with nearly every transaction—every purchase or sale—your business undertakes:

1. Convince your customer that there's good reason to pay you early, and not to require lengthy terms. Why might they agree to pay you earlier than they might otherwise like to? Lots of reasons:

   - You have something they can't get anywhere else. This was the case for Ryzex, as we saw in Chapter 1.
   - Your offering is superior, in *their* eyes, to that of other providers they might choose. If it's

   ❝If it's not superior in some way, maybe you should be doing something else!❞

   not superior in some way, maybe you should be doing something else! The millions of consumers who pay yearly membership fees *in advance* for the privilege of shopping at stores like Costco do so for good reasons.

- Your customer gets something extra for paying you sooner: better service, faster delivery, or whatever you can think of that's meaningful to *them*. Millions of consumers pay Amazon a yearly fee, *in advance*, to belong to Amazon Prime, which gives free shipping and other benefits to regular Amazon shoppers. Not rocket science, is it? But Jeff Bezos's ingenuity and mind-set? Yes!

2. Convince your supplier that there's good reason to give you lengthier terms than they might otherwise offer. Why might they do so? Lots of reasons here, too:

- You are a large or important customer to them. Clout matters. Walmart, Tesco, Carrefour, and other large retailers often demand and get lengthy terms from their suppliers.

- Giving you good terms enables your business to grow into a bigger and better customer, thanks to the customer funding with which you can operate and grow your business. That's good for them, and good for you, too! Getting attractive terms from its vendors and its shopping center landlords were two of the key elements in The Gap's growth strategy in its early years.

- Your credit is good (if it's not, clean up your act!). This means they can finance your paper—the 30, 60, or 90 days of accounts receivable for the terms you need—at a bank. Sure, this may cost you something in slightly higher pricing, but getting your hands on the cash may well be worth it. And getting the cash you need this way is probably lots more pleasant than pandering to your local banker or a VC!

- Sometimes, as was the case for Banana Republic with Zimm and East London's Mr. Coble, what you are buying from them may not turn into cash any faster, anyway, so they might as well give you good terms! In dealing with Zimm and Coble, whose goods might well have continued to gather dust if the Zieglers hadn't bought them, it wasn't unreasonable to ask for good terms: 30 days from Zimm in the early days, and 60 days after customs clearance from Coble.

Michael Dell had this kind of customer-funded (and customer-centered) mind-set from day one, as do many of the world's best entrepreneurs. He understood intuitively and instinctively that, in a business that hopes to grow, it's all about satisfied customers and positive cash flow.

> **In a business that hopes to grow, it's all about satisfied customers and positive cash flow.**

Of course, had Dell's customers not believed in the value of what the company offered, he'd never have been able to get them to pay in advance. That's true for your business, too, large or small, old or new. If you're not solving a genuine customer problem or filling a real need—better, faster, cheaper, or whatever—then building a customer-funded business is unlikely to work. As it turns out, pursuing a customer-funded model isn't a bad litmus test of your concept!

Mel and Patricia Ziegler, who began as novices in the world of business, had to learn both about business and the customer-funded mind-set. Fortunately, they learned these things very quickly, thanks in part to a friendly banker who taught them about the other side of the customer-funded coin—vendor terms.

What Angel Investors Will Want to Know—and Will Ask

At some point in the life of your business, if all goes well—as a result, among other things, of having put your customer at the center of your business—you may decide that you need some cash beyond what your customer-funded model is giving you. Michael

Dell eventually needed more than his customers' cash to develop his company's first proprietary PC, the Turbo PC. Fortunately for Dell, his parents coughed up $300,000, the only external capital Dell raised in his early years. The Zieglers also eventually needed more cash to get into manufacturing their own line of safari fashions. Selling the business to The Gap was their answer.

Just as Don Fisher peppered the Zieglers with "due diligence" questions that took them four months to answer to his satisfaction, so, too, will providers of external capital (okay, maybe not if they're your parents, as in Dell's case!) dig deeply into you and your business to understand as much as they can about them both. To such questions we now turn.

> **❝Don Fisher peppered the Zieglers with "due diligence" questions that took them four months to answer to his satisfaction❞**

The questions here are not about pay-in-advance models, which we examine in Chapter 4. They're about a wider set of personal traits and entrepreneurial skills and behaviors that will help an investor, even in a corporate setting, discern whether you have the chutzpah—and the mind-set—to become or continue to be a customer-funded entrepreneur. They are about the journey you will have taken to date and the extent to which what you've done on the journey puts you among those—like Michael Dell and Mel and Patricia Ziegler—about whom people say, "He (or she) is a real entrepreneur." They won't ask all these questions directly, of course. But collectively, just like Don Fisher's due diligence, these questions will pry into your substance—or not—as an entrepreneur. And if you're the angel sitting on the other side of the table, you'd better ask them!

Questions about You As an Individual

There are numerous lessons from the Dell and Banana Republic case histories that illustrate the kinds of things business angels or other investors will want to know about you and your business. If you're a business angel reading this book, these are among the things that *you* should be asking of your prospective investees, not only about their possibly customer-funded model, but about other things, too.

Do You Have the Courage—the Audacity, Even—to Ask for What You Want?

Michael Dell never flinched from asking for the order, and the cash along with it, whether it was *Houston Post* subscriptions or his early souped-up PCs. The Zieglers quickly figured out a shrewd way to get credit terms from Zimmerman, once they learned about the unfamiliar notion—to them, at least—of asking for supplier terms, which was definitely not the norm for startups with no credit history.

In addition, having the audacity to ask your *investor* for what you want, with a sensible logic for why you should get it, is something that too many entrepreneurs flinch from unknowingly. Though your investor may not give you what you want, he or she will probably admire your pluck in asking for it, and will take it as a signal that you'll ask *your* customers and suppliers for what you want.

Is Your Youth (If You're Young) or Your Inexperience an Impediment? Can You Make It an Asset?

If you are young, investors will want to know whether you are naïve, as well ("Yes to both," in the Zieglers' case; "No to the latter," for Michel Dell, who'd been selling things for years, despite his youth). If so, they'll want to know whether that's a problem or not. How will they know? If you've successfully pursued a customer-funded model and won customer traction, you'll have proven that you can build and deliver what you promise, even at your tender age. If you're a creative type, which The Gap's Don Fisher saw in the Zieglers, that trait and a fresh point of view can, at least to some degree, offset your inexperience and turn your fresh perspective into an asset. Besides, starting when you're young—Gates, Zuckerberg, the list is endless— is in some ways far less risky than starting when you've learned how the world, and your industry, really work. No mortgage, and no kids, either. Well, okay, you may have some student loans. But otherwise, when you are young you have little to lose!

> **starting when you're young is in some ways far less risky than starting when you've learned how the world, and your industry, really work**

Do You Have the Courage of Your Convictions to Ignore the Naysayers and Pursue Your Vision?

This is among the most difficult things for an angel to tease out about you. Michael Dell had the courage to cut out the middle-man, and was convincing in explaining why that made sense. The Zieglers' never-say-die attitude got them through one scrape after another. Who says you can't get good vendor terms for a startup with no credit history? These kinds of stories *about you* can only be told once you're some way down the track. But they'll speak volumes about your qualities as an entrepreneur. If you're in a large organization, of course, too much of this sort of behavior may cost you your job!

Are You the Sort of Person Who Turns Lemons into Lemonade?

Murphy (of Murphy's Law) is alive and well on every entrepreneur's management team. Angels will want to know if, when things go wrong, you somehow manage to turn them to your advantage. Such a skill is one that differentiates ordinary people from the best entrepreneurs. Patricia Ziegler made a habit of turning unwanted surplus

> **Angels will want to know if, when things go wrong, you somehow manage to turn them to your advantage.**

items—even size-32-only Gurkha shorts—into must-have-it clothing and accessories, and Don Fisher noticed.

Do you Underpromise and Overdeliver? Or (Sadly) Vice Versa?

Every angel investor can regale friends with outlandish stories of what their investees promised, and what was delivered (less). It goes with the territory. But some entrepreneurs build among their customers, if not their investors, a reputation for overdelivering.

The first customer who ordered from Banana Republic, a man in Bend, Oregon, was sent, along with his Short-Armed Paratrooper Shirt, a certificate embossed with a company seal appointing him Honorary Consul of Banana Republic in Bend, Oregon. Thereafter the first customer in each new town was similarly appointed. Later, Mel or Patricia would scrawl personal notes to their customers and put them in the outgoing boxes, signed by a random minister of the Republic, perhaps the Minister of Progress or the Minister of Propaganda. They made stamps to stencil sayings on the tissue paper wrapping the garments: "In Surplus We Trust" or "One Man's Bush Jacket Is Worth Two Designer Jackets." Checks were stamped "Warning: Contributions to struggling young countries are not tax deductible." The goal was to endear themselves to their customers in ways that normal retailers did not. The Zieglers say it best: "Your customer is your best asset. So over deliver. Our clothes were always better than they needed to be. The fabrics were so good, people are still wearing them 30 years later."[28]

> **Your customer is your best asset. So over deliver.**

Questions about Your Business Sense

The Dell and Banana Republic case histories illustrate additional things that business angels or other investors will want to know about you and your business, including your business acumen.

Do You Understand the Difference between Cash Flow and Profit?

Michael Dell, already an astute if fledgling businessman, understood from the beginning that getting his customers' cash in advance was crucial to growing his business. Cash was what mattered, though gross profit margins mattered, too. The importance of cash was understood by the Zieglers, too, but for a different reason: They simply had no cash to fall back on. They had to build their business on the $1,500 they had scraped together. Their early education about the importance of terms, from their friendly local banker who turned down their loan request, was a pivotal turning point in Banana Republic's journey.

Alas, too many entrepreneurs simply don't understand the difference between cash flow and profit—and too many angels, as well, most of whom have learned about business in large companies or investment banks, where most people are incentivized to earn profit, not cash flow. There, cash is something that comes from the corporate treasury when you ask for it, provided of course that you can show that the return on your project will exceed the company's hurdle rate.

> **❝too many entrepreneurs simply don't understand the difference between cash flow and profit—and too many angels, as well❞**

If you are an entrepreneur, find a backer who understands the importance of terms and the difference between cash flow and profit. If you're an angel, find out whether your aspiring entrepreneur understands that difference. If he or she has been on a customer-funded journey, you can bet your bottom dollar that he or she does. If not, beware.

Do You Have the Courage to "Break the Rules" and Do Things Differently? Or Are You Just Copying What Somebody Else Has Done?

Michael Dell quickly saw the benefits of cutting out the middleman. The economic and other benefits to his company were both obvious and explainable. Even more importantly, there were benefits for the customer of doing so, too, like the lower price and the fact they could get exactly the PC they wanted. At Banana Republic, although the 400 initial catalogs were sent out for free, when WOR Radio called, Patricia quickly priced them at a dollar apiece, knowing how crucial it was that every activity at Banana Republic had to pay its own way. When investors see an entrepreneur who is as careful with their money as the Zieglers were, you can almost feel the relief in their eyes. Investors want their money cared for, too!

Can You Delegate? Or Will You Be a Control Freak?

When Michael Dell made his move into his company's first office that didn't include his bedroom, he still held the keys. Only when someone came to him complaining about having lost a quarter in the Coke machine did Dell fully grasp the importance of delegating. "At that moment I learned the value of giving someone else the key to the Coke machine," Dell recalled.[29] Investors want hands-on founders, but they don't want control freaks. Obsessive control by the founder can get in the way of growing.

> **At that moment I learned the value of giving someone else the key to the Coke machine.**

Have You Identified Your Company's Core Strengths, and Built a Reputation around Them?

Michael Dell went to great lengths to build a reputation for both great customer service and great products. Price was secondary, though it certainly helped. Banana Republic built a reputation for having unique, not-found-anywhere-else merchandise, a tradition it maintained even after the sale to The Gap, as Patricia and the team she put together learned to design Banana Republic's own unique styles. Experienced angels will be calling your customers and asking them why they buy from you. If they get a set of consistent answers that spontaneously say what you stand for, that's good news for you, as it means your company has begun to stake out a reputation for something. If the answers are all over the place, so is your reputation, and your pitch is likely to go straight into the bin.

Have You Built upon and Extended Your Innate Personal Capabilities? In Short, Exactly What Do You Bring to the Party?

Before formally starting his business, Michael Dell had been selling things for years—subscriptions to the *Houston Post* and stamps from his stamp collection, for which he earned $2,000. Selling was in his blood. And that's what his business did: it *sold* PCs, one by one or a few at a time, mostly over the phone in Dell's pre-Internet days. When Don Fisher—a fabulous entrepreneur himself by that time, who knew one when he saw one—was grill-

> **❝ Don Fisher wanted to know what Mel and Patricia brought to the business ❞**

ing the Zieglers at their first meeting to take their measure, he wanted to know what Mel and Patricia brought to the business. "Your store is so creative," he observed. "Do you think you'll be able to keep coming up with new ideas?"[30]

"Ideas are not our problem," Mel replied, redirecting the question.[31] Patricia continued, noting to Fisher a more pressing concern—that they needed to manufacture their own line. Surplus alone was no longer sufficient to meet the growing demand. She knew The Gap, which had by then turned from retailing Levi's to designing its own line of jeans and casual apparel, had already developed and was refining those capabilities. The Zieglers' creativity—Mel's inventive, captivating catalog prose and Patricia's fashion and design sense—was obvious to Fisher, and didn't need to be stated. The fact that Mel had identified the key business problem at that time spoke volumes about whether the two highly creative individuals would be a safe investment.

Questions about Your Target Markets and Marketing

At the end of the day, your fledgling business will be all about customers—identifying the right customers, reaching and attracting them, and somehow convincing them to buy. Investors will want to know—and must ask—whether you deeply understand, and even have empathy for, your customers and their problem that you plan to resolve. And they'll seek evidence—just as Don Fisher did with the Zieglers—that you've already been successful at doing all of the above things.

Do You Know Who Your Target Market Really Is? How Do You Know?

Michael Dell quickly learned that his customers were businesses, mostly small ones at first—doctors, lawyers, and the like—who saw the benefit in getting what was probably their first or second PC, but wanted to save some money in doing so. Small businesses, small budgets. Other customers—larger businesses and government entities, and eventually educators and consumers—came later. The Zieglers saw their target market as individuals of various ages who dressed with a purpose. They wanted authenticity and a sense of adventure in their apparel, from whatever source it was available, even a flea market or secondhand store.

How did Dell and the Zieglers come to know these things? Patricia worked in the first store herself—no hiring a bunch of teenagers seeking afterschool jobs. Michael Dell and his early team sold directly to their customers. The daily sales reports, together with feedback from their direct customer contact, provided detailed information about what Dell's customers were and were not buying.

Have You Segmented Your Market in Sensible Fashion, and Targeted the Right Segment?

Not all customer segments are created equal. Why ask for a difficult sale when the low-hanging fruit is easier to reach? Michael Dell got started with small businesses as his target segment because such people could make their own buying decisions—no bureaucratic pro-

> **Why ask for a difficult sale when the low-hanging fruit is easier to reach?**

cesses there—and because he thought they would value what he had to offer. Only after he'd proven—to himself, most importantly—his capability to deliver did he reach out to other target segments. The Zieglers, once they began to understand their customer, both at the initial Mill Valley store and from tracking zip codes of their catalog customers, knew just where to locate store number two to reach the authentic adventure set in San Francisco.

Investors will ask exactly who your target market comprises. If you'll be selling to businesses, they'll ask to see their names, addresses, phone numbers, and e-mail addresses, too. And if they're smart, they'll call some of them!

Have You Managed to Make Your Business Look Bigger and More Credible Than It Really Is?

When Michael Dell made the decision to offer a then unheard-of 30-day money-back guarantee, he was signaling to his market that his company was credible, and signaling his products' reputation for reliability, too. On the Zieglers' foray into Zimm's competitor's warehouse, her charade as a trust-fund heiress was buttressed when she replied to a request for a Dun and Bradstreet credit report on her company with the rejoinder, "The family prefers not to reveal its assets."[32]

In a Consumer Business, Are You Quirky and Inventive Enough to Get Noticed by the Media?

Marketing, if you have to pay for it, is extremely expensive, and risky, too, as you never know whether the audience will respond. As the

> **Marketing, if you have to pay for it, is extremely expensive, and risky, too**

old saying goes, "I know I'm wasting half of my advertising budget, I just don't know which half!" Investors don't like financing your advertising—and maybe not your sales force, either—for these very reasons. If you've followed a customer-funded model in a consumer setting and developed traction, you've probably done so, at least in part, by finding a way to get noticed in the media, and then playing that notice for all it's worth.

The Zieglers' quirky ways, quirky brand, and quirky merchandise, too, suggested to Fisher that Banana Republic would continue to get noticed. Perhaps Patricia's quirkiest—and most noticeable—gambit came early, not long after the opening of the Mill Valley store. In July 1979, the failing—and soon-to-be falling—American spacecraft Skylab was in the newspapers every day, as it was expected to soon fall into the Earth's atmosphere and scatter 77.5 tons of debris in a shower of flaming metal. An alarmist press, working hard to sell newspapers, of course, had people wondering if such a fragment would end up in their backyard, or worse, in their bedroom one night while they were fast asleep!

Unfortunately, the Zieglers had unintentionally bought at auction a large lot of authentic flight suits that had been buried at the bottom of a container that held some other things, too. Alas, the suits were a bit *too* authentic, containing large and strategically placed rubber gaskets at the breasts and groin, where the tubes for oxygen and other vital functions would have been hooked up. There was no way anyone would have been caught dead in such a suit, Patricia knew. But when *Time* magazine ran an article on Skylab's impending fall, she anonymously called every TV station in the Bay Area, telling them that Banana Republic in Mill Valley had "Skylab Protection Suits" available on a first-come first-served basis. That night Banana Republic was on every TV news show at 6 and 11 PM. No flight suits were sold, but the store was packed for a couple of weeks thereafter!

The Entrepreneurial Process

Neither Michael Dell nor the Zieglers started their businesses by the conventional process sometimes taught these days in school. They didn't write business plans. And they didn't search for investors to provide the cash they would need, minimal though it was, to start their businesses. Instead they just got started, with their own meager resources and their customers' cash, and learned by doing as the journey unfolded. "There were obviously no classes on learning how to start and run a business in my high school," recalls Dell. "So clearly I had a lot to learn. The more mistakes I made, the faster I learned."[33] By offering what their customers wanted and were willing to pay for—sometimes in advance, and *always* before their suppliers were paid—both companies were able to prove to their founders and eventually to others that their businesses held enormous potential.

> **The more mistakes I made, the faster I learned.**

The lessons we've just gleaned from their journeys that began in 1978 and 1983—summarized in the checklist that follows—are no different, really, than the lessons that twenty-first-century entrepreneurs are learning today. As both case histories show, getting cash from your customers before your suppliers must be paid is a time-tested strategy that's certainly not new. But it's no mirage, either—the vast majority of today's fast-growing companies are started, financed, and grown in this manner, not with venture capital!

Happily, today's entrepreneurs have invented creative twists on age-old customer-funded practices, and it's now time to turn our attention to their stories and the lessons they hold for *you*, whether you're an aspiring entrepreneur, an angel, or someone trying to get your slow-growing company moving again. The next five chapters address each of the models, one at a time. And as this chapter has done, they tease out questions that angel investors (perhaps even corporate treasurers, too) will ask with regard to each of those models—or should ask, if they wish to be among the relatively few angels who actually earn decent financial returns from their investments. Are you ready for the journey? Is your mind-set right? Might one of the five models work to get *your* business, or that of one of your prospective investees, off the ground? Read on!

John's Business Angel Checklist—The Mind-Set of a Customer-Funded Entrepreneur

Questions about You as an Individual

- Do you have the courage—the audacity, even—to ask for what you want?
- Is your youth (if you're young) or inexperience an impediment? Can you make it an asset?
- Do you have the courage of your convictions to ignore the naysayers and pursue your vision?
- Are you the sort of person who turns lemons into lemonade?
- Do you underpromise and overdeliver? Or (sadly) vice versa?

Questions about Your Business Sense

- Do you understand the difference between cash flow and profit?
- Do you have the courage to "break the rules" and do things differently? Or are you just copying what somebody else has done before?
- Can you delegate? Or will you be a control freak?
- Have you identified your company's core strengths, and built a reputation around them?

- Have you built upon and extended your innate personal capabilities? In short, exactly what do *you* bring to the party?

Questions about Your Target Markets and Marketing

- Do you know who your target market really is? How do you know?
- Have you segmented your market in sensible fashion, and targeted the right segment?
- Have you managed to make your business look bigger and more credible than it really is?
- In a consumer business, are you quirky and inventive enough to get noticed by the media?

3

Buyers and Sellers, but Not *Your* Goods: Matchmaker Models

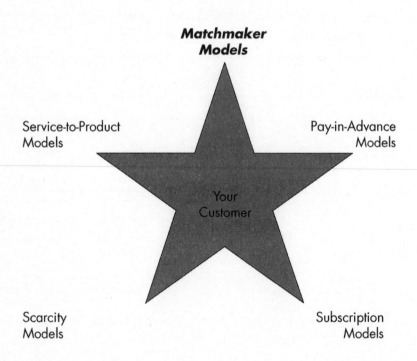

Matchmaker Models

Service-to-Product Models

Pay-in-Advance Models

Your Customer

Scarcity Models

Subscription Models

E very business sells something, of course. Wouldn't it be nice if, in your business, you didn't have to pay anything for what you sell? If you think about it, even for a moment, you'll conclude that doing business this way isn't rocket science. After all, this is what real estate agents and many other kinds of brokers have been doing forever. They don't *buy* the house you want to sell, or the apartment that you want to rent to others. But they do help you sell it, or rent it, and when they have done so, we pay them a commission or fee for their services.

Let's think about such a business from the Realtor's perspective. What sort of investment does he or she need to get into that business? Some business cards, a cell phone, and a network that will provide some properties to sell or rent and generate some prospective customers. Total investment? Other than the founders' time, virtually nil.

Matchmakers (sometimes called marketplaces), like the proverbial Cupid on Valentine's Day, do exactly what a Realtor does. *Matchmaker models are those in which the business, with no or limited investment up front, brings together buyers and sellers*—without *actually owning what is bought and sold*—and facilitates and completes transactions, earning fees or commissions for doing so. Those commissions or fees can, in theory at least, come from either the seller, the buyer, or both parties. As the power of the Internet became apparent in the late twentieth century, visionary entrepreneurs built matchmaker companies like eBay and Expedia, and they built many of them with virtually no investment to get started, because they had no need to buy what they were going to sell. Most were customer funded.

In Chapter 3, we examine the case histories of three twenty-first-century matchmakers, each of which has harnessed the power of the Web in inventive ways to bring together buyers and sellers in the markets they serve. As the cost of software development has plummeted, and as easy-to-use templates have become available on which to build these and other kinds of Web-based businesses, it has become extremely inexpensive to launch such a business. And if you can write code yourself, it may cost nothing at all!

"if you can write code yourself, it may cost nothing at all!"

Airbnb, as practically anyone under 40 knows, brings together buyers who need a place to stay or vacation and sellers who have such places they wish to rent, anything from a bed or a spare bedroom to an island villa in the sun-soaked Caribbean. DogVacay brings together pet-owner buyers who need their pet cared for temporarily (perhaps while they are away on an Airbnb holiday!) by trusted pet lovers who would be happy to look after other people's pets. ProFounder sought to bring together—past tense here, as they failed, for reasons we'll soon see—young companies that needed funding with sources of funding. Each of their stories holds lessons to be learned, not only for entrepreneurs seeking to build new matchmaker companies, but also for angel investors who are asked to back them, as well as for those in established companies who would be well placed to bring buyers and sellers together in this way.

For established companies, if you think about it, nearly every such company, whether it sells goods or services, has both buyers (its customers) and is a seller. But most of the time the seller either makes or buys whatever it sells. Such companies stand to be disrupted by Web-based players with lower cost structures that don't own the goods or services they sell, like eBay and Airbnb. The good news is that these companies already have the networks of customers they need—their current customers—to start a matchmaker business and do their own disrupting. What they lack are other providers on the sell-side—their competitors. Could some of these companies—yes, perhaps *yours*?—be the disrupters of their own cozy or not-so-cozy industries? Time will tell, but it might be worth considering building a matchmaker model and being the disrupter, rather than the eventual disruptee!

From Airbeds on the Floor to Silicon Valley Darling: Airbnb

In August of 2007, Joe Gebbia and Brian Chesky were struggling to come up with the rent soon due on their San Francisco apartment. If you're young and in the arts world, and don't have real jobs, coming up with the rent money each month isn't always easy. Drawing on the "creativity can solve problems" mantra of the Rhode Island School of Design, from which they had graduated a few years earlier, Gebbia and Chesky found a problem they thought they could solve, and earn some rent money in the process.

A large design conference was coming to town, and San Francisco simply didn't have enough hotel rooms to accommodate everyone. The city was already booked solid. Chesky tells the story: "We thought we could make some money if we rented out our place and turned it into a bed and breakfast. We got three airbeds and created a website called 'Air Bed and Breakfast.' People signed up to rent the airbeds, and we cooked them breakfast every morning and acted like tour guides. We didn't mean to start a business. It just sort of happened. There was no flash of genius. In the beginning, we didn't realize that this would be the big idea. It was the thing that would pay the rent until we thought of the big idea."[1]

Getting Customers Who Will Part with Their Cash: More Difficult Than It Appears

Several additional—and largely disappointing—launches later, and despite the addition of a third founding partner, programmer and friend Nathan Blecharczyk, there was little to show for their efforts, and Chesky had racked up $15,000 on his credit cards.[2] Their hoped-for customers and their cash were proving very hard to get! Launching a website is easy, the trio discovered.

Inexpensive, too, if you write your own code, as Blecharczyk did. And if your launch goes nowhere, the good thing is you can launch again! And again! But if nobody notices your site, then what's the use? For the design conference in San Francisco, they had sent news of their first website to design bloggers, a tactic that had worked well enough to get noticed by the three guests they hosted. But getting visibility for conferences they knew little about was proving more difficult. Matching buyers and sellers looked great in concept, but getting the attention of either group wasn't easy, they were learning.

> **if your launch goes nowhere, the good thing is you can launch again!**

Getting Attention

In 2008, the team decided that the upcoming Democratic National Convention in Denver in August might provide an opportunity to jumpstart their struggling business. With 100,000 visitors expected, many of them youthful and enthusiastic supporters of candidate Barack Obama, it seemed like a good thing to do. With only 30,000 hotel rooms available, plus lots of press coverage expected, perhaps there was a chance they could attract more listings and users and obtain some sorely needed PR. They enlisted a small army of locals to sign up spare bedrooms and prepared for the expected onslaught of delegates and other visitors.[3]

Getting publicity does not happen by magic, however. The media are in the business of bringing attention—hence readership—to their newspapers, broadcasts, blogs, and so on. In doing so, they are always on the lookout for quirky, offbeat, and newsworthy stories that will break through the clutter and get their readers to share what they've read with other readers. If they do so successfully, *their own* audiences grow, just as the Airbnb team was hoping to grow its own following. So, how might a company like Airbnb break through in Denver?

Recognizing that the business was in dire need of not just PR, but funding, too, the team came up with a creative—and customer-

> **the business was in dire need of not just PR, but funding, too**

funded—scheme: selling keepsake boxes of breakfast cereal. But not just any breakfast cereal. Co-founder Joe Gebbia explained, "We made 500 of each (Obama O's and Cap'n McCain's). They were a numbered edition on the top of each box, and sold for $40 each. The Obama O's sold out, netting the funds the team needed to keep Airbnb alive. The Cap'n McCain's—"a maverick in every bite," as the box proclaimed—"they didn't sell quite as well, and we ended up eating them to save money on food." [4] But after Gebbia was interviewed on CNN about the quirky stunt, things started to look up.[5] Fortunately there was a lot of publicity about the fact that getting a hotel room was nigh on impossible, and word started to spread to other media about Airbnb's business, too.

Though this stunt had nothing to do with their core business—other than the second "b" in its name suggesting they might deal in breakfast—it served its purpose of providing some customer funding to continue operations! With their number of listings rising and a little customer-provided cash now on hand, they decided to go on a national tour and talk with their growing but still very modest community of users, in an effort to spur word-of-mouth communication, which was all they could afford.[6] A short while later, they applied to join the winter 2009 class at the elite seed accelerator Y Combinator back in California. In accepting them and providing Airbnb's first external equity investment of $20,000, Paul Graham noted that it was the story of the Obama O's and Cap'n McCain's that convinced him that the Airbnb team had the chutzpah to do whatever it would take to build a successful business.[7] Some quirky promotion, a couple of maxed-out credit cards, and a very modest amount of their customers' cash had taken Airbnb this far. Being quirky can work out nicely with investors, too!

> **Being quirky can work out nicely with investors, too!**

Takeoff at Last: The VCs Pile In!

In the fertile soil of Y Combinator and Silicon Valley, life soon got better for Airbnb. Sequoia Capital invested $600,000 in a seed round in April 2009, and then followed with a Series A round in November 2010, alongside several other investors.[8] These investments permitted the team to invest in growing their list of properties for rent, and their renter base, too. In July 2011, they raised a further $112 million from Andreessen Horowitz and Amazon's Jeff Bezos, among others, at a lofty valuation of $1 billion.[9] Some of these funds were then spent on acquisitions of mostly copycat companies in other regions, rapidly expanding Airbnb's reach.

Why did a young company that had struggled in its early years become the darling of Silicon Valley so quickly? *Fortune* technology writer Jessi Hempel says it's all about their ability to generate cash from customers efficiently: "Financiers insist that they were drawn to Airbnb's revenue model and growth potential, not its glam factor. Unlike a number of other social websites, Airbnb generated cash right from the start. Why? A very modest cost structure—building and maintaining a website doesn't cost much these days—and no inventory, either, as Airbnb didn't own the spaces that it booked. It charges a commission of 6% to 12% on every transaction, landing it a reported $500 million in 2011 revenue."[10] As Y Combinator's Paul Graham points out, "They're very capital efficient. They would make an investor's money go a long way."[11] Capital efficiency is something investors love!

> **They're very capital efficient. They would make an investor's money go a long way.**

Contrast that with other social businesses like Facebook or Twitter, which needed years to figure out how to monetize their admittedly very large audiences. But the investments in Airbnb never would have happened without the company's earlier customer funding from fees charged to happy Airbnb customers, along with judicious use of the founders' credit cards, and of course their creativity and willingness to do whatever it took, including selling cereal to cover expenses.

By December 2013, Airbnb listed more than 500,000 properties in 34,000 cities in 192 countries—for spare bedrooms, villas, yurts, and the occasional tree house.[12] At one point, there was even a tent available at the front of the line awaiting the opening of an Apple store for its newest iPhone release.[13]

Matchmaking Works for Dogs, Too: DogVacay

When their owners are away, Rambo and Rocky, like most dogs, would rather spend their time almost anywhere else than in a cramped chain-link cage at a kennel. Like other dogs, they love to take walks, run, or play with others, whether dogs or people. In 2011, Rambo and Rocky's owners, who were planning yet another short trip away from their dogs, found a dog trainer who was watching dogs and had a big yard. Aaron Hirschhorn recalls how much better that experience was for him, for his then partner and now wife, Karine, and for their two rambunctious dogs. "It was great. I loved it, the dogs got socialization and were in a social environment. They are, at the end of the day, pack animals. We thought to ourselves, this would be a great idea to try out on our own."[14]

Aaron's business background—an MBA from UCLA and a few years in the venture capital industry in Los Angeles—was enough to pique his interest in the pet industry. He had "looked at some other related businesses like kennels, so it was in the back of my mind but I wasn't deep in the process."[15] His research showed that there were 78 million dogs in the United States, and that $5 billion was spent on pet sitting, of a total U.S. pet-related trade valued at $51 billion—all in a highly fragmented market.

Karine jumped at the idea, not least because she and Aaron were about to marry, and these days, weddings don't come cheap! Their personal need for better dog accommodation when they traveled, the apparently large potential market, and their love of dogs led them to decide they wouldn't mind having some more dogs around—up to six at a time—in exchange for some extra income. So they put a listing on Yelp offering dog-sitting services, and "all of a sudden we were getting five or six calls a day," Aaron recalls.[16]

With no marketing spend, the couple earned $30,000 in customer cash in just eight months. Aaron's Dog Boarding, as the couple's service was known, won glowing reviews on Yelp from dog owners like Wendy, an early customer of what would become DogVacay: "Our beagle is very important to us, and we couldn't have been more impressed with Aaron and Karine! They have such a warm and loving environment. While of course safety and comfort is of utmost concern for my pets, knowing that they're being loved and given affection is a HUGE priority. Thank you for taking care of our baby!"[17] But there was a limit to how many dogs the Hirschhorns could care for themselves, so they soon got to wondering if they could build a business connecting dog lovers who could care for another few dogs with their traveling owners.

> **With no marketing spend, the couple earned $30,000 in customer cash in just eight months.**

A Genuine Consumer Problem to Solve

"You're a dog owner," explains Aaron, "and when you travel you have two options. One, is you can go and put your dog in the kennel, which tends to be overpriced, where your dogs are generally in a cage 23 hours a day, and where the owner feels really guilty. That's option one. Option two, is you can ask friends or family members to pet sit. Although that often works out, you're having to call in a favor, which makes you feel bad, you might have to drive a lot, and there's guilt associated with doing that as well."[18] Kennels were very expensive, too. "Would you rather spend $55 a night to put your dog in a cage with 50 other yapping dogs with not a single person consistently taking care of them?" Hirschhorn asks. "Versus $25 a night in a real home with a family and three walks a day?"[19]

"It was how much demand there was for the service and how much people were willing to pay that boggled my mind," Aaron recalls, still somewhat amazed. "Not only that, the fact that it was so easy to set up. It didn't need anything. *At all!* We didn't spend a penny on marketing and we just put up a Yelp listing. We didn't need to invest any money into dog proofing or anything like that. How many businesses are there where you don't need to do anything to set up, you're following the same routine you follow with your own dog and you make money without spending on marketing."[20]

> **How many businesses are there where you don't need to do anything to set up?**

The positive response to their offering encouraged Aaron and Karine to move forward. As Aaron describes, "We started unraveling our jobs, building a prototype product, making a little video and getting the word out there. Once you do that and people start to see that you've left an opportunity because it's your passion to build this business then you start to get a bit of reception."[21] Given Aaron's experience in the venture capital industry—and having already drunk the VC Kool-Aid—he figured he could switch to the other side of the table and raise some seed capital. A new incubator in Santa Monica, in the heart of the growing entrepreneurial cluster known as Silicon Beach, saw merit in the Hirschhorns' idea.

Seed Capital

Science, as the incubator was called, had set out to put into place a systematic process to build startups, and to bring more venture capital money to Los Angeles. It wanted to focus on companies that would actually deliver revenue from the get-go, unlike many dot-com investors—and entrepreneurs, too—who figure it's all about eyeballs and users, leaving revenue as an unimportant detail to be worked out later. Describing the experience of Triple Thread CEO Allan Jones, whose company joined the incubator in 2012, TechCrunch says, "The program's focus is to help build businesses that have meaningful revenue. And where they are doing this, he adds, is in industries that are stale and boring and often overlooked."[22]

Having already demonstrated the power of his business to generate meaningful cash from its customers, Aaron thought Science, which had raised $10 million in 2011, would be a perfect fit to finance the next stage of his journey. Taking a small investment from Science in November 2011, he set about building a real business with his investors' support. His new team began building a website and creating a blog that would be chock full of content: how to prepare to be a DogVacay host, how to take care of multiple dogs, and more. He struck a deal with VCA Antech, the country's largest provider of veterinary services, in case a dog had an emergency medical issue while being cared for by a DogVacay host.[23]

As with the original pair of Airbnb founders, the Hirschhorns probably could have found a Nathan Blecharczyk and gone it alone, since they already had evidence that customers would be willing to pay, and as we've seen, that's a recipe for a customer-funded model. But as Aaron saw things, the value of having Science help develop the idea was twofold:

- First, Science helped him build an actual, usable product and interface. Writing code and building websites were not part of his skill set, nor was selecting someone who could do that job well.
- Second, the credibility and connections Science brought for fundraising turned out to be extremely valuable.

Hirschhorn expected to find himself at some point in a race to reach scale.

But Would You Trust Your Dog with a Stranger?

As dog lovers themselves, the Hirschhorns knew that entrusting a stranger with the care of a much-loved pet was going to require far more trust than a typical Internet transaction. "This is not like finding someone on Craigslist," said Aaron.[24] With

> **❝This is not like finding someone on Craigslist. ❞**

trust in mind, and with the capabilities of Web 2.0 well understood, both technically and in the marketplace, the team built a system to verify the qualifications of their hosts and to perform other important functions.

- First, Facebook Connect and LinkedIn would be used to verify identities—for the dog owners and hosts, of course, not the dogs—and would help identify prospective customers for new hosts who signed up.
- Training would be provided to hosts using online instructional videos and multiple-choice tests.
- Host credentials—such as CPR certification, relevant professional associations, or vet tech backgrounds—would be posted, and hosts interviewed as well.
- DogVacay would provide insurance, too.

Post-transaction, there would be reviews of the hosts and their homes, as well as reviews of the guest dogs! Aaron explained the rationale: "This dog barks a lot, so maybe you shouldn't book that dog if your neighbor complains. Or maybe it's not a problem if the dog barks a lot, because you are in a big open ranch. With those things layered together, we believe we can really help owners and hosts make the right decision on how to take care of their pets. On top of that, if things look great but you really want to meet first, we support that as well. We have a meet and greet function where you can schedule a meeting, introduce the dogs to each other, see the home, and that way have complete peace of mind."[25]

Launch and More Funding

Concurrently with the launch of the DogVacay website (following the earlier Aaron's Dog Boarding Yelp page) in March 2012, DogVacay was able, thanks to the customer traction already seen and the investors' belief in the opportunity overall, to raise $1 million in seed funding from Andreessen Horowitz (fresh off of Airbnb's $112 million round less than a year earlier) and other investors. Hosts were free to set their own prices according to their experience, the type of accommodation they offered, and characteristics of the dog(s) they would care for, though fees for a small apartment were likely to be lower than fees where there was a large meadow to roam. The site charged a 3 to 10 percent fee of each transaction on the site, depending on user reviews for the host and frequency of use. For its "star" hosts who generated a large number of positive reviews and more frequent use, DogVacay took a fee at the lower end of the range.

The Sellers—Dog-Sitters—Like DogVacay, Too

It's not just the dogs and their owners who benefit from DogVacay. The dog-sitters love it, too. Sabrina Hernandez, a student at San Francisco State University, charges $40 per night to sit for dogs in her apartment. She earned $1,200 per month on average during the fall semester of 2012, cramming all of her classes into two days each week to free up the rest of the week for dog-sitting. She likes her new job a whole lot better than her old one as a barista at Starbucks. And it pays a lot better, too![26]

More Fuel in the Tank

Eight months after its launch, in November 2012, DogVacay raised a Series A round of $6 million, this time from Benchmark Capital.[27] By its one-year anniversary in March 2013, DogVacay had paid out more than $1 million to its hosts, who according to the company earned an average of $500 per month for hosting some 12,000 stays averaging about five nights per stay.[28] In October 2013, a Series B round of another $15 million followed.[29]

DogVacay's founders have been careful about launching into new cities, to ensure there is sufficient supply when they go live. As Aaron notes, "We want to make sure we have enough qualified hosts in every area for consumers when we open the door. We want them to have multiple options and choices. The second thing, is that because these are regular people, plans change. Sometime, they have to make a last minute cancellation, and you never know what can happen. So we establish a set of first responders in each area, who we can effectively call upon if someone cancels at the last minute, if someone has to be picked up and moved . . . Our approach is to really go city by city so that we can be sure."[30] After a blitz to line up sufficient supply, they quickly launched in New York, just six weeks after their West coast (San Francisco and Los Angeles) launch. By the end of 2013, with the business still less than two years old, the DogVacay website listed more than 10,000 hosts in more than 100 U.S. cities, and some in Canada, too.[31] Clearly, the Hirschhorns have uncovered a matchmaker model with legs—four of them—despite having abandoned their initial customer-funded approach in favor of the siren song of venture capital.

A Missed Opportunity for a Customer-Funded Matchmaker Model: ProFounder

Stanford Graduate School of Business classmates Jessica Jackley and Dana Mauriello wanted to start a business together, and their complementary backgrounds led to a novel idea. Jackley, co-founder of Kiva, a thriving online peer-to-peer microlending organization that connects projects and small businesses in the developing world with lenders in the West, had already learned how to utilize the Web to build a matchmaker business. Mauriello had grown up in a family that had started and run a number of small businesses.

Jackley recalls the initial inspiration for their venture. "We started thinking of how to better serve small businesses in the United States and realized there was a big gap in an easy way for small businesses to get the funding that they needed to succeed. Yes, there were loans and a lot of people might think at first blush why don't you go to a venture capitalist or angel investors or get a line of credit? But it turns out the vast majority of private companies are funded by friends and families, and there's really no easy or clean way to do this."[32] At business school, in the heart of the entrepreneurial hotbed of Silicon Valley, they were also witnessing classmates raising seed capital from one another. Some quick desk research confirmed that the friends-and-family market for startup capital was a large one, to the tune of more than $100 billion annually in the United States alone.[33]

> **We started thinking of how to better serve small businesses in the United States.**

Thinking Big

So, in the summer of 2009, Jackley and Mauriello got to work. Their first several months were spent understanding the thicket of laws—both federal and in all 50 states—that governed how and from what other parties a startup was allowed to seek capital. Or, to put it more accurately, how and from whom *not* to raise capital.

> **it seemed that a startup was generally not allowed to widely solicit others for capital**

Simply put, it seemed that a startup was generally not allowed to widely solicit others for capital, without an extraordinary amount of cumbersome documentation and legal expense. The idea behind these regulations was to protect the ordinary person from unscrupulous entrepreneurs who might take their money, never to be seen again. In situations where entrepreneurs *were* permitted to ask others for capital, they could only attract a small *number* of investors, and those investors were required to be, in lay terms, already well heeled.

But Jackley and Mauriello found an opening in the regulatory jungle. The U.S. Securities and Exchange Commission (SEC), in Rule 504, Regulation D, did permit offers of securities (i.e., startup capital) to an unlimited number of unaccredited investors (i.e., not already rich), provided that three conditions held true:

1. The business would raise not more than $1 million over a span of time not to exceed 12 months.
2. The funds would be raised entirely from people with whom the entrepreneur had a "substantial and pre-existing relationship." Family and friends were okay. Strangers, or high-net-worth individuals you met in an elevator, were not.
3. The capital-raising activity violated no state laws in the state(s) in which it was raised.

This regulatory opening would make it possible, they believed, to build a Web-based business that would facilitate the process of raising capital from one's friends and family, the $100 billion market that the two had discovered. ProFounder would provide a "pitch creator tool" and template documents that were compliant with the laws at both state and federal levels. More importantly for the entrepreneur, it would provide a platform where entrepreneurs could host their offering; invite their friends and family via e-mail to invest, on terms that were specified by the entrepreneur (based on a revenue-share model where the "investor" would get a small percentage share of future revenues, not equity); and collect the funds. ProFounder would track the e-mails, for easy follow-up; keep track of the number of investors who signed up in each state, which was regulated in some states; and make sure the entrepreneur knew which forms had to be filed and what fees had to be paid, and to whom. In short, ProFounder would take all the hassle out of raising a friends-and-family round, as long as it was for less than $1 million.

> **❝ProFounder would take all the hassle out of raising a friends-and-family round ❞**

Notably, other crowdfunding sites that were coming onto the scene, like Kickstarter and Indiegogo, did not offer to raise funds where equity or other financial obligations were given in return, as they either had not discovered or had chosen to ignore the opportunity made possible by the Rule 504 loophole.

Proof of Concept

To prove to themselves their idea would work, Jackley and Mauriello set out to facilitate some deals. By November 2010, they had helped five entrepreneurs raise a total of $155,000 from 108 investors.[34] In December they formally launched the ProFounder site, and by April 2011 they had facilitated 14 deals for more than $350,000 in aggregate. Another 530 pending deals were listed on the site at that time.[35] This sounds like a very good start, but ProFounder's deal with its investors was to take about 5 percent of funds raised. So revenue, based on the modest sums raised for its customers to date, amounted to only around $25,000. It was customer funding, to be sure, but not very much of it.

Was ProFounder Really Pursuing a Matchmaker Model?

With family and friends as ProFounder's fundraising targets, one might ask whether theirs was actually a matchmaker model. After all, weren't the "matches" with family and friends already in place? Was Profounder, instead, a provider of simpler legal paperwork and compliance advice that costly lawyers otherwise would have had to provide? In fact, was it really a customer-funded business at all? An enormous amount of legal due diligence, along with building a website to reflect and comply with federal and state requirements, was necessary if they wanted to enact their plan of launching on a 50-state basis. In Jackley's words, the model "is going to be something we can perpetuate far and wide,"[36] and in Mauriello's, their goal was "to empower as many people as we can to pursue their dreams through entrepreneurship."[37] That work was funded by an early $1.35 million of seed capital, not by customers.[38] But all that legal and systems work, and the funding to support it, meant that ProFounder was not really a matchmaker business, as defined in this book. A marketplace? Yes, it was. But a customer-funded matchmaker? No.

> **"was it really a customer-funded business at all?"**

A Pivot to Plan B

In May 2011, with progress still modest, Profounder launched an additional fundraising structure for family and friends, once again permitted by Rule 504.[39] But changing the details of the product did not solve ProFounder's problem, and on February 17, 2012, ProFounder announced that it was shutting down. As the founders reported on their blog, "Despite our progress, the current regulatory environment prevents us from pursuing the innovations we feel would be most valuable to our customers, and we've made the decision to shut down the company."[40]

Why Didn't ProFounder Succeed?

When businesses fail, that usually means there is too little cash coming in or too much cash going out. In ProFounder's case, the key cash flow problem was on the revenue side. There just weren't enough transactions to provide a meaningful source of revenue,

❝In ProFounder's case, the key cash flow problem was on the revenue side.❞

given the small slice that Pro-Founder would take of what turned out to typically be an average friends-and-family round of only $25,000 to $30,000, a far smaller typical raise than the founders might have imagined. Too few transactions for too-small ticket sizes spelled disaster for ProFounder.

Could ProFounder have been successful had it followed a different, customer-funded strategy? One never knows what the road not taken would have brought, of course. But it is at least plausible that, by starting with a much narrower focus (say, only California) like DogVacay's focus on one city at a time, they could have avoided most of the complex legal and systems investment required to do business in 50 states. Further, the web-savvy and entrepreneurial California culture might have seen such a venture as cool. Was it an opportunity missed? We'll never know the answer, of course, and as we saw in Chapter 1, the jury on equity-based crowdfunding remains out.

What Angel Investors Will Want to Know—And Will Ask

Some readers may be thinking around now, "Actually, ProFounder wasn't really a customer-funded business. So why

❝Not all marketplace businesses are customer fundable.❞

is its story here?" Good observation, and an important one. Not all marketplace businesses are customer fundable. Those that *are* capable of becoming a customer-funded matchmaker business are those that can get by with little up-front investment to begin matching buyers and sellers. Writing (or buying) code that can get the matchmaking underway costs little these days, so that part is usually easy. For ProFounder, though, the dream was to provide its service in all 50 U.S. states, an ambition that demanded a considerable effort in legal due diligence, alongside an extensive IT system that would ensure that any given match was legally compliant, both federally and locally. Those efforts were too much to fund with a couple of MBA students' credit cards or the proceeds of the first customers' matches.

Fortunately, there are plenty of verticals that have not yet been addressed by the likes of Airbnb in accommodations or DogVacay in pet-sitting. Thus the door is wide open for *you* to discover a vertical that's right for you. The case histories examined in this chapter point to some fundamental lessons about matchmaker models:

- Matchmaker models, as least when delivered online, are winner-take-all businesses. One or at most a very few players will likely dominate any vertical. Thus achieving liquidity—the solution to the chicken-and-egg problem that you can't get users without having inventory to sell them, but you can't get sellers without an audience that will buy—is crucial.
- Such models are best driven by network effects, where players—on the buyer's side, on the seller's side, or ideally on both—have natural incentives to bring more players to the party.
- Trust is important, but it's more important in some match-making settings—someone using your home (via Airbnb), for example, or driving your car (via a car-sharing website like RelayRides)—than in others, such as somebody buying your well-used BBQ grill on eBay.

These realities of matchmaker models will lead those from whom you may seek investment at some point to ask some probing questions. They also mean that, with so many aspiring entrepreneurs eager to imitate eBay or Airbnb, it's likely that you'll need to raise capital, perhaps sooner rather than later, in order for *you* to win the race in your chosen vertical. Having proven your model with customer traction will surely help you do so. Airbnb raised its first investment capital only 18 months after its initial market test on its founders' apartment floor; DogVacay did so within a few months of the Hirschhorns' completion of the eight-month test of Aaron's Boarding Service. Customer funding, and for Airbnb a couple of maxed-out credit cards as well, got both businesses well enough down the track that investors soon stepped up. So, what will angel investors want to know when *you* come calling, with early signs of customer traction in hand?

❝ So, what will angel investors want to know when *you* come calling, with early signs of customer traction in hand? ❞

Why Is Your Business Likely to Be the Winner That "Takes All"?

Odds are that somebody down the street or up the coast has the same idea you have, perhaps with the same customer traction you've achieved when you get around to seeking capital. DogVacay got its first million dollars of external capital in Los Angeles in March 2012. Rover.com, a very similar business based in Seattle, won $3.4 million in VC backing one month later. The footrace was on!

You'll almost surely need capital if you're to win the footrace, so experienced investors will want to know why it is *you* who will win. The key is liquidity, and whether *you* can achieve it. As Greylock Partners' Simon Rothman notes, "Liquidity isn't the most important thing. It's the only thing."[41] Liquidity, as Rothman defines it, is "the reasonable expectation of selling something you list or finding what you're looking for."[42] Since you will, hopefully, via your early customer-funded efforts, already enjoy some level of customer traction by the time you seek capital, here are some benchmarks Rothman says make sense, so that you—or your prospective backer—can discern whether the likely winner is *you*:

- Conversion rates between 30 and 60 percent (among buyers seeking to make a match) are reasonable to expect. If the average selling price in your vertical is relatively high, then a conversion rate in the lower part of this range may be acceptable.
- If it is difficult to find your goods elsewhere, a conversion rate in the lower part of this range may be acceptable.
- If prices in your vertical are widely dispersed, that's an indicator that liquidity has not been achieved.

Almost always a key challenge in achieving liquidity is getting enough sellers on board to attract buyers to your site. Perhaps counterintuitively, an intensely narrow focus can help conquer this challenge—serving design professionals headed for San Francisco on a particular weekend, or dog owners in Los Angeles. When your target includes "everybody" it's much more difficult to reach them, and it's less likely that buyers looking for matches will fund sufficient depth in the right kind of sellers to make them—a host in one city does a dog owner in another city no good. Investors will want to know that you can think—and act— narrowly, but also that your scope has the potential, as with DogVacay's now 100-plus cities, to get much wider very fast.

To What Extent Are You Addressing a Compelling Problem for at Least One Side of the Buyer–Seller Dyad, As Evidenced by Network Effects?

You're likely to get referrals, and thereby "go viral," either on the buyer's side or the seller's side, if you are solving a genuine problem for buyers, sellers, or ideally, both. "Are you seeing net- work effects?" angels will ask.

ßß Are you seeing network effects? Evidence, please! ϩϩ

"Evidence, please!" Airbnb, in its early days, provided lodging where it was otherwise undersupplied. Moreover, Airbnb put cash into its hosts' pockets during a crushing recession, a problem that cash-starved hosts were eager to solve and whose solution they shared with their similarly cash-starved friends.

DogVacay worked similarly, solving a problem of where to put Rocky and Rambo that was real for dog owners. Indeed, early DogVacay investor First Round Capital's managing partner, Howard Morgan, said, "First Round Capital looks for innovative ways the web can disrupt large and inefficient markets, especially those with high rates of dissatisfaction like dog boarding. With DogVacay, we see a very unique way to leverage a passionate community of dog lovers into a collaborative network that gives dog owners a better solution to the $10 billion pet services market."[43] As with Airbnb, DogVacay puts cash—sometimes a considerable amount of recurring cash—into its hosts' pockets. In the case of Sabrina Hernandez, it beat working for Starbucks!

On the other hand, ProFounder arguably wasn't addressing a compelling problem, either on the buyer's or seller's side. Due to SEC regulations, they had to rely on their entrepreneurs' existing networks, which the entrepreneurs probably didn't need a web platform to tap. No compelling problem there. What about the supposed legal complexities of taking friends-and-family money? Was this as difficult as the Profounder founders had assumed? "Assume" is always a dangerous word. In the words of an entrepreneur, it usually means, "I don't have any real evidence for this, but . . ." Was there evidence to that effect, or did they simply *assume* it was so? Probably no compelling problem there, either. Last, it is difficult to imagine what benefit, if any, they were bringing to the capital provider on the other side of the deal table. The best matchmaker opportunities, like DogVacay, solve genuine problems on *both* sides of the transaction. Does *yours*?

> **❝The best matchmaker opportunities solve genuine problems on *both* sides of the transaction. Does *yours*?❞**

Is There an Overpriced and Poor Existing Market Structure That You Plan to Disrupt?

Part of DogVacay's early success was probably because the existing behavior—putting your dog in a kennel—is both unsatisfactory to dog owners *and* expensive. Offering an alternative that is *both* materially better *and* significantly cheaper isn't good just in matchmaker businesses, of course. But for matchmakers, it helps get early customer traction to fund a nascent business.

What Level of Trust Will Be Necessary in Your Vertical, and How Will You Ensure It?

The long-run success of matchmaker businesses requires that there be fair dealing and minimal risks as transactions take place. But, for Airbnb's hosts, clearly there are risks, like the time an Airbnb renter ransacked the host's apartment, causing extensive damage.[44] In another case, two Swedish women unknowingly rented their Stockholm apartment to what turned out to be a pair of well-dressed prostitutes, who were happy to have a place of business from which to operate while the Swedes were on a month-long vacation.[45] If the renters had not been busted, and the police not left them a note, the hosts probably would never have known about how their apartment had been used!

Establishing trust is central, but it also brings other upsides, including the ability to establish a trusted platform from which other goods or services can be offered. As Michael Jones, CEO of DogVacay's first backer Science, says, "By establishing a trusted community of dog-lovers, it's inevitable the site will roll out other unique products and services."[46]

Repeat Purchase Behavior: What Will Prevent Repeat Customers from "Going Direct" for Future Purchases?

Matchmakers need to worry about whether they can keep their buyers doing future business through the matchmaker, or whether buyers will simply go around them and deal directly with a seller they discover they like. This behavior is more likely in a frequently purchased situation—like housing your dog while you are away—than one in which purchases tend to be one-off, like buying something on eBay. This is one of these rare instances in business where repeat purchases are actually bad news, at least for the matchmaker. Airbnb and DogVacay take steps to mitigate this problem, like lower commissions for high volume and highly rated hosts, but whether those steps will suffice over the long run remains unclear.

> **repeat purchases are actually bad news, at least for the matchmaker**

Is Your Market Fragmented on Both the Buyer's and Seller's Sides?

Where matchmaker models work best is in fragmented markets where there are many buyers and many sellers. Consider eBay or Craigslist, which bring such sellers together with ease. In the case of ProFounder, the buyer's (investor's) side of the transaction was not fragmented at all; in fact, the precise number and identity of targets for any given offering were already known. Where that's the case, there's probably little need for a matchmaker's services.

Are You Targeting Narrowly or Widely at the Outset? Are You Building a Honda or a Mercedes-Benz?

In almost all entrepreneurial pursuits, it is advantageous to start with an extremely narrow target market whose (presumably unmet or poorly served) needs you can serve better than other existing solutions. Most often, you can serve those needs better—and frequently with a relatively simple solution—because you have an intimate understanding of them that your competitors lack. Philip Knight and Bill Bowerman started Nike, today's athletic footwear leader, to serve the needs of elite distance runners, which they themselves were (runner and coach, respectively)—a narrow target market if there ever was one.

A related notion is that your matchmaker business doesn't need to do *everything* better. It needs to do *something* vastly better, however. So it is with getting customer traction—hence customer funding—for a nascent matchmaker model. DogVacay

> **❝ Your matchmaker business doesn't need to do *everything* better. It needs to do *something* vastly better, however. ❞**

could have targeted all pets, not just dogs. Wisely, they didn't. They can target cats and other pets later, if they choose to. Airbnb targeted convention-goers at the outset, because such users had a clear problem—no hotel rooms in cities that were already fully booked—and were reachable through industry bloggers. When *you* seek funding to begin ramping up, angels will want to see that you're able to target narrowly and also build something simple (like the Hirschhorns' Yelp website)—a Honda Civic that gets you from here to there. The luxury automobile and other target markets—like Nike's advance across other sports than running—can come later, once your concept is proven and better funded.

A Question *for* Your Angel Investor: Can They Follow Their Money and Lead You to More?

Once you've proven customer traction for your matchmaker model and are ready for angel or VC funding, you—perhaps more than those pursuing other kinds of customer-funded models we'll see in this book—will need investors who can follow their money or lead you to more money. Part of the problem is that your slice of any single transaction is likely to be very thin, typically a single-digit percentage. Thus it's going to take lots of transactions before your slice amounts to very much. If you're in a footrace—think DogVacay versus Rover—in what could turn out to be a winner-take-all game, scale will win, and the best-funded player will have the best chance of getting to scale. So I suggest you choose your prospective investor *carefully*!

Making Matchmaker Models Work

Before wrapping up this chapter, it's worth noting that in the crowdfunding arena, one of the settings in which matchmaker models appear to be taking hold, it is said that successful offerings are usually the result of the project's proponent providing an initial network of target donors who donate and then spread the word to their own networks. As Wharton School Professor David Hsu, a keen observer of the crowdfunding phenomenon, argues,

> **It's usually necessary to 'bring your own crowd,' with the hope that your crowd will get excited enough to tell their crowds, too.**

"It's usually necessary to 'bring your own crowd,' with the hope that your crowd will get excited enough to tell their crowds, too."[47] We saw Corrado Accardi successfully bring his own crowd for his Pizza Rossa startup back in Chapter 1. Your direct access to the right networks—on one side of the transaction or the other, and ideally on both—is an asset that angel investors should and will look for, too.

With the case histories of Airbnb, DogVacay, and ProFounder now under our belts, I've examined and brought to life the first of the five types of customer-funded models, matchmaker models. More tangibly for you, if a matchmaker model fits the kind of business you want to start—or, as a business angel, you want to back—I've also identified a series of due diligence questions that should, and in all probability will, be asked, whether by angels, VCs, or by your senior management in an established business setting.

As I'll do in each of the following four chapters, I'll put this chapter to rest by summarizing those questions in the handy checklist that follows. But before you decide that a matchmaker model is right for you, you just might want to turn the page and consider the next of the five types, pay-in-advance models.

John's Business Angel Checklist—Matchmaker Models

- Why is *your* business likely to be the winner that "takes all"?
- To what extent are you addressing a compelling problem for at least one side of the buyer–seller dyad, as evidenced by network effects?
- Is there an overpriced *and* poor existing market structure that you plan to disrupt?
- What level of trust will be necessary in your vertical, and how will you ensure it?
- Repeat purchase behavior: What will prevent repeat customers from "going direct" for future purchases?
- Is your market fragmented on both the buyer's and seller's sides?
- Are you targeting narrowly or widely at the outset, and are you building a Honda or a Mercedes-Benz?

4

Ask for the Cash: Pay-in-Advance Models

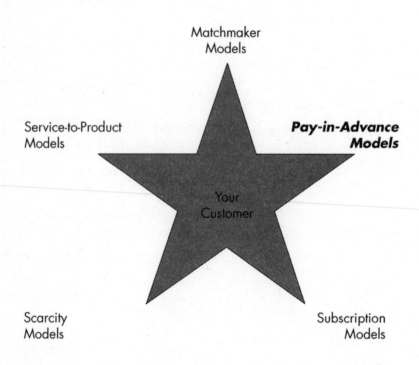

Matchmaker Models

Service-to-Product Models

Pay-in-Advance Models

Your Customer

Scarcity Models

Subscription Models

M y daughter's family shops at Costco from time to time. But not just anyone can. To shop at Costco, you'll need to become a member, and to become a member, you'll have to pay, from $55 to $110 in the United States or from £24 to £66 in the UK.[1] Why on earth would anyone *pay* to shop in a store? We willingly pay for what we pile into our shopping cart, but do we ever pay for the privilege of shopping in somebody's store? At Costco we do. Why?

> ❝Why on earth would anyone *pay* to shop in a store?❞

Millions of families are willing to pay to shop at Costco because of the benefits they get in return:

- Rock-bottom prices—they save enough to more than pay for the annual membership fee
- Huge selection—everything from food to apparel to consumer electronics
- And the eye-opening treasure hunt that any visit to Costco brings, due to their ever-changing assortment. Live Maine lobsters one week, electric pianos the next, and always well priced.

What Costco has shrewdly figured out is that by asking its customers to pay in advance for the privilege of shopping at Costco, the company can earn enough on the membership fees alone—some two-thirds of operating profit in most years—that it can run the business on gross profit margins much lower than those of any of its competitors.[2] Costco's pay-in-advance model funds rapid growth, too, having enabled the company to grow incredibly fast over its entire 30-year history, surpassing the $100 billion mark in revenue in its year ending September 2013.[3]

Pay-in-advance models are the most straightforward of the five customer-funded models explored in this book. Very simply, *pay-in-advance models are those in which the business asks (and convinces!) the customer to pay something up front*, whether in full or in part—*before* they receive what they've bought. It might be a membership fee, as at Costco, or a deposit, or some amount structured in some other way. Contractors who remodel people's kitchens work this way, requiring a deposit before they get started. So, too, do the designers or architects who plan that work. Pay-in-advance models certainly aren't new!

We've already had a look at two pay-in-advance models, those of Dell and Banana Republic, in Chapter 2. In Chapter 4, we examine the stories of three innovative twenty-first-century companies whose ingeniously designed pay-in-advance models enabled them to grow quickly using their customers' cash in their formative years, then grow even faster once they accessed additional capital to scale their businesses.

Threadless, named the "Most Innovative Small Company in America" by *Inc.* magazine in 2008,[4] is a community of artists and designers and a crowdsourced e-commerce website that produces and sells its community's designs: T-shirts and other products, as selected by the Threadless online community. Via.com, a fast-growing B2B travel network that serves India's brick-and-mortar travel agencies with real-time ticketing and other services, has grown from a standing start in 2007 at an astonishing rate. Loot, originally a consignment-based retailer of casual clothing in India, changed its business model and grew very fast, but then very nearly failed. All three companies offer important lessons for entrepreneurs—as well as for their fellow innovators in established companies—who are seeking to create customer-funded pay-in-advance models. We'll also learn lessons for the angel investors or corporate treasurers who may at some point back them.

From a T-Shirt Design Competition to Crowdsourcing Poster Child: Threadless[5]

"Threadless was never intended to be a business," begins co-founder Jake Nickell in his book about the company's evolution.[6] "When Jacob DeHart and I started out, it was all just a hobby—a

fun thing to do for the other designers we were friends with."
In 2000, Nickell (in Chicago) and
DeHart (studying at Purdue
University, two and a half hours'
drive away) were web developers,
students, and designers involved

> **❛❛Threadless was never intended to be a business. ❜❜**

in a community of peers who shared ideas about art, computers,
and coding. In a competition leading up to a New Media
Underground Festival in London in November of 2000, Nickell
posted a T-shirt design on the dreamless.org forum. Though the
winning design among nearly 100 entries—his!—was never actually printed, and no prize money was awarded, the competition
gave Nickell an idea.[7] "It would be fun to have an ongoing
competition where people could always submit T-shirt designs,
and we would print the best ones."[8]

From Idea to Implementation in Just an Hour

"Threadless started about one hour after coming up with the
idea,"[9] Nickell recalled. That very night, Nickell and DeHart
posted their first call for entries on the dreamless.org forum. They
picked the winners—5, out of nearly 100 entries. They then built
a website on which to sell the first batch of tees, later adding a
voting system so the user community could vote on which were
the best designs. Printing the first batch would cost money,
though, so they each threw in $500 to cover the printing and
T-shirt costs, and to pay a lawyer to incorporate the fledgling
business. They—actually DeHart's aunt, a screen printer who did
the printing[10]—printed two dozen of each of the five designs, and
offered them to the dreamless community for $12 each. They sold
out quickly. Do the mathematics. Two dozen each of five designs,
sold at $12 each, or $1,440 in total, enough customer funding to
more than cover the $1,000 in initial costs. A customer-funded
business was born, in a manner not unlike the origins of Banana
Republic, as we saw in Chapter 2. Nickell and DeHart—in it for
the fun, not the money—didn't realize it just yet.

From a Part-Time Sideline to a Real Business

The Threadless contests became a regular thing. "For the first two years of Threadless, every penny from selling tees went into printing more tee designs. We didn't even take a salary or cut of sales."[11] For Nickell, who had been developing websites professionally since 1996 at age 16, it was completely natural for him to spend lots of time working on the Threadless website, redesigning it every few months, just for fun.

Nickell began to build a community by posting news of the Threadless contests on every design blog he could find. As the Threadless community grew, new designs were always arriving, and the best of them were garnering votes. As soon as one batch of tees sold out, there would be enough customer money in the bank to print another batch, based on the latest winning designs. And so Threadless went, printing a new batch every couple of months

> **As soon as one batch of tees sold out, there would be enough customer money in the bank to print another batch, based on the latest winning designs.**

in 2001, then more frequently as the community expanded. In 2002, there was enough business—10,000 community members and $100,000 worth of T-shirts sold that year[12]—that the duo moved the business out of Nickell's Chicago apartment into a 900-square-foot office.

Along the way, both Nickell and DeHart did web developer jobs, and undertook their own other projects, too. Threadless was a sideline, but their sideline gradually grew to the point where, in 2004, they quit their jobs and fired their outside clients. New tees were being printed every week, and the business, after moving into a larger warehouse and hitting $1.5 million in sales by year's end, wasn't looking like just a hobby any more. "Threadless had huge potential to become a significant business," Nickell discovered. "We started to focus more on it."[13]

Business Model Validation

Soon thereafter, researchers at the MIT Sloan School of Management were studying new forms of business made possible by the Internet, including innovation driven by users, instead of producers. They called this new business model "crowdsourcing," and about the only company they could find that was really doing it was Threadless. So they invited the Jakes to speak at a conference on the topic, presenting their business model to leading business executives from *Fortune* 500 companies, among others. For the pair of artists, the MIT presentation provided some welcome confidence to anchor 2005, Threadless's first year as a "real" company.

Threadless continued to grow, fueled in large part by Nickell's commitment to building a community first, and letting the community's success take the business where it might go. He explained, "Threadless is a community of people first, a T-shirt store second."[14] Sales responded, jumping to $6.5 million in 2005, more than a fourfold increase over 2004. Threadless had been discovered. Customer funds from the Threadless community were financing and growing a thriving business.

Adding Expertise and Venture Capital

Managing such fast-paced growth is never easy, and for a business started—and to some degree still run—as a hobby, there were challenges. Shipping delays were rampant. In 2006 Nickell and DeHart (who was by then CTO) decided the business needed some professional help, and that some funding wouldn't be a bad idea, either. As Nickell recalled, "We decided to get someone who knew what they were doing invested in our success."[15] The result was selling a minority stake to Insight Venture Partners. Besides having been allowed to

> **We decided to get someone who knew what they were doing invested in our success.**

take some money off the table in the transaction, which he and DeHart did, Nickell quickly saw the benefits of that decision. Insight's Jeff Lieberman turned out to be, in his words, "an amazing source of knowledge when we don't know what to do; not to mention full of awesome ideas we never thought of."[16] Lieberman, too, was enthusiastic about the deal: "We were excited by the way they were merging content and commerce together on the Internet. We saw a totally unique company."[17]

The additional funding enabled yet another move into new space, this time going from a 6,000-square-foot facility to 25,000 square feet. Thanks to the additional space and some new hires in a few key areas, by the end of 2006 things were running much better. According to Nickell, "Orders were shipped the same day most of the time; always within a couple of days. International shipping got way cheaper and way faster. We got better at making the right amount of stuff to sell. Woo-hoo!"[18] In 2008, Nickell stepped aside as CEO, appointing himself Chief Community Officer, and brought in Tom Ryan, a veteran of one of the music industry's early Internet startups, to lead the company going forward. By 2010, the company cruised into its 10th year firing on all cylinders.

Fast-forwarding to 2013, Threadless was serving 2.5 million customers, and offering 10 new designs every Monday.[19] And because its community members tell Threadless which designs they want to buy, the major source of capital that has funded the company's growth remains its customers' funds. Will Threadless go public any time soon? Nickell and Ryan have little to say about that. As Ryan put it, "Our mission is to get the world's creative minds to make and sell great artwork."[20] Nickell added, "Respect the artist. Trust the community. And don't let ourselves trip up by getting in the way."[21]

Why Has Threadless Been Successful?

In Nickell's words, "The best thing we did is to trust our community. To constantly ask them for advice, to show them we are listening,

and to change things based on what the community is feeling. We also wholly invest ourselves in being members ourselves."[22] The 1.5 million Threadless followers on Twitter and 150,000 **❝The best thing we did is to trust our community. ❞**
fans on Facebook offer compel-
ling evidence of the results of his company's community-first focus.[23] And a consistent stream of its customers' cash didn't hurt, either!

Bringing India's Mom-and-Pop Travel Agents into the Twenty-First Century: Via.com

In 2006, the travel industry in India was abuzz with the potential for online and mobile solutions that could revolutionize the industry there, as had already happened in much of the rest of the world. Starting in a small garage on 9th A Main Road in Bangalore in early 2006, Wall Street executive–turned–entrepreneur Vinay Gupta saw a fragmented and inefficient travel industry that was ripe for change. But the change he had in mind was not what the rapidly growing number of well-funded online travel websites was pursuing.

On July 28, 2006, having secured membership in the International Air Transport Association (IATA), which gave his company access to real-time ticketing and flight availability, Gupta and Amit Aggarwal launched Flightraja.com as a way to book air tickets via mobile phones, of which there were 170 million in India at the time, with forecasts predicting that 350 million Indians would have mobiles by 2010. The consumer would simply send a text via short messaging service (SMS), requesting flight options for the destination and the date of travel, and Flightraja would reply with availability and pricing. The e-ticket for the chosen flight would then be issued and charged to the consumer's credit card. Simple, easy, and fast.[24]

But there were a couple of problems with Gupta's Plan A. First, while mobile phone penetration in India was growing fast, credit card penetration was not. Gupta soon discovered that only 23 million Indians held credit cards, a very small number in a country of more than 1 billion people.[25]

❝there were a couple of problems with Gupta's Plan A❞

Flightraja's SMS solution was predicated on consumers having credit cards. The dearth of credit cards was also an indicator of the second challenge Gupta's new venture faced: India was a cash-based economy, and Indians simply preferred to pay for most things, travel included, with cash.[26]

Getting to Plan B

Gupta's vision wasn't simply to build a mobile-enabled consumer-facing business, though. He knew that Indians who traveled—still a relatively small market segment, but one that looked like it would grow, thanks to India's burgeoning middle class—mostly bought their tickets from mom-and-pop brick-and-mortar travel agents. Most of India's travel agents, however, were not IATA members and lacked access to real-time ticketing capability. "Come back tomorrow, and I'll tell you when you can fly and at what price," was the refrain their customers would hear when asking to book airline tickets. So Gupta pivoted, starting a B2B concept that would serve travel agents. In exchange for a rolling $5,000 deposit against which tickets would be issued in real time, Gupta gave the agents a computer and a connection that provided them with IATA-certified real-time flight availability and ticketing capability—and better commissions, too.[27]

Customer Funding Adds Up!

Very quickly, Gupta's Plan B, funded by his customers' deposits, signed up 110 travel agents in Bangalore and another 70 in Chennai, and was booking 200 tickets per day.[28] Do the mathematics: 180 travel agents at $5,000 each—nearly $1 million! It was customer funding on a substantial scale, and raised in less than two months, too! Progress was sufficient to convince Ashwini Kakkar, angel investor and former India CEO for global travel giant Thomas Cook, to take a small stake.[29] More important than his modest cash investment, however, were Kakkar's industry knowledge and connections.

By June 2007, Via had enrolled more than 3,000 agents in 290 Indian cities and was issuing 5,000 tickets per day.[30] Flightraja was the largest travel network in India, with over 3,000 registered agents in 290 cities.[31] Thanks in part to Kakkar's connections, and to the value the travel agents saw in Gupta's proposition, word had gotten around the Indian travel agent community that signing up with Flightraja was a good way to go. The company's progress and potential convinced venture capital investor NEA IndoUS Ventures to come on board that June, with a $5 million Series A investment to enable the company, renamed Via at that time, to expand into hotel, rail, and bus bookings.[32] "But they really didn't need our money," NEA's Managing Director Vani Kola

They really didn't need our money, and it's nearly all still in the bank!

recalled two years later, "and it's nearly all still in the bank!"[33] Why? Its two key sources of customer funding, the rolling pay-in-advance deposits from the travel agents and Via's margins on the tickets it sold (yes, Via was a matchmaker, too!), were largely sufficient to fund its rapid growth.

Customer Funding and More

Despite the global economic slowdown of 2008, Via continued to grow rapidly, both by expanding its network of travel agents using the Via platform and by growing beyond air travel to sell bus tickets, hotel stays, and train journeys, with its customers' cash still funding most of the growth.[34] Having come out of the downturn unscathed, Gupta began thinking really big. He wanted to raise another investor round to further grow the business within and beyond India, leading to a hoped-for public offering in the near future.[35] The result? Sequoia Capital India came on board, investing $10 million in a Series B round in December 2009.[36] By early 2011, Via had established a presence in more than 1,700 Indian cities and towns and had expanded into the Philippines and Middle East.[37]

But that's not all Via did with its new capital. It launched a consumer-facing online booking business, to reach the market segment that had online access and preferred to shop for tickets that way. Gupta also saw an opportunity to build a presence in numerous other countries with airline connections into India. So his next step, in November 2011, was to use some of his new capital to acquire a travel consolidator, TSC Travel Services, to take advantage of TSC's relationships with numerous international airlines and its 500-strong network of travel agents in the north of India. Gupta explained the rationale for the deal: "We have always been looking out for growth opportunities: both organic and inorganic. TSC provides us a perfect platform to further strengthen our position in North India and boost our operations here. TSC will also play a key role in increasing our overall international travel business."[38]

Gupta even placed a bet on the domestic pilgrimage tourism market, investing in a fleet of luxury Volvo buses. When you've got plenty of cash coming in, not everything needs to be customer-funded! Via's chief marketing officer, John Kuruvilla, explained, "There is a huge potential in this sector, with close to 50,000 people visiting Tirupati every day. Our surveys have shown that 40 buses arrive at the temple town every day from Andhra Pradesh and Karnataka and another 30 from Tamil Nadu."[39]

> **When you've got plenty of cash coming in, not everything needs to be customer-funded!**

Then, in December 2012, having grown its overseas network to more than 150 cities in the Philippines and 75 in Indonesia, Via struck a deal with Singapore's fast-growing Tiger Airways to become its exclusive distributor in India.[40] The commercial director of Tiger Airways, Kaneswaran Avili, valued the positive reputation and network that Via had already established: "By tapping on Via.com's extensive pool of travel agents, we are thrilled to offer Indian travelers good value travel deals, greater accessibility and a more convenient payment system."[41]

In January 2013, Gupta stepped upstairs into the chairman's role, having led his business from its origins in a small garage in Bangalore to the largest player in India's domestic travel industry in less than seven years.[42] Via's customer-funded, pay-in-advance model, along with a couple of timely and easily raised doses of venture capital along the way, has served it very well!

Loot Stores: From Small Consignment Retailer to 155 Stores—and Back Again![43]

Jay Gupta knew he wanted to be an entrepreneur. "Belonging to a small business family, I had always looked up to my father and seen his dealings and day-to-day activities. That's when the passion of doing something unique on my own developed."[44] He had already seen the craze for fashion among his friends in college. Witnessing the ease with which style-conscious young shoppers were parting with wads of cash for new Western-style clothes, Gupta felt he had the answer. "Retail was within reach for me. I felt that the apparel sector would be the easiest for me to organize. I wanted an easy life— to start my own business and live well."[45] Gupta plunged into apparel retail while still in his first year of college in Mumbai, via an apparel exhibition sale.

> **❝I wanted an easy life— to start my own business and live well. ❞**

The 1994 Exhibitions

In India, temporary exhibitions were a common way for budding designers and entrepreneurs to display their products to a local audience. Gupta took this route and launched an exhibition in Vashi, a suburb of Mumbai. The exhibition product assortment was deeply discounted and ranged from traditional Indian outfits to denim jeans and T-shirts. Gupta, who lacked the capital to start a sizeable business but could scrape together enough cash to rent a small space, took the goods on consignment from vendors in order to learn the business of apparel retailing without incurring too much risk. This meant that the ownership of the goods remained with the vendor until the goods were sold by the consignee, Gupta, at which point he paid the vendor for the goods. Unsold goods could be returned to the vendor. It was a classic customer-funded—and vendor-funded—pay-in-advance model. The customers paid Gupta for the fashions they bought, after which Gupta paid his vendors. Cash needed to get started? Other than the modest rent, virtually nil.

❝Cash needed to get started? Virtually nil❞

Though his first exhibition ran only four weekends, it offered a lot of learning to Gupta, and he made good money, too, with his customers' cash more than sufficient to cover his expenses. He was able to identify the fastest-moving product categories, sizes, and brands; count foot traffic and assess buying behavior; and understand the licenses and permits required to do business. Gupta held three more exhibitions in the same space, initially renting and then finally purchasing the tiny 200-square-foot space in 1995. The purchase was financed through a bank loan and the sale of an inherited family property. Now, with a series of successful exhibitions under his belt and favorable market research also in hand, Gupta decided that apparel retailing was, indeed, for him.

Casual Plus

Leveraging the trend for Western-branded casual wear, Gupta invited heavyweight foreign brands such as Adidas and domestic brands such as ColourPlus to give him a franchise. These brands had already proven their success in India and were looking for the right partners to increase their distribution. However, no one was willing to provide exclusive terms to a young, inexperienced college student operating a tiny suburban store. So Gupta had to settle for a multi-brand model, with a smaller selection from each brand, a relatively low-risk proposal for the vendors. His Casual Plus store opened in 1997 and featured Western brands such as Reebok athletic shoes and Lee Cooper jeans, plus Indian brands Spykar and Haute Cotton.

Once again he managed to convince his apparel vendors to give him the merchandise he needed on consignment, but Gupta's earnings from his earlier exhibitions weren't sufficient to cover the other costs of opening his store, which he financed through loans from the federal bank, family, and friends. The customer-funded model that had gotten him started, while still in place, was not able to fully fund the new store.

> **The customer-funded model that had gotten him started, while still in place, was not able to fully fund the new store.**

Soon the young Gupta discovered that a few of his vendors would give him a 5 percent discount if purchases were paid in cash up front, instead of providing the goods on consignment. Punctuality on payments was something Gupta took seriously: "When your payments start getting in on time, the brands start trusting you."[46] But his changing terms meant that the cash from his customers' purchases was no longer sufficient to fund his entire inventory, even though his margins had improved. Profits were up, but cash flow was down. A local bank, seeing a profitable and growing business, filled the gap, agreeing to finance most of Gupta's inventory with a credit line.

The Casual Plus format was successful in sales and profitability, but Gupta observed that customer conversion was only around 7 to 8 percent of those who entered the store. By personally interviewing and observing his customers, he concluded that consumers wanted a larger range of product choices in a larger shopping environment. Encouraged by his success and improved credibility, Gupta approached the new domestic clothing brand Provogue, which had just started opening franchised stores in cities across India. Trendy, fashion-focused, and urban, Provogue would no doubt be a hit with young shoppers. Gupta persuaded the brand to let him launch an exclusive franchised outlet.

Single-Brand Stores

The new Provogue store, opened in early 1998, was the first of three single-brand franchised formats that Gupta pursued for the next several years. The gross margins in these franchised stores were a healthy 25 to 28 percent, and goods were usually taken on consignment, avoiding the need for much cash up front, so Gupta was able to get by without very much cash other than what his customers (and his generous bankers) provided. He wasn't entirely customer funded, but his consumers paid cash when they bought, and "sitting on the float" before he had to pay his consignment vendors helped make ends meet.

But Gupta was always on the lookout for the next opportunity. An informal survey of his own stores and Adidas's retail outlets in Mumbai led Gupta to an insight that transformed his retail philosophy: "I saw that 95% of customers in these Western sportswear and casual apparel stores wanted discounts."[47] This observation captured a curious contradiction about Indian consumers: They were definitely brand conscious but still remained bargain hunters at heart. Gupta wanted his retail formats to satisfy both demands simultaneously.

A Turning Point: Factory Outlet Stores

In search of a retailing format that could offer customers discounts as well as variety, Gupta opened the first franchised factory outlet store for the international footwear brand Adidas in Chembur, another growing suburb of Mumbai, in 1999. As a factory outlet, Gupta's store was selling excess or off-season stock, and sometimes "seconds," which were damaged or defective in minor ways. First-year sales soared to almost four times the store's break-even level, more than tripling Gupta's forecast, and the store's productivity was the highest among all Adidas stores in India. Although Gupta was already operating a full-priced franchise store for Adidas in an upscale shopping area in Mumbai, he soon directed most of his attention to the factory outlet store, as he believed this format held the most promise.

Despite lower gross margins in the factory outlets (15–20 percent), over the next three years Gupta opened five more factory outlets for Western apparel and footwear brands Levi's and Nike, as well as leading Indian apparel manufacturers Provogue, Colour-Plus, and Weekender. Gupta continued his practice of taking goods on consignment, limiting both his inventory risk and need for cash. His portfolio of 10 apparel stores now contained three different formats: the multi-brand Casual Plus store, three full-price franchisees, and six factory outlets, with all but Casual Plus selling, for the most part, consignment goods.

The Loot: "Great Steals on Big Brands"

Although the factory outlet format was working well for Gupta, his conversations with his customers indicated that they always wanted more. "They wanted the environment, an exchange policy, first-quality products (not factory seconds), air conditioning, and trial rooms," recalled Gupta.[48] This led him to envision a multi-brand store that featured factory outlet prices with the shopping environment of an exclusive-brand, full-price store. Gupta opened his fourth retail format, called The Loot, in late June 2004.

Gupta selected the name because "loot" has the same meaning in both English and Hindi. He liked the idea of "stealing" great deals from aspirational brands and passing them on to fashion-minded yet bargain-hunting consumers. Gupta recruited famous Bollywood villain Gulshan Grover to become the brand ambassador and to give credence to the modern-day Robin Hood feel of the brand. Grover's image peered ominously from a sign behind the cash counter outlining what The Loot stood for: no fakes, no seconds; guaranteed price; guaranteed product; and 25 to 60 percent off, 365 days per year. The trial room where customers could try on their clothing looked like a prison cell, and outside the trial room was a ramp imprinted with a large barcode slashed with The Loot's logo, where customers could show off their selections.

> **❝Gupta recruited famous Bollywood villain Gulshan Grover to become the brand ambassador❞**

One Catch: The Loot's Business Model Was Changing

Gupta knew the success of the concept would depend on his ability to source aspirational Western brands and coveted domestic brands cheaply. "Companies, on an average, have 45 per cent of production as surplus," Gupta explained. He began paying up front to obtain large supplier discounts on surplus products that had already been imported into the country, but in a sharp departure from his factory-outlet store model Gupta refused seconds or defective goods. "The brands were not happy with me!" exclaimed Gupta.[49] This ownership also gave Gupta more flexibility in terms of product selection, display, and distribution across stores, as some consignors had been putting restrictions on the placement of products. "It was great not to be dependent on any one brand, to buy the products ourselves and put them wherever we wanted, and to fully own the business model," he said.[50] But by abandoning his largely customer- and vendor-funded consignment model, Gupta had altered his business model more fundamentally than he realized.

Focused primarily on young men's casual clothing (jeans, tops, shoes, and sportswear), The Loot format clearly resonated with shoppers. In its first two months, his new store generated dramatically more revenue than any of Gupta's previous store openings. "Though at 2,000 square feet it was twice as large as my other stores," Gupta recalled, "I knew I was onto something really big." Emboldened by the response to the store, Gupta decided to convert most of his other factory outlet and franchisee stores into The Loot format. "We went to the brands from which I had taken franchises and told them to take over management of their stores or give us permission to turn them into The Loot."[51]

During autumn 2004, Gupta converted eight of his existing stores to The Loot, bringing the total to nine Loot stores and leaving just two of the full-price franchisee stores. "Suddenly we had real impact on the Mumbai retailing scene. More important, with nine stores operating under the same format, we now had the buying power that we sorely needed. Finally, I felt that we had a formula that worked."[52]

> **❝We now had the buying power that we sorely needed. Finally, I felt that we had a formula that worked.❞**

But What about the Business Model?

Consignments were a thing of the past, so not only did Gupta have to buy inventory up front—a new cash outflow that had previously been the brands' responsibility—but he also had to face the risk of excess unsold inventory that could not be returned. Fortunately, Gupta had convinced his banks to increase The Loot's credit lines, which had been very modest earlier and always repaid per their terms, to support the company's growing and profitable sales, now nearly $2 million per year. Despite a small infusion of cash from his father-in-law and some income from his two remaining franchise stores, at the end of the fiscal year ended March 2005 Gupta was seriously stretched for cash. This was new terrain for Gupta. "I'd always worked with profits and I always had the cash I needed to operate. I failed to appreciate the difference between

> **❝I had failed to appreciate the difference between profits and cash flow.❞**

profits and cash flow." With his original consignment model now long gone, "it shook me up to see the cash disappear when I started flipping the stores and adding corporate overheads."[53] The Loot was walking on a knife edge, and the banks were holding the knife. The risky situation did not bode well for the future of The Loot.

Chhabra to the Rescue

R. P. Chhabra, the recently retired father of one of Gupta's closest friends, had spent his entire career in finance in the public and private sectors, and enjoyed chatting with Gupta about his journey with The Loot. Chhabra knew, and taught this to Gupta, that the bank lines he had relied on to that point were badly stretched and inadequate for the next stage of growth.

In 2006, Gupta began to receive inquiries from financiers eager to invest in the fledgling business, which had received considerable press coverage. A prominent news publication gave The Loot a sizeable valuation, and Gupta suddenly saw the opportunity to validate the value he had created. He made a presentation to ASK Raymond, a joint venture between a local financial services company and U.S.-based Raymond James Financial. ASK Raymond made an offer immediately, with Gupta accepting 60 percent of the amount offered, to prevent too much dilution of his ownership. Besides the immediate liquidity, Gupta saw that the external investment from a professional financial institution gave The Loot credibility in the eyes of banks, suppliers, and regulators. "The ASK people were good, demanding in the right way," said Gupta.[54]

A New Customer-Funded Model: Franchising!

As the company's reputation grew, Gupta began to get inquiries from businesspeople around India interested in operating The Loot as a franchise. When he figured out that franchising would once again give him the customer's cash in advance—the customer this time being The Loot's franchisee—Gupta jumped at the chance. By mid-2010, there were 155 Loot stores around India, of which he was running only 40 directly, mostly in Mumbai and Delhi, with the rest owned and managed by franchisees.[55] The customer cash generated by the franchise operation had been used to finance the opening of the additional company-owned stores. Inventory in his warehouse and the 40 company-owned stores was still being financed by banks, but the other costs to grow the business, as well as the franchisees' inventory, were borne largely by the franchisees.

The Loot Unravels[56]

While Gupta's foot was pressed firmly on the accelerator from 2008 through 2010, some new taxes were imposed on companies like Gupta's. First came a value-added tax on garments (4 percent) and shoes (12 percent); then a tax on services (12.5 percent), which was imposed on most of The Loot's operating cost structure, including rent and the store and warehouse labor Gupta had been sourcing from a staffing firm; finally, a new excise tax at 4 percent of manufacturers' retail price, which meant an 8 percent tax rate at The Loot's average discount pricing. Worse, the new excise tax was due at the time the goods were purchased, not at the time they were sold!

> **the new excise tax was due at the time the goods were purchased, not at the time they were sold!**

The entire Indian chain-retailing industry was up in arms over the new taxes. The retailers asked for—and were granted—a stay while the issue was deliberated. They argued that it would be impossible to pass the costs on to their cash-strapped customers and to remain competitive with the local *kiranas*—the traditional mom-and-pop stalls that still comprised more than 90 percent of retailing in India. Fully expecting the taxes to be rescinded, many players, including The Loot, proceeded with business as usual. But in October 2011, their hopes were dashed. The verdict was announced: All back taxes were now due. For Loot, this amounted to approximately 30 percent of the prior three years' sales, due overnight. For Gupta, who had not been expecting this turn of events, there was simply no way to pay.

But that wasn't all. Many of the franchisees simply closed their stores, finding the new taxes untenable. Some, finding it prohibitively expensive to buy Indian or Western goods taxed per the new laws, resorted to selling untaxed merchandise smuggled from China. The Loot's sales to its franchisees came to a screeching halt. Even worse, the legislation required landlords to collect some of the taxes from their retail tenants. When tenants like The Loot or its franchisees couldn't pay, landlords simply put locks on their stores and grabbed whatever was there—jeans, T-shirts, store fixtures, and more—in an effort to cover the taxes that were due. Amid all the turmoil, The Loot ran out of cash, and its banks called the loans. For Jay Gupta and The Loot, a downward spiral ensued, taking the company back to its roots, as it closed all but five of its company-owned stores by February 2013. His quest for "the easy life" remains unfulfilled.

The Loot's Precarious High-Wire Act

The Loot's journey to the heights of Indian retailing and back demonstrates how precarious a customer-funded business can sometimes be if one is not careful. During The Loot's early years, when Gupta bought his merchandise on consignment and returned to his vendors whatever he didn't sell, his pay-in-advance model worked well, financed largely by his customers' cash and his vendors, who were willing to wait for their cash. Thus his pay-in-advance model and his generous vendors had given him a great start and had lowered his risk. Once Gupta himself started paying in advance, however, even

> **❝ The Loot's journey demonstrates how precarious a customer-funded business can sometimes be if one is not careful ❞**

though that got him better discounts, things changed for the worse in his business model. No longer were his customer's purchases and his franchisees' payments sufficient to fund his increasing inventory, which at times exceeded six months of stock as he made opportunistic purchases to obtain merchandise in advance of new store openings. Suddenly he needed banks to do so.

Relying on banks is fine when things are going well, but if a shock hits the system, such as new taxes in India, watch out! Gupta had the pedal to the metal while things were balanced precariously, during a period when things were going well. But once a shock hit the system, the party was over. That's the way it is with debt. If the world changes around you and the banks get twitchy, you're asking for trouble.

But the risk that comes hand in hand with debt—financial risk, as it's called, as opposed to the normal commercial risk your business faces every day—is only one part of The Loot's downfall. The larger lesson for those pursuing customer-funded models, whether in early-stage companies or established ones, is that once you change from a customer-funded model to one that requires more cash, perhaps in an effort to grow faster, the cash has to come from somewhere. There are essentially two choices: equity, from the likes of VC investors; or debt, from banks. We've seen Airbnb, in Chapter 2, and Vinay Gupta's Via in this chapter make successful transitions from customer-funded models to investor-backed models in order to pursue rapid growth. Such transitions may well be likely in *your* customer-funded business, too, and the great start that customer funding gives you will help you obtain the capital you'll need, whether equity or debt. Jay Gupta elected not to seek a transition to venture capital, and he paid a heavy price. Many well-funded retailers have survived the change in India's tax regime. Sadly, The Loot didn't.

> **❝the risk that comes hand-in-hand with debt is only one part of The Loot's downfall❞**

What Angel Investors Will Want to Know—and Will Ask

We've seen the case histories of two fast-growing retail businesses in this chapter, The Loot and Threadless. You may be wondering, "Aren't most retail businesses 'pay-in-advance'?" You're right: they are, as most of the time, we pay our money—whether online or at a store—and we *then* receive what we bought, albeit moments later in physical stores at least. So most retail businesses are, indeed, pay-in-advance, but—alas—many of them are not customer funded. Why not? Because there's a store to build or lease and fit out (whether a digital one or the bricks-and-mortar variety), inventory to buy, and so on. Pizza Rossa's founder, Corrado Accardi, who we met in Chapter 1, chose a crowdfunding campaign to finance these costs as well as a central commercial kitchen. In most cases, the retailers who start or grow new retail concepts—whether entrepreneurs or well-established retailing firms—spend money up front, sometimes lots of money, doing these things before they really know whether customers will buy what they propose to offer. Is there another way?

By heeding the lessons of this chapter, and those from Banana Republic in Chapter 2, many of these budding retailers could perhaps find ways to start their businesses with little or no up-front investment (just $1,500 for Banana Republic, $1,000 for Threadless), and fund their proof of the concept (Or not!) with their customers'—and their vendors'—cash. Even Accardi hopes to borrow an underutilized kitchen in London, rather than fitting out his own, at least at the outset, and until customer traction for Pizza Rossa is proven. So what will prospective investors in pay-in-advance models want to know about *your* business, once you've proven traction with your pay-in-advance start?

You've Been a Customer-Funded Business to Date. Why Do You Need Capital Now?

There's a straightforward answer to this question: "Something has changed." For Threadless, when Nickell and DeHart decided in 2006 that they needed "someone who knew what they were doing," sales had jumped fourfold in the prior year. With shipping delays rampant, they knew that, as managers, they were now in over their heads. They needed help—*and* money—which came along with the help. More importantly, they were transparent and courageous enough to acknowledge the gaps in their skills. They didn't pretend that "everything is wonderful" when it was not.

> **they were transparent and courageous enough to acknowledge the gaps in their skills**

At Via, what had changed when Kakkar came on board was that Vinay Gupta had shifted from his first SMS-driven B2C strategy to a B2B model, one that could take particular advantage of Kakkar's travel industry network. And the new model was working! Then when NEA came in with a Series A round, Gupta's vision had grown wider—not just air travel any more, but trains and buses, too. The opportunity was there to add fuel to the tank! At The Loot, Jay Gupta's capital—probably not enough capital, in hindsight—came from ASK Raymond at a time when his business model had changed from buying on consignment to buying in advance. That simple but crucial change in the manner in which his company bought held enormous implications for the cash needs of the business.

Note that in two of the three cases, Threadless and Via, it was a need for real value added—more than just money—at particular moments in time, that provided the impetus for the first external financing round. Angel investors will ask, "Why now?" when you ask for their support and their expertise, as well as their money. If you're an entrepreneur, you'll need to have a convincing answer.

What's Different about Your Proposition Compared to Others?

It is sometimes said—and often observed—that early-stage investors, whether angels or VCs, are like lemmings. Once their peers have an investment in one kind of company, they want a similar one, too. But we all know what happens to lemmings (or we think we know, for it's actually a misconception), as in the 1958 Disney film *White Wilderness*: they follow one another, jumping off a cliff and into the sea to their death.

❝❝early-stage investors, whether angels or VCs, are like lemmings❞❞

The best of breed, whether angels or VCs, are one step ahead of the curve, though, and are looking for entrepreneurs who are genuinely breaking new ground. Via's Vinay Gupta was doing exactly that—first with his SMS system for using mobile phones to book tickets (rather than the Internet, which others were pursuing), and then with his travel agent play—amid a much wider rush to Expedia and Travelocity knockoffs. He was very clear about doing so. "We used a different market entry strategy based on consumer and market needs without blindly copying a model that existed in other countries."[57] Threadless's Jake Nickell, with his community-first ethic, was differentiated, too. So, if you want the best investors on your side—and you do!—they will be looking for evidence that you, too, are a contrarian, and that you are not simply following the current crowd.

Would You Like to Take Some Money off the Table?

It's a question most VCs don't ask, but it's worth pursuing. When Insight Venture Partners invested in Threadless, they allowed the Jakes to take some cash off the table, by putting some of their capital into the business and some of it into Nickell and Dehart's own pockets. It's unlikely angels will allow you to do this in your early years (Via's Kakkar did not), but if your customer-funded model gets you far enough along the road, as was the case with Threadless, venture capital or private equity investors will sometimes permit this.

Their logic is that you've already proven your commitment by bringing the business this far (six years, at Threadless) and it's not unrealistic to think that the entrepreneur should get at least some payout for having done so. And, because they want in to your already proven business, they have an incentive to make it worth your while to let them in. That's not the case if you try to *start* your business with investor money, and it's usually a long wait—until *their* exit—before you get to take anything out.

> **❝If you try to *start* your business with investor money, it's usually a long wait before you get to take anything out. ❞**

Do You Genuinely Understand the Difference between Profit and Cash Flow? Or Have You Simply Stumbled into a Customer-Funded Model?

Too many entrepreneurs—and many angels and corporate executives, too—don't fully appreciate the difference between a profitable business and one that generates cash as it grows, versus consuming it. I said so at the end of Chapter 1, and I'll say so here, too. The Loot's Jay Gupta stumbled into a customer-funded model by taking goods on consignment, but because he didn't fully understand its implications, he inadvertently got away from it when he flipped his stores to The Loot's new model. He ultimately paid a heavy price.

> **❝Too many entrepreneurs don't fully appreciate the difference between a profitable business and one that generates cash as it grows ❞**

Making Pay-in-Advance Models Work: Ask for the Cash, and for Good Terms, Too!

The founders of this chapter's examples share one very important thing in common: They all had the audacity and persistence to ask for what they needed to start their business in largely customer-funded fashion. For Threadless it was getting people to buy winning designs before they were printed, then waiting to run another contest until the previous one had generated enough customer cash. For Via, it was the travel agent's $5,000 rolling deposit. For The Loot, it was the cash-at-the-till nature of retailing plus consignment terms from his vendors that enabled Jay Gupta to get started. We saw the same behaviors from Rud Browne at Ryzex in Chapter 1 and from Michael Dell and Mel and Patricia Ziegler in Chapter 2. There's a pattern here, one that

❝There's a pattern here❞

speaks volumes about the customer-funded mind-set I hope you'll soon have!

Whether you're an entrepreneur just getting started or a leader in a growth-starved company, if you start *your* new venture with a pay-in-advance model or find a way to change your existing business to one, you may at some point decide that additional funding might be helpful. If so, you might want to give the questions posed above—and summarized in the checklist that follows—careful consideration. You may or may not need to raise external capital eventually. Whichever route you take over the life of your business, though, asking your customer for the cash you need—and your vendors for the terms you need—and convincing them to give them to you is a hallmark of many of today's best entrepreneurs and other successful businesspeople, in companies of every size and in every industry. Do it and thrive!

John's Business Angel Checklist—Pay-in-Advance Models

- You've been a customer-funded business to date. Why do you need capital now?
- What's different about your proposition compared to others?
- Would you like to take some money off the table?
- Do you genuinely understand the difference between profit and cash flow? Or have you simply stumbled into a customer-funded model?

5

Recurring Revenue: Subscription and SaaS Models

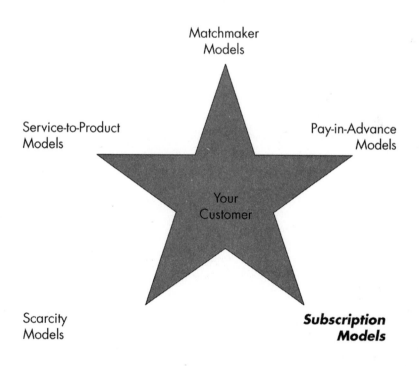

Matchmaker
Models

Service-to-Product
Models

Pay-in-Advance
Models

Your
Customer

Scarcity
Models

*Subscription
Models*

For many of us, subscriptions are something we rarely pay much attention to, but benefit from every day. We get our videos from a subscription to Netflix, and many of our newspapers and magazines by subscription, too, in print, online, or delivered on our mobile

> **❝ subscriptions are something we rarely pay much attention to, but benefit from every day ❞**

devices. Our cell phone service and our cable or satellite TV programming come via subscriptions. The gas and electric utilities that heat and light our homes come that way, too. Even organic vegetables, in some places, arrive each week by subscription, in a box delivered to our doorstep.

Why do people choose to obtain such goods and services via subscription, rather than renting DVDs from a store or grabbing periodicals from a newsstand or organic produce from the local supermarket? Three major reasons:

1. Their demand for what they subscribe to is regular and predictable: They want it every day, week, or month (though in some settings, like utilities, the quantity may vary).
2. It's easier than having to remember to get it another way, or to make a special trip to get it.
3. Often, it's also cheaper than buying the goods or services individually.

Subscription models are those in which the customer agrees to buy something—a good or a service—that is delivered repeatedly, whether physically or digitally, over an extended period of time. Sometimes payment is made at the beginning of a relatively lengthy period— for example, a one-year subscription to your favorite magazine. At other times, payment is made more often, perhaps monthly, as with most utility and Netflix bills. As we'll see in this chapter, subscription models have, in recent years, been applied in some surprising settings, so much so that one observer wondered whether 2012 would be "The Year of Subscription Models."[1]

Subscription Models for Software: SaaS

One of the possible reasons why subscription models have moved onto the radar is that the software industry has embraced them wholeheartedly. Rather than buying software in a shrink-wrapped box, or downloading it to our PCs, it's become commonplace to simply subscribe to the software we need—software as a service, or SaaS for short—and pay a monthly or other periodic fee. Salesforce.com was an early SaaS pioneer, but in recent years the SaaS model has exploded, with software subscription revenue reaching $56 billion in the United States alone in 2012, and growing at double-digit rates.[2] Why might users prefer to buy on a SaaS basis?

- You're always running the latest version, with no fees for upgrading to get the latest features.
- It typically requires a much smaller expense up front than buying similar software outright would entail.
- Online support typically comes as part of the deal.

And why might software companies prefer SaaS models? Among the reasons are these:

- They get predictable recurring revenue.
- They don't have to spend money continuing to support old versions of their products.
- It's easier to get customers to adopt, given the lower initial cost. This makes it an attractive strategy for disrupting well-entrenched competitors.
- They can observe what features users are putting to use, and which they are not, enabling them to better serve their customers' needs.
- It's less costly to support and market software through the cloud than by other means.

Even Microsoft, the longtime leader in selling shrink-wrapped or downloaded software the old-fashioned way, introduced a subscription-based Office Home Premium product in March 2013. At a subscription price of $100 per year, it's become Microsoft's fastest product ever to hit annual revenue of $1 billion.[3]

The tricky part, for software companies considering shifting from the old model to SaaS, is that making the change generally entails a revenue hit. Adobe Systems moved its entire suite of popular creative applications—Photoshop, Illustrator, and others—to a SaaS model in 2013.[4] Though Adobe's quarterly revenue fell from $871 million to

> **❛❛The tricky part, for software companies considering shifting from the old model to SaaS, is that making the change generally entails a revenue hit. ❜❜**

$645 million in the following quarter, Adobe is pleased with the change. "We've exceeded our expectations so far," says David Wadhwani, Adobe's senior vice president for its digital media business.[5] Investors appear pleased too, as Adobe's stock price has been on a tear.[6] If you are an aspiring software entrepreneur or an executive in an established software company, SaaS models must be at the center of your strategic thinking these days. If you don't have an attractively priced SaaS offering, one of your competitors surely soon will.

In this chapter, we devote little attention to software companies, though, as the SaaS phenomenon is well understood in the software community. It's fair to say that the SaaS model has become the model of choice in today's software startup scene. Instead, we will examine the application of subscription models in other, more novel industry settings, although the lessons therein are fully applicable to software players, too, whether in nascent startups or well-established software firms. In particular, we explore the case histories of two highly inventive subscription-based businesses, both of which got their start with customer funding. In both cases, their growth rates skyrocketed once their models were proven and venture capital investors liked what they saw.

TutorVista, a provider of online tutoring for kids in the developed world—in mathematics, English, and more—has grown from a few teachers with a VoIP connection in Bangalore into the leading such provider and an acquisition by Pearson PLC, the world's largest education company. Petals for the People and H.Bloom, two subscription-based providers of cut flower arrangements for offices, hotels, and other commercial customers, started separately at about the same time—in Washington, DC and New York City, respectively—and are now one. The combined company initially grew rapidly to 10 American cities, though as I write their growth appears to have plateaued. We also briefly examine the stories of several subscription-based businesses that have stumbled. The contrasts between TutorVista and these others are telling.

> **" We also briefly examine the stories of several subscription-based businesses that have stumbled. "**

Educating the World from India: TutorVista

In 2005, a cartoon showed an irate American father telling his son, "No! You can't outsource your homework to Bangalore."[7] Outsourcing the homework hasn't happened just yet, but outsourcing some of the learning has, thanks to the power of the Internet and Krishnan Ganesh's observation in 2005 that education—particularly in mathematics—was suffering in the United States and elsewhere. In October that year, Ganesh took a small space in a business incubator in Bangalore; in November, he hired three Indian schoolteachers, who began tutoring American students more than 9,000 miles away.[8] With a headset and webcam at each end, a VoIP connection, and an "erasable whiteboard" on their computer screens on which both teacher and student could write—one in red, the other in blue—TutorVista was born.

Ganesh recalls how he conceived TutorVista while traveling in the United States in early 2005. "During my visit, I was shocked by the amount of media debate over the crisis in the U.S. school education system. My curiosity was piqued . . . When I went deeper, I found that while the public school system is good and the teachers are good, personalized education is simply unaffordable."[9]

Ganesh, a previously successful entrepreneur, was looking for a new problem to solve, and this one seemed meaningful and ripe with opportunity. "In math," he observed, "they're more than happy to be tutored by an Indian, because Indians are considered more studious and nerdy."[10] He already knew all about managing remote workers from his experience with one of his earlier companies, which did business-process outsourcing. Further, he felt that his access to the low-cost Indian workforce would be an asset. Not only were Indians' salaries dramatically lower than those of American teachers and tutors, but Indians also had a good reputation among Americans for academics.

A Customer-Funded Subscription Model: Ganesh's Silver Bullet

Thanks to his experience of having built and sold two successful companies in India, Ganesh spent the first few months tinkering with the service. He hired an American educator to train his tutors on the application-based American pedagogy—"a guide on the side" rather than "a sage on the stage"—which differed from the rote memory and repetition more common in India.[11] With face-to-face tutoring priced at $60 per hour and up in the United States, Ganesh priced his offering at $20 per hour, but he soon discovered that a subscription model—$100 per month for all the tutoring you could want, 24/7—enhanced customer adoption and retention, not to mention cash flow.[12]

> **Ganesh soon discovered that a subscription model enhanced customer adoption and retention, not to mention cash flow**

The switch from hourly pricing, paid by the customer after the engagement had been completed, to a subscription model was TutorVista's silver bullet. Not only did the subscription model mean that TutorVista was getting paid before even delivering its service, and long before paying its tutors—the essence of a customer-funded model—but the revenue stream for his customers became much more habitual and predictable, as did the level of tutor capacity and infrastructure required to service that revenue stream. It also meant the business would be, as with the other customer-funded models we've seen so far, highly capital efficient to grow!

A small amount of angel investment quickly followed, and the business, fueled by regular subscription payments from his growing cadre of American consumers, took off. Six months after launching TutorVista, Ganesh had enrolled 500 students, served by 50 tutors working from their homes in India.[13] With pricing at $100 per month, and with average renewal rates topping 50 percent following a six-month trial subscription, Ganesh had achieved the proof of concept he needed, not to mention a $600,000 run rate revenue-wise.[14] With customer traction proven, he was ready to raise serious capital so his business could grow faster.

Customer Funding Gives Way to Venture Capital

Customer funding can be a great way to start and fund the early growth of a subscription-based business, Ganesh knew. But if he wanted to grow at rocket-ship speed, and take advantage of the opportunity to the fullest, more money was needed, primarily for investment in online marketing to grow the customer base. Such an investment would have been foolhardy at the outset, as he had no idea how customers would respond

> **if Ganesh wanted to grow at rocket-ship speed, and take advantage of the opportunity to the fullest, more money was needed.**

to his offering, nor how long they would remain on board. Now, however, he knew that customers came—and, more than half the time, stayed—which enabled him to begin to understand how much a customer was worth, at $100 per month for who knows how long! "What is the biggest challenge in starting a consumer business?" Gupta asked. "In my opinion the single biggest challenge is whether you can acquire a customer profitably. The only two parameters that matter are what is the cost of acquisition of a customer and what is his or her lifetime value?"[15]

Ganesh's credibility from his past entrepreneurial successes and his early momentum led in June 2006 to a $2 million Series A round led by Sequoia Capital India.[16] A little competition also helped to secure the deal. An experienced fundraiser, Ganesh played his cards carefully. "The final straw was when [Sequoia] knew two other venture capitalists wanted to invest. It's a very small close-knit community so other VCs had spoken to them and I dropped not-so-subtle hints."[17]

Tuning the Engine While the Plane Flies

Ganesh wanted to grow quickly, partly because the opportunity was looking, by now, incredibly attractive. But there was also the possibility that someone else could do exactly the same thing—no entry barriers here. So, while much of the new funding went into a more aggressive online marketing effort, part of it

> **❝Ganesh wanted to grow quickly," but there was also the possibility that someone else could do exactly the same thing—no entry barriers here❞**

went to tune up the business and prepare it for even greater growth going forward.

Ganesh knew he had to maintain a high level of quality to keep his subscribers happy—and staying and paying!—and to facilitate the word-of-mouth marketing that was proving to be a valuable supplement to the company's online advertising. Twenty-four-hour access to tutors was a boon for parents and their busy kids, and TutorVista was happy to switch tutors until a good match was found for each client.[18] Isha Gulati of San Jose, California, age eight—working on math, science, geography, and English four or five times per week with her tutor, Bina Joseph—loved TutorVista. "It's really fun. We always talk about things I really want to know."[19]

Tutors, who were required to have a master's degree in their primary area of tutoring, received increased training in American culture and pedagogy to ensure the primacy of TutorVista's offering. Further, tutors were paid above-average wages for the local market—about double those of business-process outsourcing jobs like those at one of Ganesh's former businesses.[20]

TutorVista wasn't just a good deal for American students; it was a good deal for TutorVista tutors, too. For Bina Joseph, working for TutorVista gave her more time with her family than if she were teaching in an Indian school—and better pay, too. Other tutors felt the same way. Lalitha Venkatesan, a mathematics and English teacher in Delhi for nearly 25 years, had recently retired. She'd been a vice principal but had moved to Bangalore to look after her grandchildren. Her passion for teaching and learning hadn't died, however, and she soon found herself sitting in the morning at her computer, online with her new American students some 9,000 miles away. "The big advantage is that you can sit at home and teach," she says.[21] Her paraphernalia: a webcam, a headset, and a good computer to facilitate face-to-face interaction.

Happy Customers + Happy Teachers + Capital Efficiency = Additional Investors

With its aggressive customer acquisition strategy, customer funding was no longer sufficient to provide enough fuel for TutorVista's tanks. But with the capital efficiency of its subscription model driving the economics, Ganesh convinced Sequoia of the merit of its earlier round of investment. Sequoia contributed another $3 million to TutorVista's Series B round of $10.75 million in November 2006.[22] Lightspeed Venture Partners led the round with a $7 million investment, eager to participate because "TutorVista is building the next big Internet education company," according to general partner Ravi Mhatre.[23] This larger round enabled TutorVista to pursue more significant expansion, building on its success thus far and continuing to make operational improvements.

As the year 2007 opened, TutorVista had grown to 250 Indian tutors serving 2,000 students in 13 countries, including the United States, the UK, Canada, Turkey, Australia, and China.[24]

> **❝Ramping up his management talent was next on Ganesh's agenda❞**

Ramping up his management talent was next on Ganesh's agenda, so former dot-com entrepreneur and American educator Dr. John Stuppy came on board as president and chief executive for America.[25]

The additional capital also funded the development of TutorVista's own online platform for tutoring sessions. The company had previously been using WebEx, but that solution wasn't optimal in terms of usability for TutorVista's target audience. As Ganesh explained, "WebEx worked well for tech-savvy people but others find it slightly daunting."[26] The company's location in Bangalore enabled cost-effective, high-level technical development of a proprietary platform that soon improved TutorVista's service offering.

India's Kids Need Better Education, Too!

Teaching kids in the United States and the UK was a good thing to do, but what about kids in India, Ganesh wondered one day.

> **❝what about kids in India? Ganesh wondered one day❞**

While India's best schools were world class, much of the Indian educational system, especially in rural areas, had real problems. Literacy rates were far behind those of China and other comparable nations. There was a market for TutorVista services within India, Ganesh concluded, but not in their current form. "When we looked at opportunities in India, we decided that we cannot apply the global model here."[27] Despite its presence in 23 Indian cities with more than 800 tutors, he knew a different approach was needed for India. So, using some of its recently raised capital, TutorVista made its first acquisition in November 2007, buying Edurite Technologies, a Bangalore startup founded in 2000 that was in the business of creating content for educational CD-ROMs.[28]

The plan was to take advantage of Edurite's content to power physical centers throughout India that would deliver standardized technology-delivered curricula with in-person tutorial support. This approach would take advantage of "the propensity of Indians to spend on education, [which] is one of the highest in the world," according to Ganesh.[29] Like TutorVista's journey to date, this plan had ambitious targets: TutorVista planned to open 300 centers in the next year.[30] To continue to fuel his company's growth, Ganesh then raised an additional $18 million in July 2008.

Right Place at the Right Time

As Ganesh geared up to attack the Indian education market, Pearson, the British publishing group, was developing a strategy for doing the same thing, having already made considerable investments in China and Latin America.[31] Khozem Merchant, deputy chairman of Pearson India, said, "The entire Pearson group has a sharp eye on opportunities in India." Pearson and TutorVista began talking and, in June 2009, Pearson announced that it would take a 17.2 percent stake in Tutor-Vista for an undisclosed sum. The company said it planned to add TutorVista's online tutoring to its range of services for students in North America, the UK, and other parts of the world, and to develop new businesses for the Indian schools market. Simultaneously, Pearson announced it was buying a 50 percent stake in Educomp Solutions, a Delhi vocational education company that created software and training systems for 23,000 schools.[32]

Ganesh and his team managed the Pearson relationship well, and just a year and a half after joining forces, Pearson increased its stake to 76 percent of the company for another $127 million, and shortly thereafter to 80 percent by buying the stakes of the early angel investors. Pearson valued the company, with its 2,000 tutors serving 10,000 online students per month and a growing presence serving the Indian education system, at $213 million. This deal was significant for TutorVista's future, but also meant a lot to its earlier investors. Lightspeed Ventures and Sequoia Capital India, along with other investors, were all able to fully exit from their positions. KP Balaraj, Sequoia Capital India's managing director, expressed sentiments probably shared by all of the investors: "At close to 7× returns, this would rate as one of the very best seed investments in India."[33]

Pearson's commitment to the deal—and to India—went one step further in February 2013, when it bought from Ganesh the remaining 20 percent of TutorVista.[34] Newly appointed TutorVista CEO Srikanth Iyer remarked, "We have now 35 schools and we will increase this to 100 schools in a year or so. Through Pearson's pedigree, systems and processes, we are now a step closer towards establishing ourselves as the leading technology-enabled education services company in India, offering global standards of learning to Indian students, at affordable prices."[35]

TutorVista's customer-funded subscription model was not responsible for its entire journey, of course. But it gave the company a great start and a capital-efficient model with which to grow. In addition, the early traction it provided gave Sequoia, its first investor, the confidence to back it early, and to follow their money, too!

Petals for the People and H.Bloom: Two Startups Come Together[36]

In April 2009, Sam Pollaro was out of a job, his employer having closed his business to take a position in the Obama administration. Having long wanted to start and run a business of

""In April 2009, Sam Pollaro was out of a job""

his own, Pollaro thought, "This would be a good time to start a business"—except for one thing. "It was the worst recession in 70 years."[37] Pollaro, whose wife, Sarah, operated a small floral design business that provided floral arrangements for weddings, events, and some corporate accounts, was looking for an idea that wouldn't take much capital. Sarah already knew how to buy and arrange flowers, and the two of them wondered whether the combination of Sarah's capabilities and the power of the Internet might offer consumers a better way to buy flowers.

Neither of them knew anything about developing a website, but from Sam's perspective, "We had no idea what features and functions we needed, so it was better to teach myself how it needs to work, as opposed to 'Let's go out and build this gold-plated site where we attempt to figure out everything that people are going to need to do and hope we get it right.' In retrospect, he recalled, "It was one of the things we did right."

Launch on a Shoestring, Plus Customer Funding

In July 2009, the Pollaros launched their site, PetalsForThePeople .com, having spent practically no money—just a couple of thousand dollars on a graphic designer and some printed materials. Their customers' cash would fund the rest of their journey. Consumers could log on, create a weekly or biweekly subscription, and then either have a small bundle of cut flowers delivered or pick them up at a couple of locations in Washington, DC. A video on the website told the customers how to arrange the flowers, and the site described for the customers the sources of the flowers in that week's bundle, along with information about the species. So there was an experiential and educational element to the concept, too.

Sam knew someone at Daily Candy, a blog with tens of thousands of subscribers in the Washington area, and for the first couple of weeks Daily Candy was extolling his company's virtues. "Never again shall we search in vain for unique and affordable blooms. From this day forward, the people will receive bundles of fresh flowers each week with which to create their own unique arrangements."[38] On just one early day, 50 new customers signed up, and referrals soon followed. Word was spreading!

> **the Pollaros knew exactly how many subscribers they had, unlike a local florist**

Because the Pollaros knew exactly how many subscribers they had, unlike a local florist, who never really knew what demand would be from one day to the next, they could provide to their customers flowers that were truly fresh, and at a price at which customers could get flowers for several weeks for the price of a single high-end delivered bouquet.

By June 2010, the business, though still small, with a couple of hundred subscribers, was, in Sam's words, "running on cruise control. We had employees packing and delivering the flowers, and the rest was easy." The Pollaros' first son had just arrived, however, and Sam was beginning to realize that flowers were Sarah's passion, but not his. He began thinking about what else he could start.

Enter H.Bloom: Different Strategy, Different Funding Model, Too[39]

At about the same time the Pollaros were getting started in Washington, Bryan Burkhart left the California software company where he had been among the earliest business hires. He had risen to senior VP of global sales at age 28, but what he was selling was boring. "If I described it here, you would fall asleep," he recalled.[40] So he and a techie coworker and longtime friend, Sonu

Panda, decided to "take a year off, recharge, and spend the time to come up with a new business idea," in Burkhart's words.[41] The duo soon stumbled on an article about flowers, which argued that the market for flowers was one where there had been little technological innovation to date.

> **the market for flowers was one where there had been little technological innovation to date**

Burkhart decided it was time for a little research. "It turns out that the flower industry is a $35 billion dollar market in the United States alone. That's right, $35 *billion*. That was certainly enough to pique my interest. But I didn't know anything about flowers, so I did the only thing I could think of to learn more. I put an ad on Craigslist, saying that I wanted to buy a flower shop. I got dozens of responses, and spent the next two weeks at Chelsea Market in Manhattan, sitting in front of one of the city's best espresso stands, meeting with flower shop owners (and drinking inordinate amounts of coffee)."[42]

Burkhart quickly realized that flower shop owners were in actuality artists, creating living art from individual stems of living material. In his view, though, there were flaws in the typical retail florist's business model. First, retail real estate was expensive, especially in New York. Was a physical storefront really necessary in the day of the Internet and the iPhone? Second, the need to display a wide range of flowers created massive spoilage, as much as 30 to 50 percent of purchases.[43] Florists had to mark up their flowers substantially—as much as five times their cost, in some cases—to cover these losses.

As a global software sales executive, Burkhart had been on planes and in hotels practically all the time. And everywhere—seemingly every office tower, every restaurant, every hotel—there had been flowers! Clearly there were corporate customers who saw flowers as an essential part of decorating their premises, but, he speculated, they probably didn't really want to make a flower purchase decision every week. They would probably much prefer that the flowers would somehow miraculously appear!

As part of his research into the floral industry, Burkhart spoke in December 2009 with Sarah Pollaro, through the introduction of a mutual acquaintance. Nothing substantial came of that contact at that time, and Burkhart continued to develop his ideas. Soon, he had an epiphany.

ʻʻWe can get into the flower business and change its fundamental economics. ʼʼ

"We can get into the flower business and change its fundamental economics by offering subscriptions primarily to corporate customers."[44]

The business would have predictable revenues (just like Petals for the People) and would have an advantage over the competition by reducing spoilage.

Subscription Model? Yes. Customer Funded? Not!

Fresh from his experience in Northern California, where raising money from investors is just what you do, Burkhart prepared a pitch showing how a subscription model with its predictable revenue stream and its ability to revolutionize the industry by reducing spoilage had potential, especially in a market the size of cut flowers. In April 2010, with $1.1 million in seed funding from a small group of angel investors, he launched H.Bloom in New York City, saying, "We're the Netflix of flowers. We enable customers to sign up for luxurious flowers with convenient delivery at really affordable prices."[45] Fresh-as-a-daisy flowers for $29 and up, beautifully arranged and delivered automatically. It looked like a good deal.

Sonu Panda came along as co-founder—despite being allergic to pollen!—contributing his technology expertise to complement Burkhart's business development skills.[46] He quickly set about building proprietary technology for H.Bloom to handle accounts, place orders, and coordinate deliveries.[47] The pair decided that they would run all operations themselves at first to ensure the quality and customer satisfaction they thought essential for the luxury brand they intended to build.[48]

In June 2010, Burkhart got a call from the Pollaros, who had been alerted to their New York–based counterpart by a friend. After a few months of discussions, in November the two companies reached an agreement whereby H.Bloom bought the assets— mainly the customer list—of Petals for the People, and hired Sarah Pollaro as H.Bloom's creative director. Washington instantly became H.Bloom's second market.

Taking stock, the Pollaros saw that they had spent 15 months building what was still a modest but cash-positive business that, except for the first couple of thousand dollars, had been funded entirely by its customers. The deal with H.Bloom turned those 15 months of effort into a small nest egg with which to pursue Sam's next idea. Better yet, he'd learned a great deal—a customer-funded education, in a sense—about building an Internet business. For Burkhart and Panda, with customer traction now apparent in two markets, from commercial customers in New York and from consumers in Washington, the acquisition gave them the momentum to raise a round of $2.1 million from Battery Ventures to fund further technology development and organic growth.[49]

Revving Up Operations at H.Bloom

With two markets up and running, and their investors' expectations growing by leaps and bounds, the challenge for Burkhart and Panda was to grow, and grow fast! Burkhart explained the key: "The subscription model was the silver bullet. It would allow us to buy only what someone had already subscribed for, thus reducing spoilage almost completely."[50] The key benefit they offered their customers, however, was a price advantage, so operating the business efficiently was also critical. Panda's team of software engineers took charge of building an efficient back end.

> **❝The subscription model was the silver bullet.❞**

They built systems to tell the flower buyer how many calathea cigar or amaryllis red lion stems she needed (and when), which of the 500 varieties of red roses were in season and at what prices, and which suppliers were sending too many damaged flowers. Software was used to plan delivery routes that took into account where customers were located. Even the flower arrangers across the hall from the engineers used software to help decide which kinds of lilies to use in next week's arrangements.[51] The company's software-driven approach was appealing to investors, too. Brian O'Malley, a partner at Battery Ventures, explained, "Because they're measuring everything, as it gets bigger it will only get better."[52]

By September 2011, H.Bloom had made considerable progress in automating the business and continuing its growth. Spoilage was running at 1.2 percent, a far cry from the industry's 30 to 50 percent. Sales were up in both New York and Washington, and the business was on track to do $2 million in revenue in 2011, up substantially from the $342,000 it had done in its first partial year.[53] H.Bloom's investors were pleased with the progress, which led Battery Ventures to lead another round of financing for $4.7 million, with other investors participating as well.[54]

Ready to Grow Faster

With more funding in the bank, H.Bloom opened its third market, Chicago, that same month,[55] followed by San Francisco in February 2012.[56] Growth was crucial for several reasons, not the least of which was that others, including those already in the floral industry, could easily choose to do something similar. As with many subscription-based businesses, this one was easy to copy, technology aside. As was the case for TutorVista, there were no entry barriers here, either. Equally important, though, was the opportunity to begin

> **As with many subscription-based businesses, this one was easy to copy**

gaining economies of scale. Burkhart explained, "Getting to a certain volume allows price breaks that you just can't get as a sole proprietorship."[57]

But adding new markets was no trivial task, much more a traditional bricks-and-mortar than an Internet play. Each new city required "feet on the street" to win commercial accounts and take them away from the customers' current suppliers. A simple distribution facility in each city, where flowers were sorted and arranged, and a small fleet of vans for deliveries were also essential. And in each city it was essential to connect with a top floral designer, a crucial talent that was essential for H.Bloom's luxury positioning. Choosing the right one, with an already happy set of commercial customers, could get a new market off to a fast start.

Washington, with a growing number of satisfied commercial clients like the Sofitel Hotel, tripled its sales in its first year of operation, evolving from "someone's basement" to "a bustling space that's half-office, half-botanical gardens," according to Burkhart.[58] It was on track to deliver $1 million in sales for the 2012 year. Chicago hit its one-year anniversary in September, also having generated $1 million in its first year of operations.[59] And Dallas, the company's fifth market, was just launching.[60]

Despite its success in growing its top line and in raising capital, H.Bloom was still a modest, though growing, business doing just a few million dollars in sales. More cash was needed to fund the costs of expansion and further development of the technology-driven systems that comprised the heart of the business. So in April 2012, its investors stepped forward once again, with another $10 million of funding, bringing total capital raised to date to $18 million. Shasta Ventures led the round, with Battery Ventures and other earlier investors contributing more capital, and a few other new investors signing on.[61] Of course, the primary goal remained H.Bloom's expansion into new cities; the company was now targeting a total of 25 markets served within a year.[62]

By July 2013, Boston and Atlanta had been opened, and Los Angeles and Las Vegas were launching that month.[63] By targeting major cities H.Bloom was able to better and more efficiently serve customers like Sofitel and Four Seasons, which had properties in most of them, as did many of H.Bloom's high-end luxury retailers like Chanel, Burberry, and YSL, and its property manager customers with national office building portfolios.[64] True to its Petals for the People roots, H.Bloom was beginning to more seriously pursue the luxury consumer market, too. But why, one might ask? Was this an indicator that all was not well in the commercial market segment? Despite the 2012 infusion of additional capital and the company's aggressive plans, by March 2014 only Miami and Philadelphia has been added to H.Bloom's roster of service areas, and the company's PR output had slowed to a trickle. Another bad sign?

❝Was this an indicator that all was not well?❞

In the early days of the business, it had apparently not been clear to Burkhart that many of his brick-and-mortar competitors already operated subscription models for their commercial accounts, where weekly deliveries were already the norm. The competitors just didn't do it online. Presumably, they, too, experienced little spoilage in the commercial, subscription-driven portions of their businesses. Does technology give H.Bloom a genuine competitive edge in the commercial market, where others with lower cost structures also pursue subscription models? Will Burkhart and his team be able to successfully confront the challenges of rolling out a technology-based but people-intensive business, and grow fast enough to deliver the returns his investors expect? Time will tell. As the company's voracious appetite for capital makes clear, though, its customer-funded model disappeared very early; in fact, for H.Bloom, unlike Petals for the People, it was never really there at all.

When Subscription Models Fail

The TutorVista and H.Bloom stories reveal some of the benefits of pursuing subscription models. Because such models are inherently attractive in many ways—predictable revenue, customer payment up front, and the fact that many customers just stay on board without even being asked—they became something of a darling for Internet entrepreneurs looking for the next big thing, at least for a while. But as Forrester Research e-commerce analyst Sucharita Mulpuru observed in late 2012, "Subscriptions were the hot trend in the last year, but I think some of that energy has really flattened."[65] Let's consider some additional examples.

Do men really need Manpacks. com, which has the presumably brilliant idea to deliver socks, underwear, and other men's essentials on a quarterly subscription basis?[66] I don't know about your underwear, but mine, unlike the flowers on our dining room table that will soon perish, lasts a long time. Or take shoes. Do women, even shoe addicts, really need a subscription to a business like American TV personality Kim Kardashian's ShoeDazzle, which offers a new pair of shoes each month? In late 2012 ShoeDazzle was struggling, having replaced its CEO and laid off employees, calling into question the wisdom of the new breed of subscription-based businesses, despite the millions of VC funding they attracted from some top-tier VC funds.[67] Some such businesses, like ShoeDazzle, rocketed to large numbers of early subscribers and impressive sales numbers. But for many if not most, the novelty has quickly worn off, and they've had to pivot to other, hopefully more sustainable propositions.

> **Do men really need Manpacks. com?**

There were more. GuyHaus offered (apparently unselective) guys what founder Jesse Middleton called the "magic" of toiletries that "just show up," with a monthly subscription for certain products, without specifying the brands.[68] Were they thinking men would drink or eat the stuff? Lollihop sent a box of presumably carefully reviewed healthy snacks to subscribers each month for $22.75.[69] Is it really that difficult to find healthy snacks for your kids at the supermarket, probably at lower prices, too? Both GuyHaus[70] and Lollihop[71] went under by early 2012.

Clearly, subscription models are no panacea that can take the place of the fundamentals of building viable businesses. So let's examine some of the questions that business angels will ask about *your* idea for a subscription-based business.

> **Clearly, subscription models are no panacea that can take the place of the fundamentals of building viable businesses.**

What Angel Investors Will Want to Know—and Will Ask

If you are reading this chapter and putting it to good use, you may have already gotten your early customers to fund your subscription-based business. Whether you're an entrepreneur or someone building a subscription-based business within a well-established company, perhaps you are thinking that now is the time to add some fuel to the tank, just as TutorVista did, in order to invest in better underlying technology or to acquire customers at a faster rate to stay ahead of the pack that's probably nipping at your heels. What will angels or other investors—even corporate investors—want to know about your progress to date and what it says about your potential for the future?

Does a Subscription Model Make Your Offering Both Better *and* Cheaper for Your Target Customer?

For H.Bloom, the main benefit of its subscription model is said to be savings in reduced spoilage, some of which are passed on to the customers, and some of which are eaten up in building proprietary technology and putting a sales and operations team on the ground in each city. But brick-and-mortar florists should also be able to forecast their demand for the subscription-based commercial parts of their businesses, too. Is there really a material competitive advantage here? Is H.Bloom *better*, in the customers' eyes? It's difficult to tell. And how much *cheaper* is it? Local florists who serve commercial customers probably don't take the newcomer lying down! Thus, the long-term viability of H.Bloom's model probably rests on whether the savings from reduced spoilage, if in fact they are real, sufficiently outweigh by a dramatic margin the other costs of operating the business. If they don't, and if the price advantage turns out to be modest, local mom-and-pop florists will probably continue to compete just fine. Disrupting a market is easy to talk about, but difficult to deliver. H.Bloom is still a young company; whether it will thrive over the long term remains to be seen.

> **" Disrupting a market is easy to talk about, but difficult to deliver. "**

For TutorVista, on the other hand, its subscription model offered significant savings over face-to-face tutoring, to be sure. But more important, perhaps, was the 24/7 access it offered and the parents' peace of mind that if one's kids were stuck on a math problem while Mom and Dad weren't home, someone would be there to help at a moment's notice—better *and* cheaper![72] If your customer-funded business offers something that's both better *and* cheaper, it's a lot more compelling—to customers and investors—than just better *or* cheaper. And if it offers neither—like Manpacks or ShoeDazzle, some would argue—you are probably in for a difficult journey.

What Is It Costing to Acquire Each Customer, How Quickly Does That Investment Pay Back, and What Is His or Her Lifetime Value?

As an experienced entrepreneur, Ganesh identified the key to TutorVista's profitability as keeping the acquisition cost per customer lower—probably significantly lower—than that customer's lifetime value to the company.[73] Decisions related to target customers, for example, were guided by projections of a certain group's likely evolution with the company. Ganesh reasoned, "I'd rather take a lower amount per month and keep someone for several years. What is the lifetime value of an 8th or 9th grade student? How much can I up-sell him as he goes through high school, college and onward?"[74]

Most investors won't want to invest in marketing expense without clear evidence already in hand that it pays back very quickly, probably in weeks or months—not years, an even more stringent test than Ganesh was applying. Of course, early in the life of your business, you won't know how far into the future your customers will remain with you and continue to spend. But your renewal rates to date, like TutorVista's early figures north of 50 percent, will give you some information, the quality of which will improve over time. Your renewal rates are a key metric that every angel will want to know and understand, probably in considerable detail. Analyzing what happens to each of the monthly cohorts of new customers you acquire, how many of them renew, and how much they spend over time is the best way for you to understand—and communicate to investors—whether your model is working or not. And needless to say, when you measure the value of your customers' lifetimes to date or going forward, you should measure their contribution margin, after the costs of selling to them and servicing them, not just the revenue you get from them.

Are You Selling Perishables, Consumables, or Durables?

Unlike items from startups such as Manpacks, with its regular deliveries of underwear and socks, "Flowers die and you actually want more," Burkhart says. "You're going to need a new shipment every week or the week after."[75] The same was true for Diapers.com, which built a successful business that was sold to Amazon for a tidy sum. Building a subscription

> **Flowers die and you actually want more.**

business for a durable good is probably much harder, and may be nigh on impossible, than for something that either perishes like flowers or gets consumed very quickly—the faster and the more predictably, the better! Sure, Manpacks offers toiletries such as cologne, too. But the rate at which most men use cologne is neither fast nor predictable. In contrast, numerous entrepreneurial companies, like Abel & Cole in the UK, have built successful businesses that deliver boxes of organic vegetables to their customers' doors. Veggies spoil or get eaten, of course, and need to be replenished very quickly, a good reason why many such businesses have thrived.

Is There Any Evidence to Believe Your Subscribers Are Helping You "Go Viral"?

Ideally, you'll want your subscribers to be telling their friends about your wonderful subscription-based business. Subscriber referrals helped Petals for the People quickly reach break-even cash flow. Is there something about what you offer that makes it likely that your customers are telling their friends? Are you measuring it? Do so!

Are You Building Technology Because You Can, or Because Your Business Depends on It?

H.Bloom, thanks to Sonu Panda's vision and skills, invested heavily in technology to support its operations and growth. That technology may well turn out to be a fixed cost that, once it gets leveraged over a sufficiently large number of cities, becomes a real source of sustainable competitive advantage for H.Bloom. Alternatively, there is always the risk in technology-driven ventures that—like the carpenter with a hammer in hand, to whom every problem looks like a nail—fancy technology is built not because it is needed, but because the team can (and loves to) build it! Angels will—and should—look carefully to see in which camp the business you are building falls.

Making Subscription and SaaS Models Work:
Final Lessons

We began this chapter with a cursory look at SaaS models, which are taking today's software industry by storm as I write. The set of angel investor questions I've just identified offer some imperatives for software businesses using SaaS models, just as they do for the examples in other industries that we've studied more deeply in this chapter. Be better *and* cheaper, in the customers' eyes. Get the balance right between the cost of acquiring a customer and the customer's lifetime value or payback period (measured by margin contribution after variable costs, not by revenue). Software is neither a consumable nor a durable—it's a service, and software as a service is clearly working in many settings. No issue there. And is your offering "going viral"? If not, maybe it's not as compelling for your customer as you had hoped.

> **Get the balance right between the cost of acquiring a customer and the customer's lifetime value or payback period**

Before we wrap up this chapter, it's also worth taking a look at what's happening in one of the world's oldest subscription industries: newspapers. The venerable newspaper industry, which has been under siege for years by online media, is showing signs of regaining its footing. The *New York Times* now gets more revenue from subscribers—both print and digital—than from advertising.[76] Paywalls, requiring digital subscribers to pay for some or all of the newspapers' online content, and used by the *Times* and others, seem to be working. And, surprisingly, perhaps, Warren Buffett's Berkshire Hathaway has spent $344 million buying 28 newspapers over the past couple of years.[77] Why?

Buffett says this about why his newspapers will be money-makers: "Newspapers continue to reign supreme in the delivery of local news. If you want to know what's going on in your town—whether the news is about the mayor or taxes or high school football—there is no substitute for a local newspaper that is doing its job. A reader's eyes may glaze over after they take in a couple of paragraphs about Canadian tariffs or political developments in Pakistan; a story about the reader himself or his neighbors will be read to the end. Wherever there is a pervasive sense of community, a paper that serves the special informational needs of that community will remain indispensable to a significant portion of its residents."[78]

Local newspapers are probably better, as a way to keep people informed, than other alternatives. And probably cheaper, too, than having to gather local information yourself. Buffett's newspapers' challenge will be to provide local information that people want, but don't get, via broadcast media. Whether his newspapers provide it in print or online or on a mobile device doesn't really matter, as long as the content is made available when and how the consumer wants to get it. And, though Buffett doesn't talk about it openly, his newspapers' capital-efficient subscription models give Berkshire Hathaway recurring revenue, something Buffett loves!

Perhaps the most important lesson of this chapter, for both entrepreneurs and angels, and for those investing in new ventures in established businesses, is that just because you *can* sell something on a subscription basis— tutoring, shoes, men's underwear, or whatever—doesn't mean you *should* do so! Selling durables, I suspect, probably won't work, though numerous entrepreneurs are trying to prove me wrong. Selling perishables or other consumable goods and services can work, providing doing so via a subscription model is both better in the consumer's eyes, *and* cheaper, too.

> **just because you *can* sell something on a subscription basis doesn't mean you *should* do so!**

The questions you've learned in this chapter to ask about subscription models, summarized in the checklist that follows, are intended to provide a flashing caution signal, because the history of subscription models—of the B2C dot-com variety, at least—is decidedly mixed. But if you're a dot-commer looking for a customer-funded business *you* can pursue—or if you're a business angel seeking some flashy dot-com investments to talk about at cocktail parties—subscription models might fit the bill. But hold your horses, as we'll see some more dot-com examples in the next chapter, on scarcity models. Will you like them any better? Turn the page and read on!

John's Business Angel Checklist—Subscription and SaaS Models

- Does a subscription model make your offering *both* better and cheaper for your target customer?
- What is it costing to acquire each customer, how quickly does that investment pay back, and what is his or her lifetime value?
- Are you selling perishables, consumables, or durables?
- Is there any evidence to believe your subscribers are helping you "go viral"?
- Are you building technology because you can, or because your business depends on it?

6

Sell Less, Earn More: Scarcity and Flash Sales Models

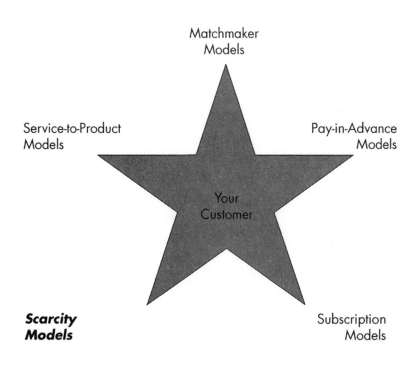

Matchmaker
Models

Service-to-Product
Models

Pay-in-Advance
Models

Your
Customer

**_Scarcity
Models_**

Subscription
Models

Scarcity models, of the five types in the book, are perhaps the most ingenious of all and the most difficult to pull off successfully. As we'll see in this chapter, though most of them generate lots of customer cash, some have been difficult to make profitable over the long term. Scarcity models are nothing new, of course, because purveyors of high-end designer apparel and other luxury brands have been "doing scarcity" for years—you won't find Prada or Gucci on every street corner. Even eligible singles sometimes use scarcity tactics—"Really sorry, I can't make it on Friday," they tell their suitors—to make themselves more appealing to the mates they covet.

But Zara, the Spanish fashion apparel chain, took the scarcity idea to new heights and, in so doing, defined a new model. Unlike most sellers, which seek to sell as much of everything as they possibly can, in scarcity models sellers actually restrict what is available for sale, in time *and* in quantity. When it's gone, it's gone. And there won't be any more, either! The implication, of course, is that "you'd better buy now, or you'll miss your chance!"

❛❛you'd better buy now, or you'll miss your chance!❜❜

Zara, as every young fashionista knows, does just that. It follows "who's wearing what" on stage and on the fashion runways—even on the streets of London or La Coruña, the small Spanish town where Zara got its start[1] —and copies it (quickly!). A knockoff of what was worn by the Spice Girls at London's O2 Arena at a Saturday night concert can hit the stores in as little as a couple of weeks. But Zara won't reorder that same style, so its young clientele know how shopping at Zara works:

- They'd better visit Zara often, or they'll miss out on something they might want.
- If they see something they like, they'd better buy it now, as it will soon be gone.
- Given Zara's limited inventory of any single style, they are unlikely to find someone else wearing the same garment, heaven forbid!

Thus, *scarcity models are those in which what's for sale is restricted by the seller to a limited quantity for a limited time period, with no reorders, with the seller's supplier being paid* after—*sometimes long after*—*the sale is made.* Scarcity models can be applied in a variety of industry settings, especially those where there is fast-paced product obsolescence. So, whether you are an aspiring entrepreneur or a leader or innovator in a company in such a setting, this chapter is for you.

In this chapter, we examine the case history of a fascinating and inventive customer-funded business, vente-privee, whose scarcity model created an entire new category of retailing into which untold numbers of copycats have jumped: flash sales. Vente-privee used its customer-funded model not to start its business, which already existed in another format, but to grow it. Then we examine some of the flash sales copycats, exploring the fact—and the reasons behind it—that for so many of them, and for flash sales retailing as an industry, this model has delivered decidedly mixed results.

Vente-privee Invents the Flash Sales Model

For years, Jacques-Antoine Granjon and his partners, all with well-established roots in the distribution of manufacturers' overstock inventory, had been performing the delicate task of moving unwanted excess inventory of Parisian fashion designers, through a variety of events that would not disrupt the carefully honed brand images of their upscale suppliers. They served an important function for these suppliers because, like anyone in the fashion industry, sometimes the designers got it wrong and made more of a style, or bought more of some fabric, than they should have.

In 2001, connecting the dots between their business experience and the Internet's ability to create a virtual store that offered the potential to move volumes of discounted merchandise without diluting the brands' images, Granjon and his team came up with a simple idea.[2] From time to time, an e-mail would sent to the "members" of vente-privee (the French phrase *vente privée* means "private sale" in English), giving them 48 hours' notice of an upcoming "sale event." The e-mail would be accompanied by a video that not only presented the (overstocked, excess, and unwanted!) merchandise in the best possible way but also gave the brand confidence that its image was not being tarnished. Two days later, the merchandise, of which there would be a limited quantity—always the case for closeouts, which was the real problem that vente-privee would be solving for its suppliers—would go on sale. But not for long. The sale would last for just three to five days, with the goods priced 50 to 70 percent below what they would have sold for on the Champs-Élysées. The brands wouldn't mind, for several reasons:

- They needed a way to get rid of unwanted inventory.
- Vente-privee would present the merchandise in an appealing way.
- The discounted price would not be available to the public, but only to the members that vente-privee could attract.

When the sale event was over, vente-privee would place its order with the brand for what it had already sold (and been paid for, the classic hallmark of customer-funded models!). Last, vente-privee would pay the vendor (sometimes several weeks later) for what it had bought and sold. Just as businesses with pay-in-advance models do—like The Loot, which bought on consignment from its suppliers, as we saw in Chapter 4, or those with matchmaker models like Airbnb or Expedia in Chapter 3— so, too, do those applying scarcity models "sit on the float" for as long as their vendors will let them.

> **those applying scarcity models "sit on the float" for as long as their vendors will let them**

Vente-privee's scarcity model is a unique combination of exclusivity, price, and value-added merchandising. Success rests on vente-privee's deep understanding of brands and their values and needs (more than selling on the cheap), and on the fact that each event's scarcity—both in duration and in quantity—gives vente-privee its eager customers' cash before it pays its vendors. It never has any of its suppliers' inventory on its own books. If the sales ran on forever, the system just wouldn't work. "We are selling discount products, a product that people don't want," says Granjon. "But we're selling it in a high fashion way. Which means we are a luxury site selling discount products. That is the paradox. It's the key of our success."[3]

Understanding the Brands: Why Customer-Funding Might Work

Granjon explains his early insight: "I had the products in brown boxes in a warehouse. I thought let's give life to the products— let's do this with a lot of creativity, and create a model on the Internet where offer is less than demand."[4] His experience with the wholesale and overstock businesses provided the understand-

> **I had the products in brown boxes in a warehouse. I thought let's give life to the products.**

ing of the brands' needs to sell off excess merchandise without compromising their own brands. And his insight about the power of a customer-funded online scarcity model gave him the opportunity to ramp up his then-small company's growth.

As well as limiting the audience, vente-privee ensured that there would be no public record of its Internet sales after a 72-hour period. This protection meant that, after the sale had ended, Internet surfers wouldn't stumble upon discount offers of a luxury brand's goods when searching online. The arrangement satisfied the brands' needs to unload stock without countering their efforts to stay exclusive and somewhat elusive. Xavier Court, one of vente-privee's eight co-founders and the man responsible for marketing, says, "The way we are dealing with overstock is a revolution for branded products. It is extremely efficient, protects the image of the brand, and brings in new customers on- and off-line."[5]

The strategy Granjon and the vente-privee team developed to help the brands generate revenue from overstocked fashions without diluting their luxury appeal was to establish vente-privee itself as a luxury brand from day one. "It is very expensive," says Granjon. "I could have sold all those products without doing that. I would not have created vente-privee, I would have created a discount store. But by doing that I created a brand."[6]

Indeed, vente-privee has been so successful at establishing itself as a luxury brand in its own right that more than 600 exclusive brands, including Dolce & Gabbana, Cacharel, and Givenchy have supplied merchandise to vente-privee.[7] Before long, vente-privee was ranked as France's fifth most popular brand, ahead of the ultimate French fashion icon, Chanel.[8] CEO Granjon is keenly aware of the mutually beneficial relationship between his company and the brands it serves. "Our relationship with brands is completely win-win. If we don't perform for them, they leave."[9] He also believes his company has been built for the long run. "In the future, all brands will be using companies like us. It's the best way to get rid of excess inventories discreetly."[10]

Customer Funding Wins Venture Capital Backing

Because it received its customers' cash before it paid its vendors, vente-privee grew steadily in its early years, without the need for institutional capital. In 2004, a particularly successful lingerie event pushed vente-privee into the limelight, and in 2005, its revenue quintupled, happily still funded by its customers' cash. In 2007, as others began copying the vente-privee formula, Granjon decided to sell a 20 percent stake to private equity firm Summit Partners to provide fuel for launching in seven other European countries. "Vente-privee.com has created an entirely new channel for brands," said Summit's Christian Strain, who was thrilled with the deal.[11]

The company used its new hoard of cash to fund an aggressive program of European expansion. First it went into Spain and Germany, followed by Italy and the UK, and then Belgium, Austria, and the Netherlands. In 2008, its invitation-only sales events were attracting an average of 1 million unique visitors a day, with sales of some 40,000 items. By 2010, vente-privee was operating in eight European countries, and was doing $1.28 billion in sales.[12]

New Geography? Not Easy!

While vente-privee was enjoying some success in its new geographies, in 2010 it still generated more than 70 percent of its revenue in France.[13] Why? For anyone with supplier relationships and the ability to build a website, its model was incredibly easy to copy. More than 70 copycat businesses were up and running in France, and others had beaten vente-privee to market in most other European countries.[14]

> **others had beaten vente-privee to market in most other European countries**

Further, each of these markets had become dominated by a local or multinational version of vente-privee. Spain's Privalia, also VC-backed, with some 5 million members, was the leader in Spain, Italy, and Germany, and in Mexico and Brazil, too.[15] In those markets the originator of the flash sales concept, vente-privee, was seen as the copycat, and it struggled to gain market share. Simon Chinn, a retail analyst in London, explained this phenomenon: "It's not a unique business model any more."[16] Indeed!

Crossing the Pond

Struggling to win dominance in European markets other than France, vente-privee decided to cross the pond to the United

States in pursuit of additional growth. But Granjon didn't want to go it alone, so in late 2011, vente-privee established a joint venture with American Express to facilitate an entry into the U.S. market. AmEx's 30 million cardholders and its existing partnerships with 1,450 brands were seen as invaluable assets to increase the chances of success.

Granjon said of AmEx, "It's a very big brand. I had always said that I wouldn't be going to the U.S. without a partner. It's a very mature market. Discount shopping here is very structured, with companies like TJ Maxx and others making billions in revenues each year."[17] He contin-

❝There's tons of competition. We have to be very humble. ❞

ued, "This is the U.S. There's tons of competition, there's an entrepreneur everywhere, there's always someone who can do what you do better and cheaper. We have to be very humble."[18]

But in the United States, too, vente-privee was a latecomer to the flash sales party, with well-funded Gilt Groupe and Rue La La having gotten their starts in 2007 and 2008, respectively. Both were direct copies of vente-privee, so the market was already very crowded and the American fashion vendors already well served. Perhaps not surprisingly, given vente-privee's experience in the rest of Europe, the going was slow.

By 2012, having removed the requirement to be "invited to join," vente-privee had reached 16 million members in Europe,[19] who were logging on to the company website or mobile app to the tune of 2.5 million daily unique visitors,[20] and buying more than 110,000 items daily.[21] But all was not well, at least in its markets outside of France. "Right now our revenue is 78 percent France and 22 percent Europe," Granjon said in an interview. "I want to go 50–50. I want to be a huge European company. In France we are, but I want to be the same in Europe."[22] And in the United States? "In the U.S., we basically don't exist yet. We are so small. Maybe we'll never be really big here, because this is the country of discounts. So we have to be very creative. It is an adventure."[23]

Even for the originator of the flash sales business, and despite the capital efficiency of its still largely customer-funded model (vente-privee has taken no further institutional capital), growing the geographic reach of the business was proving difficult. Entrepreneurs and investors, take heed!

Gilt Groupe: Large, Capital Efficient, and Growing, but Profitable?

In mid-2007, serial entrepreneur Kevin Ryan observed what was happening in Paris with vente-privee and with its flash sales copycats elsewhere, and saw outside his New York City office the excitement—not to mention the 200-person queues!—that the city's designer-sample sales brought to fashion-focused women. "All I could think was, if there are 200 people who are willing to stand in this line, that means in the United States there are probably hundreds of thousands. They don't live in New York, they're busy right now, they just can't do that. And I can bring this sample sale to them."[24]

Ryan knew next to nothing about fashion, though, and his previous Internet businesses had not been in e-commerce, so he found two style-conscious Harvard Business School MBA students with whom to found the business. Alexis Maybank had worked in e-commerce at eBay and her classmate, Alexandra Wilkis Wilson, brought experience from designer brands Louis Vuitton and Bulgari, along with some other vendor relationships that Ryan and Maybank knew would be useful.

> **he found two style-conscious Harvard Business School MBA students with whom to found the business**

Maybank recalls Gilt's launch in late 2007: "We sent invites to a list of about 15,000 people—friends, former colleagues and classmates, dating back to grade school!"[25] Word of Gilt's great deals spread quickly. Better yet, four months into the launch, Gilt and its great deals were mentioned on a TV show by a concierge specialist, Michael Fazio. As a result of the segment, Wilson recalls, "We went from 20,000 members and after a few hours of being mentioned, we went to 80,000 members."[26]

Growth Takes Off

The business grew quickly, fueled in part by the recession that sank its teeth into the American economy in 2008. The makers of designer apparel were stuck with too much inventory, and Gilt was ready to help them out, at deeply discounted prices, of course. Timing is everything!

After having raised a Series A round in late 2007 to fund the launch (this was *not* a customer-funded business!), Gilt raised a Series B round of $43 million in August 2009, then another $35 million in May 2010, and a whopping $138 million in May 2011, at a billion-dollar valuation. Gilt skyrocketed from a 15,000-person e-mail solicitation at its 2007 start to 5 million members in the fourth quarter of 2011.[27] Manufacturers' overstocks weren't the only thing fuelling Gilt's astonishing growth—a boatload of venture capital did the rest, in part because Gilt's model was, in fact, proving to be not very capital efficient. Why?

Along the way, Gilt had branched out from selling women's fashions to a collection of brands selling everything from menswear to travel to home fashions, even specialty foods, always to exclusive high-end customers. Cross-selling was the buzzword that drove Gilt's growth. And the business had gone from selling virtually all its goods at discounted pricing to selling nearly two-thirds at full price.[28] Was this a sound replication of vente-privee's model? Was the company losing its way?

Not So Fast

By late 2012, it was clear that the company was stumbling, and that many of its new initiatives and merchandise categories were doing poorly. Gilt's customers, unlike those at vente-privee, weren't happy either, with Gilt among the worst performers in

"By late 2012, it was clear that the company was stumbling."

online shopping satisfaction in the critical Christmas holiday selling season in 2012.[29] Ryan and his board agreed that he would step down as CEO, in favor of someone with operations and e-commerce skills.[30] Nearly 10 percent of Gilt's staff were laid off in January 2013.[31] By summer 2013, with new CEO Michelle Peluso, Gilt's fourth CEO in five years, at the helm, Ryan announced that Gilt had "reached profitability, _excluding_ some expenses"—my italics, not Ryan's; if you exclude enough expenses, _any_ company becomes profitable!—"and that the business is starting to generate cash—a huge turnaround since losing $50 million last year."[32] Sales for calendar 2012 were $550 million, up from 2011's $450 million (excluding sales of businesses that were discontinued).

But did Gilt's problem lie in its earlier adventurous moves, or was it in Gilt's original flash sales business? According to Peluso, "Flash is our core."[33] Other observers, however, weren't so sure that the flash sales model is all it's been cracked up to be. "People are pretty negative on flash sales right now," said VC investor Brian O'Malley of Battery Ventures. "Gilt has probably taken longer to become a profitable business than any of them would have liked. It was probably the poster child of this space, but they expanded and got faced with some complexities they weren't expecting."[34] Adds Silicon Valley observer Tom Taulli, "The big concern for Gilt is that the flash-sales business is a fad," he says. "Many companies in the space have already refocused their businesses."[35]

Whether Gilt will get back on track, as Peluso expects, or whether its days as a dot-com high flyer are numbered is yet to be seen. In early 2014, Gilt reportedly engaged Goldman Sachs, an early Gilt investor, to manage a planned IPO.[36] Will Gilt be able to convince the public market that it merits being a public company? If it manages to get its IPO away, will Gilt thrive, or will its share price, like Groupon's, tumble, as we saw in Chapter 1? Time will tell.

As we've seen in this chapter, flash sales businesses can be—perhaps should be—customer-funded, but attempting to grow too fast, too soon, or straying from the model means the customers' cash isn't sufficient to cover the costs. It's a similar lesson we learned about H.Bloom's subscription model in Chapter 5. Entrepreneurs and investors of all kinds, beware! While we wait to see how the Gilt story turns out, let's search for more clues by examining some other early flash sales players.

Totsy and Zulily: Flash Sales for Little Kids' Moms

Totsy, a flash sales site for eco-conscious moms, got its start in 2009, at the height of the flash sales craze in the United States. Like its predecessors vente-privee and Gilt, Totsy sold manufacturers' unwanted inventories of goods. Totsy's focus was on goods for babies and children aged neonatal to seven at deeply discounted prices. Shortly after launch, and after acquiring the 82,000 member list of bTrendie, a similar business that had failed, Totsy raised $5 million in a Series A round in November 2010 from DFJ Gotham and Rho Ventures.[37] True to the flash sales mania that prevailed at the time, its investors then ponied up another $18.5 million in August 2012, followed by another $11 million three months later.[38] By November 2012, Totsy had more than 100 employees serving 3 million members.[39] Things looked bright, but not for long.[40]

> **By November 2012, Totsy had more than 100 employees serving 3 million members. Things looked bright.**

These events were occurring alongside the progress of Zulily, a 2009 Seattle-based flash sales startup that was raising prodigious amounts of capital for an almost identical business targeting young moms and their kids. Zulily's founders, Darren

Cavens and Mark Vadon, both veterans of successful Internet diamond merchant Blue Nile, saw flash sales as an attractive opportunity. They were able to quickly raise $10.6 million from August Capital and Maveron. Then, only 22 months after launch, in August 2011, Meritech Capital Partners invested a whopping $43 million at a lofty $700-million-plus valuation.[41] Zulily already had 5 million users and 240 employees.[42] Totsy wasn't running in an open field.

In May 2013, Totsy crashed, laying off all of its employees, the number of which had already dropped to 83. Its membership list appears to have been acquired by women's flash sale operator Modnique.com. Totsy's revenue in 2012 had only reached $16.9 million, and it incurred $22.9 million in losses. Why? Totsy was spending aggressively to expand its member base, but its new members weren't turning into paying customers quickly enough to make the customer acquisition costs profitable in the short run. Over the previous 24 months, only 10.8 percent of those who signed up as Totsy members had actually become paying customers.[43]

Zulily, on the other hand, raised yet another round, in November 2012, this one from Andreessen Horowitz for $85 million at a valuation of $1 billion, bringing its total VC haul to over $138 million. Zulily passed the 10-million-member mark and was running as many as 35 flash sales offers each day, generally for 72 hours each. It brought its fulfillment activities in house, and built new distribution centers in Ohio and Nevada to enable faster shipments to its customers.[44]

Why has Zulily apparently prospered while Totsy has died? Zulily CEO Darrell Cavens explains. "When you've got a solid business with real revenues and growth, I think there is money willing to invest in that. From day one, we've had the vision of building a real retailer focused on driving revenues, driving engagement, driving member growth. And all of those things are the foundations of a great business."[45] It's also arguable that Zulily's product category enjoys an inherently built-in scarcity, due to a relative paucity of retail channels to give manufacturers, many of them very small independent businesses, adequate market access. In November 2013, Zulily went public, with its hot stock nearly doubling on day one to give Zulily a whopping $4.8 billion valuation. Its investors were very happy, as they took more than $110 million off the table.[46] Not bad for a barely profitable company that had launched less than three years earlier!

Lot18: Flash Sales for Wine

If flash sales work for fashion apparel in Paris and for kids' stuff in Seattle, why not wine? Lot18 was launched in November 2010, with $3 million in capital added to an earlier $500,000 seed round to kick-start the business. Co-founder Philip James, already a veteran of the online wine lovers' community Snooth, had a formative—not to say traumatic—experience while climbing Mount Everest that led him to take the plunge and start the company. "As an entrepreneur, you have to ignore the doubters . . . You always have people telling you, 'This idea is stupid.' I hear it all the time. That belief in what you're building and then kind of head down, everyone else get out of my way, I'm building this. That's what Everest taught me."[47] But was this the right lesson to take from his Mount Everest experience?

> **But was this the right lesson to take from his Mount Everest experience?**

Performance: Not!

Lot18's first six months were promising, with 200,000 new members, thousands of bottles sold each week, and monthly revenue quickly topping $1 million. More funding came in, first $10 million, then another $30 million in November 2011[48]; and Lot18 acquired Vinobest, a similar French business, just a year after launching. The company was off to an excellent, though not customer-funded, start!

But then, in January 2012, just weeks after the Vinobest acquisition, Lot18 laid off 15 percent of its employees.[49] A few months later, four senior executives departed.[50] Then, via the acquisition in early 2013 of Tasting Room, another online wine merchant with a different approach, Lot18 pivoted to a subscription model (we've already seen some of the problems with that model in Chapter 5!). By May 2013, after yet another round of layoffs, the company was down from more than 100 employees[51] to 36, and both of its co-founders had departed.[52] As one unhappy former employee characterized it, "I finally left after one of the most frustrating experiences I've encountered in the tech industry."[53] In July, the company closed its UK office, which it had opened a mere four months earlier.[54]

Why all the turmoil? As in some other settings, the flash sales model simply didn't work in the wine business, where tastes don't

> **❝the flash sales model simply didn't work in the wine business ❞**

come and go in the same way they do in the world of apparel. Wine is a much more stable product category than fashion, with tastes, trends, and reputations established over long periods. The fashion volatility just isn't there, so scarcity really doesn't play very well; it is more difficult to create a sense of urgency with such merchandise as compared to fashion, which can go from "not" to "hot" and back again in a matter of months. Worse, wine is a heavily regulated business in which regulations differ from state to state, country to country. Scaling a business with that kind of complexity is no simple task.

Flash Sales: A Difficult Game

Whatever the eventual fate of some likely survivors—venteprivee and Zulily among them—the flash sales industry has proven, in its short existence to date, to have been brutally unforgiving. Unlike Zara's version of a scarcity model, it's far too easy to imitate—bad news for sensible entrepreneurs, and widely understood by more corporate types, who rightly prefer

❝the flash sales industry has proven to have been brutally unforgiving❞

businesses with more proprietary advantages. Worse, it's hampered by too much competition for vendors' limited supply of the right (i.e., discounted!) goods to sell. It has attracted far too much capital, thereby exacerbating the supply problem and encouraging vendors to simply produce more merchandise for their eager flash sales customers. Scarcity, gone! And consumers appear to be tiring of the daily bombardment of daily deals in their inboxes, too. As Rue La La founder Ben Fischman reflects, "This is a hard business, with a low barrier to entry but a high barrier to success."[55]

But none of that has deterred a plethora of entrepreneurs from starting and continuing to believe in flash sales businesses. Fischman's Rue La La, a Gilt lookalike, launched in 2008 and has passed through the hands of several owners, including eBay, which acquired it when it bought another online retailer, GSI, in March 2011. EBay didn't want Rue La La and promptly spun it out, retaining a 30 percent stake just in case they were wrong. In early 2012, with Fischman saying the company was still committed to its flash sales model, Rue La La laid off 85 people.[56] But Fischman puts a positive spin on his situation. "When we were spun out, it was kind of a 'died and gone to heaven' scenario. We became a private company, with no institutional or venture investors or private equity . . . I love the flexibility that we have. We can do with the business what we believe is most important . . . And we think consolidation is really interesting . . . We look forward to playing a role as a consolidator."[57] In other words, Fischman, one of the flash sales industry's veterans, believes a shakeout is coming.

Will Any Flash Sales Players Survive—and Thrive?

Vente-privee's Granjon insists his business is profitable and has been since 2004. And he argues his competitors are not. "They thought they understood the business and raised lots of money and are still not profitable,"[58] he says of his U.S. rivals. They are all privately held, though, so nobody outside their boardrooms really knows. Granjon is not happy with the competitive environment, however, something he might not have foreseen back in 2001. "Everyone is fighting for the same raw material, the inventories of brands. If too many are fighting, it drives the prices up. The funny thing about this business is that the more people there are buying the inventory, then we will all die. If you drive the prices up, you will not sell. Remember, the inventory is what people did not want to buy the first time. So we have to sell at low price."[59]

Given the abundance of VC and private equity funding that's gone into this industry around the world, one might expect to have seen several exits by now— either IPOs or successful sales (not fire sales) to large companies. Why hasn't that happened very often, aside from the Zulily IPO

> **one might expect to have seen several exits. Why hasn't that happened?**

and the sale of HauteLook to Nordstrom in 2011? One can only conjecture, as no investor likes to admit any of its deals are struggling, but a few reasons appear plausible:

- Given the capital efficient and (if you don't try to grow too fast) potentially customer-fundable model that Granjon invented and others have followed, it's possible that there's not been much pressure on these companies' cash. So fire sales haven't had reasons to happen. But Totsy's demise suggests that, at least in their case, this wasn't the case. As one Totsy vendor commented in June 2013, around the time of Totsy's closure, "Totsy is going out of business fast! They are not paying any vendors at all for their products and collection agencies will not take the case because they say it's a no win situation. Totsy has burned many, many people!"[60]

- Another plausible answer is that optimistic VCs figure they can take their companies public at some point, as Groupon did in 2011, followed by Zulily in 2013, despite no or minimal profits. So they keep supporting them, hoping for an IPO payday. This may be what's happening at Gilt Groupe. Time will tell.

- Perhaps some players see a shakeout coming, which may give them a chance to acquire rivals' membership lists or other assets at fire-sale prices. This appears be the game Rue La La is playing.

- Or, perhaps most likely, most companies' money-losing performance is simply inadequate to support IPOs or high-value trade sales at this time. As one entrepreneur remarked, "Entrepreneurship is the art of staying alive until you get lucky!"[61] For the underperforming companies in this industry, simply staying alive may be the right strategy for today.

Granjon appears to concur. Though he remains upbeat about vente-privee's prospects, he is less sanguine about those for the rest of his industry. "Flash sales are about doing events for businesses. Flash sales happen because a brand has a problem, so you do an operation to solve that problem. It's a completely different business. And when Gilt says they're going to open new verticals, and open full-price e-commerce sites, they're becoming just another e-commerce company. What we want is for something to happen every day that's so special that people come. And with those daily events, we create an addiction. We don't do e-commerce, we do events."[62]

What Angel Investors Will Want to Know—and Will Ask

If you're running a perhaps struggling flash sales business today, or—perish the thought—planning to start one, whether as an entrepreneur or inside an established company, you may at some point decide you'd like some capital to enable your company to grow faster, whether organically or by buying up the membership lists or other assets of others who will inevitably fail. Or maybe you, like Zara, have created another scarcity model that appears to be working. If either of these is the case for you, what are the questions that the case histories of this chapter suggest you'll be asked?

What Is the Depth of the Vendor Relationships You and Your Team Bring to the Table?

The real strength of vente-privee's business lies in its trusted, deep, and lasting vendor relationships. These relationships enable it to procure merchandise that is in genuinely scarce supply, at least in its home market, France. Perhaps its lack of such relationships elsewhere is a contributor to what Granjon acknowledges as disappointing performance in the other countries it has entered.

If you are "just another flash sales merchant," the vendors will probably sell you some goods—after all, they are in business to grow, just as you are. But what they'll sell *you* won't be what they sell to the likes of vente-privee, with whom they probably already have a long-term relationship. They'll tell you, of course, that you're getting a big discount. But your customers will soon discover that their claims just aren't credible.

If you're an angel or other investor pondering a flash sales deal, maybe you shouldn't! But if I have not yet dissuaded you, at least be certain that deep and lasting vendor relationships are in place at the heart of the business you are considering and that the

> **If you're an angel or other investor pondering a flash sales deal, maybe you shouldn't!**

scarcity underpinning your business is genuine and likely to remain.

Is Your Venture Easy to Copy, Thereby Making New Competitors Likely?

Sadly, if yours is a flash sales business, the answer is yes. Unless you can convince an investor that you are the right player to win in the consolidation game that is likely to unfold, this means that your prospective investor's answer is likely to be "no." But the principles of this chapter don't just apply to flash sales—or to Groupon-style daily deals, either—which some might regard as a scarcity model, too. (I'm not sure, though, that there's any real scarcity of deals on lunch at a nearby restaurant or discounts on car washes! Deals for these kinds of things, whether delivered online or offline, appear to be ubiquitous these days.)

Our brief look at Zara's scarcity model may hold a clue. Because Zara itself controls the supply of what it sells, if it forecasts well, it can "manufacture" and control real scarcity of the styles it creates. As much as half of what Zara sells is managed this way.[63] Contrast that with the presumed scarcity that flash sales merchants hope to benefit from. The ease of entry into this industry means that the vendors, which in the depths of the recession saw flash sales as the solution to the inventory problems they had, now see the flash sales industry as an opportunity to sell more! Many of them now produce goods specifically for the flash sales trade. Scarcity—not! So if you aren't really dealing in scarcity, your future appears cloudy at best.

Are Your Metrics about Members, or about "Paying Customers" and Their Value?

Too many Internet entrepreneurs talk about the number of users or members they have acquired, a phenomenon clearly evident in much of the business press coverage of the companies profiled in this chapter. But users or members don't pay the bills. Customers do. If you've built a customer-funded scarcity-based

❝users or members don't pay the bills. Customers do.❞

business, you'll probably also have figured out just what it has cost you to gain one more average customer, and you'll have some evidence that indicates what your typical customer is worth in margin contribution over that customer's lifetime. The relationship between the cost of acquiring a customer and that customer's lifetime value, as we saw with TutorVista in Chapter 5, is a crucial one that prospective investors will want to know *you* understand.

Is Your Plan to "Get Big Fast" or to Grow at the Pace Your Customers (Plus a Bit of Capital) Can Fund?

As we've seen in this chapter with vente-privee, when a promising new business model is discovered or invented, if the concept is easy to copy, then VC money will pile in. As we've seen, Gilt, Lot18, Totsy, Zulily, and numerous others spent aggressively to ramp up their membership lists, thanks to the war chests they were able to raise from optimistic VCs. "Get big fast," a mantra successfully applied by Amazon in the early dot-com days, has merit if the fundamentals of the business are sound. But eBay grew much more slowly in its early years, letting its customer funding drive its early growth. Too much capital flowing into any industry probably isn't a good thing!

If your scarcity model has Zara-like characteristics that make it difficult to copy, then you shouldn't need to grow at an always risky rocket-ship speed. Angels may well like such a deal. But if you're asking for funds to enable an easily copied business to get big fast, that's likely to be a much more difficult sale.

It is perhaps telling that vente-privee has grown relatively slowly in its U.S. joint venture with American Express, to a modest $40 million in sales after two years.[64] While that progress may have disappointed Granjon and his private equity investors, it may provide a clue about what may be the best way for most scarcity models to grow—slowly, at a pace at which their customers' cash can fund them!

Is Your Business Reliant on One Stage of the Business Cycle?

It was clear to vente-privee's Jacques-Antoine Granjon and to Gilt's Kevin Ryan that their flash sales models were helped on the supply side by recessionary economies. Zara, by contrast, makes money in good times and bad. Most angel investors' investment horizons turn out to be longer than they would like, so a business tailored to a single stage in the economic cycle is not likely to fare well in attracting capital. When the dust settles on the flash sales industry, it may become evident that the flash sales model generally works only when economies are in the doldrums. For other scarcity models, like Zara's, that may not be the case.

> **Most angel investors' investment horizons turn out to be longer than they would like.**

Making Scarcity Models Work: Three Final Lessons

In addition to the just-enumerated questions that business angels will ask, summarized in the checklist that follows, there are three important lessons that this chapter's case histories provide. First, at the heart of the scarcity models we've seen in this chapter is the truism that the customer must pay long before vendors are paid. Unless growth is pursued at a lightning pace, that condition is likely to be sufficient to customer-fund a scarcity-based business for some time, with one caveat: The margins that the business generates must be sufficient to cover the day-to-day costs of running the business and generate profits, too. It's easy to be blinded to the profit reality in a business where the customers always keep it flush with cash. But sooner or later, profits will be essential.

Second, the stories in this chapter of so many companies—all but Zara and vente-privee—that got their start with venture capital, followed by more of it early and often, are testament to the downsides of raising invest-ment capital too early. Some have gone under. Many have had man-agement turmoil. Some founders

> **"the stories in this chapter are testament to the downsides of raising investment capital too early."**

have been ousted. Perhaps most sadly, though perhaps not evident in these stories, all of which are still incomplete, is that the ownership stakes of the founding teams in virtually all of these companies besides vente-privee have been so signifi-cantly diluted by round after round of high-priced capital, that these hard-working and committed entrepreneurs own very little of their companies. True, they will be happy if their small stakes turn out to be slices of very large pies. This may turn out to be the case for Zulily founders Cavens and Vadon, if their stock holds its value before their lockup period ends. But the sad state of the flash sales industry suggests that, in most cases, such an outcome is unlikely.

Last, Zara's long-running success, thanks in part to its complete designer-to-shop-floor control of the quantities of the styles it sells, suggests that scarcity models can work under the right circumstances, even though most flash sales models have struggled. So whether you're an entrepreneur looking for a business model that can grow or a corporate innovator seeking to jump-start your company's growth, scarcity models—if not the flash sales variety—appear to hold consid-erable potential. It is somebody's turn to learn from Zara and create a new and better scarcity model that actually works. Is it *yours*? Or might you first want to consider the last of the five kinds of customer-funded models that we've not yet explored? If so, turn the page!

John's Business Angel Checklist—Scarcity and Flash Sales Models

- What is the depth of the vendor relationships you and your team bring to the table?
- Is your venture easy to copy, thereby making new competitors likely?
- Are your metrics about members, or about "paying customers" and their value?
- Is your plan to "get big fast" or to grow at the pace your customers (plus a bit of capital) can fund?
- Is your business reliant on one stage of the business cycle?

7

Build It for One, Then Sell It to All: Service-to-Product Models

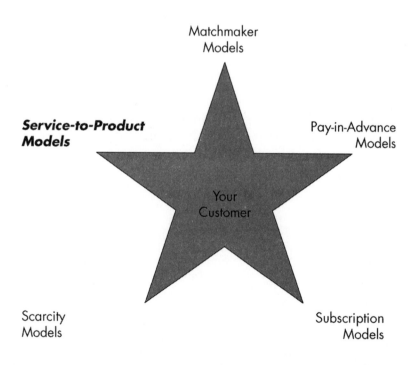

Matchmaker
Models

Service-to-Product Models

Pay-in-Advance
Models

Your
Customer

Scarcity
Models

Subscription
Models

One of the wonderful things about many services businesses—architecture firms, airlines, consultancies, and many more—is the very nature of services themselves. Services, once they've been delivered and consumed, cannot be given back, as products can. If the car you buy turns out to be a lemon, you may be able to convince the dealer to take it back and give you a different one. But if the services customer is unhappy for some reason, the services can't be given back in the same way, as the house has already been built, the airline trip has been flown, or the consulting advice delivered.

For this reason, in many services businesses it is customary for the provider and consumer of the service to agree that the provider will be paid some portion of the fee (or sometimes the entire price, as in the case of an airline ticket) in advance, sometimes with additional payments made as milestones are met along the way. This protects the seller from not getting paid (since the seller would not be able to "take back" the service if payment were later withheld) and, when payments are milestone-based, protects the buyer from shoddy service work (the work can be stopped prior to completion if the buyer does not like what he or she sees in the early stages).

For anyone starting a services business, this is great news. (If you're an executive in a services company, you know this already.) Why? Most services businesses can easily be started and run for a considerable time with their customers' cash, in the form of initial deposits and periodic payments. It's the classic pay-in-advance model in its most basic form. Up-front investment is often modest, sometimes nil!

> **For anyone starting a services business, this is great news.**

As we'll see in this chapter, though, starting a services business and eventually transforming the services into marketable products that can stand on their own is a customer-funded, cash-efficient way to start a products business, too. Just ask Bill Gates and Paul Allen. But before we examine Microsoft's customer-funded origins, let's make clear exactly what we mean by service-to-product models: *Service-to-product models are those in which businesses begin their lives by providing customized services—to meet customers' varying needs—and eventually draw on their accumulated expertise to deliver packaged solutions that stand on their own,* able to be used or consumed by the customer largely without seller support.

From Services to Products at Microsoft

Service-to-product models certainly aren't new. In 1975, Gates and Allen made a pitch to the makers of the new Altair 8800 microcomputer to develop a programming language for the new device.[1] Computer hobbyists themselves, they knew the new Altair product would be essentially worthless to most of its target market without an easy programming language like BASIC.[2] They then did similar deals to write BASIC for other PC pioneers, developing solutions for Ricoh, Texas Instruments, and others. Gates recalled how they were paid: "When we started selling to Japanese companies, we were so overpromised it was ridiculous. Ricoh licensed every language we had and paid us $180,000 up-front, which was incredible."[3] Allen chimed in on the delivery challenge: "We were so late that Ricoh finally flew a guy over whose whole job was to sit in our office day and night until we delivered."[4]

A few years later, in 1980, Gates's and Allen's experience building such software applications led IBM to hire their young company, Microsoft, to build the operating system for the secret new "personal computer" that IBM was developing. Actually, though, Gates and Allen didn't really *build* PC-DOS. They bought much of it from a nearby company, Seattle Computer Products, and hired

❝ Actually, though, Gates and Allen didn't really *build* PC-DOS. They bought much of it. ❞

the company's top engineer to make it work for IBM.[5] Shrewdly, Gates and Allen structured the contract with IBM to permit them to provide DOS for any future IBM copycats, too.[6] Gates vividly remembers his thinking: "Our goal was not to make money directly from IBM, but to profit from licensing MS-DOS to computer companies that wanted to offer machines more or less compatible with the IBM PC."[7]

As PC penetration grew, clever programmers soon figured out some things one could do with PCs: write and edit prose, for example, or develop what we now know as spreadsheets so that financial calculations could be easily changed and updated. Microsoft, having developed extensive software expertise with its services delivered to one PC maker after another, began developing software *products*—Windows, Word, Excel, and more—that came in shrink-wrapped boxes. Services had become products, and the rest is history. As we saw in Chapter 1, that's what India's CE Info Systems did in transforming its digital mapping capabilities into MapmyIndia.com.

Chapter 7 builds on Microsoft's early history to examine the stories of two twenty-first-century service providers that, after developing extensive capabilities in their respective arenas, were able to transform themselves into product companies, the benefits of which will become clear as their stories play out. GoViral, a Danish developer and distributor of online video content, was started with *zero* capital and never took a single krone or dollar of outside investment. In 2011, barely seven years after its founding, GoViral was sold for nearly $100 million. Rock Solid Technologies, a much smaller IT services company in Puerto Rico, saw an opportunity in 2010 to transform itself from a services provider to municipalities in Puerto Rico into a SaaS-based provider of turnkey cloud-based software products, and made its own service-to-product transition.

> **GoViral was started with *zero* capital and never took a single krone or dollar of outside investment**

Whether you're a budding entrepreneur or someone running an established services business, why might you want to make a service-to-product transition in your company? For a couple of good reasons:

- Product businesses are often more scalable than services businesses, which seem to require so many more people and more systems as they grow that they often lack any meaningful economies of scale. Being bigger for its own sake may not be what you want.
- Product businesses are typically less dependent on a single (or a few) individual's talent—your ability to sell *and* deliver your services offering. Entrepreneurs leading services business often wish they could clone themselves. Alas, they cannot.

A service-to-product transition isn't the only way to grow a services business, so this chapter also examines the story of a services business, QuEST Global Services, that has grown dramatically *without* making a transition to a product-based model. I've placed it here, rather than in the pay-in-advance chapter where it arguably belongs, to highlight the choices that pay-in-advance services business may have at hand.

GoViral Goes Viral[8]

GoViral got its low-key start in Copenhagen in December 2003, though formal incorporation didn't come until later. Co-founders Claus Moseholm and Balder Olrik had known each other for several years and had often talked about going into business together. Olrik, a creative type and an artist, had established a digital media agency that he had sold in 2002. Moseholm, a marketing strategist and account executive, was running a small eight-person advertising agency, which he left in the summer of 2003.

Olrik got things started that summer by producing and launching the duo's first service offering, an online video campaign, after convincing a friend to let him produce such a campaign for his business, BullGuard, which sold security software globally. Olrik drew on his diverse background as an artist and media expert and delivered the entire project, from designing the campaign to shooting and editing the video. "The campaign was a huge success," recalled Moseholm, "spreading its reach virally, as consumers passed the link to the entertaining video on to their friends."[9] In total, nearly 20 million people viewed the video, not a bad start for a fledgling company's first effort!

Later that year, Moseholm wrote an article about what Olrik had generated, which required him to do some research on viral marketing. He realized that only a few players were really focused on this kind of work. One company in the UK, The Viral Factory, had done some similar projects, but not much other conscious effort was being made to create video content that would spread organically and virally.

With an encouraging pilot in hand, and with some consulting work keeping food on their families' tables, the pair decided to take the plunge. Over the 2003 Christmas holidays, they developed a website for the business and soon began trying to sell their services. The idea was simple yet novel. They would create, produce, and distribute viral video campaigns for advertisers in Denmark. It did not bother the intrepid pair that, as far as they could tell, there was little demand for such a service among advertisers, perhaps because such campaigns hardly existed and online video was still a niche phenomenon.

> **It did not bother the intrepid pair that there was little demand for such a service**

Despite their experience in the advertising industry, success with the first client's campaign, and an apparent gap in the market, the early going was difficult. "When we talked to agencies about creating a movie for their clients that would attract two million views," Moseholm recalled, "we just got blank stares."[10] It became increasingly clear that educating the market was going to take some time to bear fruit.

Early Days

In 2004, GoViral sold two more campaigns to BullGuard, under an arrangement whereby GoViral was paid based on the sales directly generated from the campaign. Though both campaigns spread widely, GoViral earned only modest revenues, as the number of actual sales that were closed was modest. These jobs were important accomplishments and provided some cash—and performance metrics!—to fund further development of the still-small company, but getting any other traction from the advertising community was proving difficult. Something would have to change.

With the help of Henrik Busch, a friend who headed the digital side of McCann Worldgroup in Copenhagen, plus the customer reactions they'd been gathering, the duo developed a new pitch and a new way to think about online video as a medium: cost-per-view pricing. GoViral would guarantee a certain number of video "views" for a certain fee. "We guaranteed a certain volume," recalled Moseholm, "for example 100,000 click-to-play videos for a certain price, and anything on top of that would be free of charge."[11]

Becoming a Real Business: Customer Funding Leads the Charge

In February 2005, YouTube launched, and Web-based video began to gain some prominence on online users' radar. By late 2005, Moseholm and Olrik saw enough promise to register their company and officially open for business. They had delivered about 1 million Danish kroner (around US$120,000) worth of campaigns that year, with just a single programmer, working mostly with Danish advertisers to serve companies in the fast-moving consumer goods arena. This modest amount of customer cash was sufficient to cover the young company's costs for a few more months and to hire a second programmer, but the founders, who were still taking very small salaries, continued their consulting work to balance their families' books.

With YouTube beginning to prove consumer interest in online video content, Moseholm and Olrik knew they would need some help if the opportunity they imagined—to create, produce, and distribute online viral video campaigns for advertisers—became real. They began talking with Jimmy Maymann, a mutual friend, to convince him to join the GoViral team. During the 2005 Christmas holidays Maymann agreed to join GoViral, but he owed his employer a 12-month notice period before he could come on board.

Maymann proposed that the company raise its sights, setting the goal of becoming a 100 million Danish kroner company, with

❝Maymann proposed that the company raise its sights❞

a first benchmark of earning 10 million kroner in revenues in 2006. In Moseholm's view, "This ambition was audacious at best, foolhardy at worst. It was ridiculous, given that the company was all over the place, with poor technology and everything up in the air. Nothing was really working." To make achieving the goal even more difficult, it was Maymann's view that GoViral should get out of the video creation and production business, which he saw as not very scalable, and focus on distribution. Signing on to Maymann's dream, Moseholm and Olrik decided to stop their consulting work and focus all their energies on building GoViral into a successful business.

Happily, GoViral soon secured an attractive contract—more customer funding, paid in part in advance, as the team had by now come to expect—through the creative agency Leagas Delaney in London. The agency would create the videos, and GoViral would manage the distribution, placing the videos on websites that would reach the intended target market for the client, Goodyear

Europe. The campaign launched that spring of 2006, before Maymann was able to come on board. The team was thrilled, and made a conscious decision to overdeliver for Goodyear, which is exactly what they did. Moseholm explains why: "The content was really strong, so the videos got a lot of traction and delivered millions of views more than what we had guaranteed."

Getting Noticed: On Stage at Cannes

Using their industry connections, the team managed to talk its way onto the agenda to present at the Cannes Lions International Advertising Festival in June 2006. The festival was the largest and most important meeting of the European advertising industry each year. The trend toward viral and online video, accelerated by YouTube's launch the year before, was proving fortuitous for GoViral. Everyone wanted to understand this new medium, and there was growing interest in the advertising community.

The duo resolved to leverage the Cannes opportunity to the fullest extent possible. Moseholm recalls, "We prepared a 30-page booklet with facts about our work and quotes about our viral campaigns, and we got this document inserted into every delegate's gift bag."[12] The exposure in Cannes launched GoViral into position as a market leader in this emerging niche of viral online video. More importantly, it validated GoViral's work. As Maymann put it: "If you're giving a keynote at Cannes, you must be worth talking to."[13] They got invited to do more seminars on the topic, and frequently heard it

> **If you're giving a keynote at Cannes, you must be worth talking to.**

said that they "seemed like a lot more than five guys in Copenhagen."[14]

With the increased visibility and business that followed GoViral's appearance in Cannes, the team realized that the company needed a footprint in London, home to much of Europe's advertising industry. Moseholm moved his family to

London, brought along another team member from Copenhagen, rented a spare desk from a PR company, and hired a new assistant to field phone calls and prepare presentations. Maymann, having finally come on board in October 2006, after managing to convince his employer to shorten his notice period, remained in Denmark.

The London team was rarely physically at that desk, spending virtually all their time on the go, talking to media and advertising agencies about GoViral's approach and the potential of the still-new phenomenon of viral online video. Sales grew, and the 10 million Danish kroner (about US $1.2 million) that GoViral billed in 2006 was enough not only to hit Maymann's audacious target for the year, but to continue to grow the team, with head count reaching a dozen by year end. More importantly, as a services business, it was nearly always possible to convince clients to pay a hefty portion of the fee in advance. The clients' funds were now financing a nicely growing business.

Technology Matters

In 2007, with the focus of the business having turned from the creation of video content to its distribution, co-founder Balder Olrik was not entirely happy, as the creative work had been largely his responsibility and his love. In addition, Moseholm and Maymann recognized that though all three of them had strong backgrounds in advertising and media—and could sell!—they lacked expertise in the technology underlying their offerings.[15] Laborious manual processes were required each time a new campaign was run. "It just wasn't scalable," recalled Moseholm.

❝ It just wasn't scalable. ❞ Once again, changes were needed.

After a year's worth of effort to automate some of the processes, it became clear that GoViral would need to bring on a tech-savvy executive if they were to achieve their goals for the company. Serendipity connected Moseholm with Rene Rechtman on a playground in London. Rechtman was the commercial director at Tradedoubler, a Swedish company that had developed affiliate marketing programs, whose technological and commercial strategies were much like those planned for GoViral. Maymann and Moseholm set about courting him to join them at GoViral, though Balder Olrik wasn't so sure that such a move made sense. The company was growing nicely, in his view, and attracting Rechtman was sure to be expensive.

Amidst these challenges, business went on. And it went on very well, all things considered! By year end 2007, despite the technical challenges, the group had managed to double revenue to 20 million Danish kroner, providing nearly US$2.5 million of additional customer funding to cover the costs of running the business! While still a small company, GoViral had reached this milestone with no external capital, spending only the funds generated from the distribution of video campaigns that were sold.

Breakthrough

In 2007, Nissan Europe began planning the launch of a new model, the Qashqai, targeted at a youthful demographic in Europe. Moseholm and Maymann convinced Nissan that online video was exactly what the company—seen as somewhat stodgy by many consumers—would need if it had any chance to resonate with its Generation X target. Nissan quickly became GoViral's biggest single client in 2007 and 2008, providing about half of the company's revenue with substantial projects related to the launch of the new model.[16] The Nissan revenue made a huge difference, enabling the company to bring the tech-savvy Rechtman on board in the summer of 2008, along with a new CTO and some other technical talent who followed Rechtman. As a result, 2008 was the company's third consecutive year of 100% year-on-year growth, with sales doubling to 40 million Danish kroner.

The Nissan campaign was a complex one, appearing on 15,000 sites across 17 European markets. It generated 50 million views, and helped generate millions of euros in revenue for Nissan Europe. Thanks to a tech platform that was finally fully functional—though by no means perfected—GoViral was also able to provide detailed data reports and analysis for the client.[17] This success became a huge validator of the firm's capabilities, and made for a compelling case study in pitches to other global brands. Awareness was growing quickly about the potential of video as an advertising medium, and GoViral had the sales numbers—and a growing body of performance metrics!—to justify themselves as a strong bet in the field.

Underlying the Nissan success was the fact that, as Moseholm recalled, "we got a lot organized in 2008."[18] Maymann called the launch of the new technology platform a "game changer" for GoViral, allowing them to serve clients at a higher level than they would have been able to without its complex data collection and analysis capacities. The platform also enabled GoViral to handle a greater volume of customer campaigns, and hence revenue. Instead of being simply a services provider, GoViral had turned its offering into a product—a robust platform for delivering video content online—that media buyers and ad agencies could use to measure and report on their campaigns' performance. Better yet, greater efficiency in delivery meant the company was now not just marginally, but highly, profitable.

> **Maymann called the launch of the new technology platform a "game changer" for GoViral**

An Investment Partner Joins the Party

In early 2009, a confluence of the new platform and other events set GoViral onto a new and even faster growth trajectory. First, GoViral expanded its sales strength beyond its top management team, adding sales executives in key European cities. Second, the

CTO brought in by Rene Rechtman more than delivered, launching an even better state-of-the-art platform to support GoViral's customers' campaigns in mid-2009. With some tension still lingering between the company's early focus on content creation and its new focus on distribution, plus a recognition that considerable value had been created to date—and a realization that despite the technical progress, as Moseholm put it, "our technology was still not where it should have been"[19]—the company took on an investment partner, Kennet Partners.

Kennet bought out Olrik's and some of Moseholm's and Maymann's shares, allowing the team to reap some of the value they had created, and it put a stock option plan into place to help GoViral attract and retain the technical and other talent it would need to achieve its potential. No money actually came into the company, as GoViral's customer-funded model—having evolved into more of a product platform than a services business—was more than sufficient to fund its planned growth.

Setback and Setup

The 2008–2009 crash in the world economy—and especially in the auto industry—meant that GoViral's "cash cow" client, Nissan Europe, pulled back in 2009. Nevertheless, despite sales that only grew by 50 percent (to 60 million kroner) in 2009, GoViral's progress with other clients was enough to attract the attention of AOL Europe at the annual Cannes event in 2009. AOL proposed some joint work and a possible acquisition. But Moseholm and Maymann were having fun, and weren't really interested in selling their company.

At Cannes a year later in 2010, AOL made further advances, and this time the GoViral team was more receptive and agreed to sell. The sale of the company was closed in January 2011, with AOL paying 500 million Danish kroner, or $96.7 million, a multiple of five times the company's 2010 annual sales. GoViral had achieved its once "ridiculous" target of 100 million kroner in sales, and its team had created half a billion kroner of value in a company that had never taken *any* external investment. The only

> **❝GoViral had created half a billion kroner of value in a company that had never taken *any* external investment.❞**

funding that had ever come in was the revenue from its happy customers.

This sale reflected the team's early arrival to the viral online video market, its ability to package and sell an attractive and unique concept (cost-per–view pricing), and their better-late-than-never success in developing an effective technological platform to transform the business from a not-very-scalable services business to one with a highly scalable, and highly profitable, product platform. Indeed, AOL chief executive Tim Armstrong explained the GoViral acquisition as such. "GoViral has created an incredibly compelling platform that delivers highly measurable and cost effective solutions to publishers and advertisers."[20] Thanks to its transition from a provider of one-time services to providing a product platform its customers could use on their own, GoViral had achieved its outlandish objectives in fewer than eight years. Their customer-funded service-to-product transition had served them well!

From Typewriters and Carbon Paper to SaaS: Rock Solid[21]

It was January of 2000, and Ángel Pérez was looking for work. He'd wrapped up a major IT assignment, making sure that the arrival of the year 2000 would not disrupt the systems of a major automotive parts maker where he was employed. The Y2K scare passed without a whimper, and Pérez wondered what would be next. Returning to his native Puerto Rico from the United States, Pérez took a job running the small San Juan office of Rock Solid, a Texas-based provider of IT support for Microsoft products. The office and its five employees served a single Puerto Rican customer with a million-dollar service contract, and Pérez thought there was potential for the business to grow.

By 2006, through strengthening and taking advantage of his company's Microsoft certification and relationships, Pérez had built the Puerto Rican operation to 80 people, most of them supporting business and public sector clients using Microsoft software, though Dell, Citrix, Barracuda, and others were also in the mix. The growth was funded entirely by the customer cash that Rock Solid's service contracts delivered, and the Rock Solid team was becoming known as the best place to go in Puerto Rico for IT services and support, especially in the distribution industry and government, which were the mainstays of the Puerto Rican economy. But Pérez wanted more.

> **the Rock Solid team was becoming known as the best place to go in Puerto Rico for IT services and support. But Pérez wanted more**

A New Opportunity

In 2006, Pérez saw an opportunity to bring Puerto Rico's 78 municipalities (cities and towns of varied sizes) into the twenty-first century systems-wise. Most were still operating with typewriters, carbon paper, and manual ledgers. They were, in Pérez's view, both inefficient and ineffective in serving their constituents' needs. Pérez wanted to pursue this opportunity by finding a reference customer, which he found in the small trading town of Coamo, a forward-looking city of some 30,000 inhabitants that also happened to be the site of the annual San Blas half-marathon, which attracted some of the best runners in the world. Coamo's hot springs had once been rumored to be Juan Ponce de Leon's fabled fountain of youth. Coamo's mayor, Juan Carlos Garcia Padilla, was a visionary leader. "He thinks big," recalled Pérez, "and he loves to be first."[22] Coamo looked to Pérez like a good place to start.

Pérez offered to do for Coamo what would normally have cost $2 million in systems development work for half a million dollars—deposit up front, please!—figuring that what he and his team would develop by applying Microsoft's enterprise resource planning (ERP) and customer relationship management (CRM) systems, ordinarily targeted at small and medium-sized businesses, to this public sector setting would have application elsewhere. Coamo's administrative staff quickly adapted to the new systems, as work got done more easily and faster. Citizens quickly noticed a difference, too:

- Missing stop signs were replaced more quickly
- Potholes in the roads were filled
- Stray dogs were found

And those who reported such things were notified when the problems were resolved.

Completing the project and finding a second visionary mayor took another year and a half, but by 2008 word began to get around. Rock Solid had won a reputation for adapting ERP and CRM systems to municipal settings. Its systems enabled the municipalities to reduce their staffs in some functions by half, putting them and the savings to more productive uses. And better systems also made it far less likely that shady uses of government funds could occur.

Service Businesses: Difficult to Grow

Despite the consistent but relatively modest growth Rock Solid had achieved, Pérez found it difficult to convince prospective municipal customers to move their systems and processes from typewriters and carbon paper to PCs. Doing so involved much more than hiring Rock Solid to implement new IT systems. The municipalities would need PCs, servers, cabling, power backup, and more—even a new IT person to run things once new systems had been installed. Even though the savings and the improved services the municipalities provided for their residents looked promising, the capital expense—as well as the idea of small towns running their own IT systems—was daunting. These complexities, and the fact that for such projects, requests for proposals and competitive bidding were required, made the sales process for Rock Solid laborious. There had to be a better approach.

❝ There had to be a better approach. ❞

With the arrival of cloud computing, Pérez found his answer, seeing an opportunity to go to market in an entirely different manner. He would turn the services his team was delivering into products that future customers could simply run from the cloud:

- No servers
- No cabling
- And no permanent IT staff, either

Better yet, running systems from the cloud would mean that clients would incur no major capital expenditure, simply an operating budget going forward. City employees would just log onto their Internet connections. Even better, winning operating contracts required far less bureaucracy than tendering for major capital expenditure projects. A simple purchase order was all that would be required!

A Customer-Funded Service-to-Product Transition

Pérez focused on what he had learned about his customers' needs. "There were four key systems that made municipalities run better: HR and payroll, collections (from taxes to parking tickets), accounting, and citizen services (everything from ambulance service to fixing potholes in the roads)."[23] He and his team began adapting his software to run on the cloud, and by mid-2010 he had his first cloud-based municipal customer. No servers, no cabling.

Just three PCs with Internet connections, each paying Rock Solid a modest per-seat monthly fee. His IT services, delivered in customized fashion to one municipality at a time, had been transformed into products that clients could subscribe to and run largely on their own. Happily, the transition from customized client services to his new SaaS-based subscription model had been entirely funded by his customers' cash.

By mid-2012, Rock Solid was continuing to deliver its traditional services work to distributors and other clients in Puerto Rico, and the cloud-based revenue was adding 25 percent to its top-line sales at attractive gross margins, and with a scalable model, too. By late 2013, Rock Solid had signed up more than a third of Puerto Rico's 78 municipalities, and had also secured similar customers elsewhere in Latin America. Better yet, his company's profitability had soared. "Over time, the SaaS model gets better and better. We get smarter and more efficient, and the customers learn, too, so they need less of our time." Perez's service-to-product transition had turned Rock Solid into a customer-funded and highly profitable growth machine.

How Else Might You Scale Your Services Business? QuEST Global Services[24]

As we learned in Chapter 4, many services business are by their very nature based on pay-in-advance models. But many aren't truly scalable businesses, as growing the services offering or the customer base means growing the staff of service providers at an equivalent pace. If the payment terms you can get from your customers and your gross margins are sufficiently attractive, however, you may well be able to scale your business *without* transforming it into a product business.

That's what QuEST Global Services, a fast-growing provider of outsourced engineering services, has done. Ajit Prabhu and Aravind Melligeri started their company in upstate New York in 1997. Prabhu, having been entrepreneurially inclined from an early age (in his home village in India he had "leased" a fruit tree from an elderly neighbor, paying him a portion of the pro-

> **Prabhu had 'leased' a fruit tree from an elderly neighbor, paying him a portion of the proceeds from the fruit he harvested.**

ceeds from the fruit he harvested), was doing part-time engineering work for General Electric's Corporate Research and Development Center while studying for his PhD. Prabhu thought he could do a better job sourcing talent for GE, primarily among his fellow engineering students, than GE's current providers.

In 1998, Melligeri suggested that India could be a source of additional talent, at lower cost, so the duo opened an office in Bangalore. The business model was compelling, with GE paying $90 per hour and QuEST paying its Indian engineers about $5. Thanks to the world's rapidly increasing thirst for energy, and the fact that GE was a leading supplier of gas turbines for power plants, QuEST grew quickly, hitting $5 million in sales in its year ending March 2001, with GE accounting for 80 percent of QuEST's sales.

Customer Funding: Not Enough

Though QuEST's gross margins were attractive, GE's payment terms meant that the rapidly growing business could mostly, but not entirely, be funded with its customers' cash. In 2001 Melligeri, who in QuEST's early days had raised $60,000 from a family member and few business angels, thought that putting some more substantial equity on the company's balance sheet would make sense. "We should think about raising external money," he said one day to Prabhu. "It's much better to start conversations when we don't need money than when we are really desperate."

> **It's much better to start conversations when we don't need money than when we are really desperate.**

Suddenly, in December 2001, Enron, one of the world's largest energy companies and a large driver of demand for GE turbines, went bankrupt due to some fraudulent accounting; several of its leaders eventually went to jail. Despite Enron's fall, QuEST's business continued to grow, hitting $14 million in its year ending March 2002. Meanwhile, Melligeri continued his dogged efforts to raise capital, often a difficult task for a services business in which the company's key assets arrive each morning and go home each evening. Happily, his months of pursuit finally paid off. In January 2003, The Carlyle Group agreed to a $6 million investment for a 23 percent stake, and advanced the first $1 million pending closing the deal. Alas, one month later, GE announced it was opening an engineering center in India and that it would take back all of its outsourced engineering activity. Prabhu and Melligeri were stunned.

Performance Plummets, Then Recovers

GE's volume with QuEST plummeted from $17 million in QuEST's year ending March 2003 (out of total revenue of $20 million) to $10 million in 2003–2004 (of $14 million total). Suddenly, QuEST's need for capital was desperate; fortunately it had built trust with Carlyle, which went ahead and completed the deal. In Prabhu's mind, it suddenly became clear that "we have too many eggs in the GE basket. We have to win more big customers."[25] Using his company's already formidable track record for first-rate service delivery, Prabhu quickly set about finding for QuEST "another GE."[26]

As a result of its work on gas turbines for GE, QuEST was developing considerable expertise in turbine engineering. That expertise, together with Prabhu's business development prowess, brought Rolls-Royce, one of the world's largest makers of jet engines (which are in effect just another kind of turbine), on board in late 2004. By 2006, other large clients were on board, including EADS, the European maker of jet aircraft, and United

Technologies' Pratt & Whitney division in the United States, another jet engine maker whose earlier business with QuEST had grown significantly. In 2004–2005, QuEST's top line recovered to $19.6 million, and it jumped to $25.8 million in 2005–2006. Profitability rebounded, too, from a $3.5 million loss in the difficult year of 2003–2004 to profits of $2.5 million and $3.8 million in 2004–2005 and 2005–2006. QuEST was back on track.

By its year ending spring 2010, QuEST's sales had grown to $88 million, and profits to $10.7 million. The global economic downturn had actually been a boon to QuEST, helping it attract key managerial talent and encouraging its customers to expand their outsourcing, for **❝The global economic downturn had actually been a boon to QuEST❞** both cost and strategic reasons. "Recessions are a good time to pick up talent," recalled Prabhu, "and customers, too."[27] Along the way, Carlyle had exited with a handsome return, but Prabhu and Melligeri were considering whether or not to take on external capital once again. They saw engineering services as a growing but still fragmented industry, and wanted to make QuEST the unquestioned leader therein. Prabhu recalled the dilemma he presented to his management team. "As I see it, we have two options before us. One is to continue our current rate of growth, eventually pay off our debt (which all of you know I dislike) with the cash we generate and possibly go public when the time is right. The other is to take private capital now, to enable us to grow faster and pursue the vision that is within our grasp."

With offers in hand from three of the world's top private equity firms, all valuing QuEST at more than $300 million, Prabhu and his team decided to take external investment once again. Warburg Pincus invested $40 million in QuEST and paid another $20 million to the founders—a small portion to Prabhu, $10 million to Melligeri for him to use in pursuit of an entrepreneurial opportunity he had identified in manufacturing, and the rest to the early angels and QuEST management. Prabhu turned on the jets. In its year ending March 2013, sales (having crossed the $100 million mark in 2010–2011 and $160 million in 2011–2012), soared to more than $250 million. QuEST had become consistently and highly profitable.

Can Services Businesses Scale without a Product Transition?

As the QuEST story indicates, just as there is more than one way to skin a cat, there is more than one way to scale a services business. "Productizing" the business is one way, as the case histories earlier in this chapter show. Sticking to your services knitting, as QuEST chose to do, is another. But scaling a services business, even one that gets paid partly in advance, often requires more than its customers' funds. Thus Prabhu elected to raise capital to take advantage of an opportunity that was clearly at hand. Customer funding will only take most services businesses so far.

> **just as there is more than one way to skin a cat, there is more than one way to scale a services business**

In the preceding chapters, we've seen other examples of services businesses that have scaled, most of which relied on customer funding for their early growth, then took on investment when it became clear that more fuel in the tank could be put to productive use. Let's examine what angels—or your senior management if you're in an established company—will want to know if you ask them for capital to help scale *your* services business should you decide that "productizing" it is the best way forward for you.

What Angel Investors Will Want to Know—and Will Ask

If you're running a successful services business and are trying to figure out how to scale it, one way to do so may be to "productize" your offering, as we've seen in the examples of GoViral and Rock

Solid in this chapter and in CE Info Systems' transition from a mapping services provider to MapmyIndia, India's go-to source for digital mapping products, both hardware and software, back in Chapter 1. The transition from services to products may constitute a suitable inflection point at which some external capital may not only make good sense, but also may be required to fund the product development work that may be necessary. If this is a strategy that you want to pursue,

> **❝The transition from services to products may constitute a suitable inflection point at which some external capital may not only make good sense, but also may be required. ❞**

what are the key questions that your prospective investors—whether angels or others—will ask?

What Customer Insights Have You Gleaned That Will Make a *Product* More Compelling Than the Already Successful Services You Now Provide?

In the case of Rock Solid, we saw that, despite clear customer benefits, moving from typewriters and carbon paper to a twenty-first-century computer-based operation entailed challenges on both the customer's and seller's sides of the transaction. For the customer, the transition meant not only hiring Rock Solid, but also buying computers and servers, cabling, and more, and hiring an IT person to keep things running after the sale—a messy proposition at best. For Rock Solid, getting the order was a time-consuming process of educating the customer about the benefits to be had, then assisting the customer in developing a request for proposals, then winning the bid. All these challenges meant that winning new customers was much more difficult and time con-suming than Ángel Pérez had hoped. The complexity was proving to be a barrier to growth, and Pérez wanted to grow! The insights he had gained into what the municipalities' needs were, which software solutions could best meet those needs, and how the barriers to actually making a sale could be mitigated were the keys to identifying and unlocking the opportunity to move to a cloud-based product solution.

> **The insights he had gained into what the municipalities' needs were, and how the barriers to actually making a sale could be mitigated were the keys**

To What Extent Will a Service-to-Product Transition Open Up New and Attractive Market Segments?

Rock Solid used its service-to-product transition to better serve its current target market. GoViral did the same. CE Info Systems, on the other hand, used its transition to dramatically widen the market segments it could serve:

- It would be able to serve businesses of nearly any size with Web-based location services, such as providing maps to show where a business is located. In India's somewhat helter-skelter system of addresses, this would prove to be a real value to MapmyIndia customers and users.
- It would be able to target the fast-growing market for navigation systems in automobiles, one that Western providers lacked the Indian data to serve effectively.

If the transition you have in mind in your business is intended to open up new markets for you, investors will want to know why those markets are attractive, and whether yours is the right team to pursue them. They will also want to know whether such a transition places you into a new industry, with a new set of competitors, and whether that industry is an attractive place to play.[28] You'll also need to convince them that the expertise or other assets you've built in your services business provide a suitable foundation on which to build the new business that will serve the new markets. CE Info Systems had assembled a unique and unmatched repository of Indian mapping data that did exactly that, one reason why Sherpalo and Kleiner Perkins made their investments.

Do You Have the Right Talent to Transform Your Business from Services to Products?

The GoViral team excelled in understanding the advertising and media game, and knew how to sell in that familiar environment. But in their early years their business struggled on the technology side, which was not among their core strengths. Only when Rene Rechtman came on board, bringing other skilled technical people with him, did the service-to-product transition really bear fruit. Fortunately for GoViral, the business was so capital efficient that they didn't need to raise capital to make the transition.

Your company, though, may need funding to invest in product development, as was the case for Rakesh and Rashmi Verma at CE Info Systems, despite their IT

> **❝Your company, though, may need funding to invest in product development❞**

backgrounds. Unlike them, you may need help in identifying exactly who are the right people to add to your team. There are lots of people who can write code and develop software, but some do it far better than others! This is an arena where the right external investor with technology experience can add value that goes well beyond the check he or she writes.

Do You Really Want to Go from "Slow and Steady" to a Rocket-Ship Pace?

GoViral, Rock Solid, and CE Info Systems were all growing businesses at the points in time where they made their transitions from services to products. But neither Rock Solid nor CE Info Systems were growing particularly fast. Most investors aren't very interested in "slow and steady" growth, of course. The return they seek on their capital typically requires putting fuel in the tank and pressing the pedal to the metal. Investors will want to know some things:

- Is it your aspiration to build a very large business, even if that means you may be asked to relinquish your leadership role to someone who has already learned to manage faster growth?
- Or have you and your team demonstrated the ability to manage such growth yourselves?

Here, too, your investor may be able to add value—helping to find additional talent, for example, or guiding you through the inevitable and predictable challenges that rapid growth entails—that goes beyond the funds they provide.

Should You "Productize" Your Business, or Should You Scale It As Is?

As we've seen in the QuEST case history, sometimes it is neither necessary nor desirable to transform a services business into a product business. QuEST has grown in phenomenal fashion without making such a transition. Investors will—and should—ask whether upsetting your apple cart and transforming it is worth the risk and expense, or whether adding some equity to the existing business can help you scale without taking on that transition and its inherent risk. It's an important question, one not to be taken lightly.

Conventional wisdom says that people-intensive services businesses simply can't scale. For some of them, perhaps including GoViral's early incarnation as a *creator* of viral online video, that may be true. But Ajit Prabhu doesn't buy it. From zero to more than a quarter of a billion dollars in revenue in 16 years is

> **Conventional wisdom says that people-intensive services businesses simply can't scale. But Ajit Prabhu doesn't buy it.**

the kind of performance most entrepreneurs, not to mention their investors, would like to have!

Making Service-to-Product Models Work

If you've decided that a service-to-product transition is for you, the questions angel investors will ask—summarized in the checklist below—offer a useful set of points to verify that it's really worth taking that route. If so, as the GoViral and Rock Solid stories show, it's not just the Bill Gateses and Paul Allens of the world that can make it happen. With the right market opportunity, and the right team in place, maybe *you* can, too!

By now, if you've read this book in order, you'll have examined five customer-funded models that could help *you* achieve *your* entrepreneurial dreams, and do so without having to spend time courting early investors, either. But my job is not yet done, for there is another substantial set of lessons my research has uncovered from my conversations about the five models with others who've applied them. There are enough of these lessons that it will take me one more chapter to develop and deliver them and hammer them home. So whether you are an entrepreneur or a corporate leader seeking new avenues of growth, before you go out and get started putting one of the five models to work in your business, I suggest you hold your horses and turn the page to what I believe you'll find is a crucial, and once again inspiring, Chapter 8.

John's Business Angel Checklist—Service-to-Product Models

- What customer insights have you gleaned that will make a *product* more compelling than the already successful services you now provide?

(continued)

(*continued*)

- To what extent will a service-to-product transition open up new and attractive market segments?
- Do you have the right talent to transform your business from services to products?
- Do you really want to go from "slow and steady" to a rocket-ship pace?
- Should you "productize" your business, or should you scale it as is?

8

Make It Happen: Put a Customer-Funded Model to Work in *Your* Business

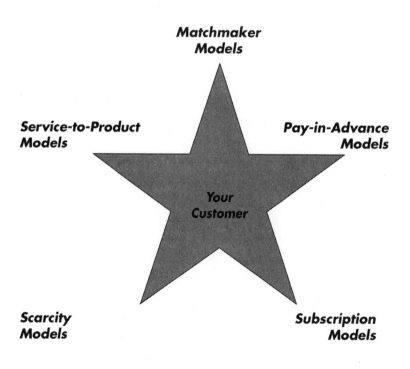

Matchmaker Models

Service-to-Product Models

Pay-in-Advance Models

Your Customer

Scarcity Models

Subscription Models

"Ring the cash register." That's what you want to make happen to get *your* business off the ground or growing faster, of course. And, as you may recall having read in the Preface ("Why This Book?" way back at the front), it's also where venture capital investor Mark Suster argues that his entrepreneurs should place *their* focus. Why? "Some businesses take time to find their magic, says Suster. "And I only know one reason companies go out of business—they run out of money. Delaying going out of business gives you way more chances at product/market fit than any other strategy I know of."[1] It is Suster's view that getting your customers' cash flowing sooner rather than later is the best way to lower your company's burn rate and defer that unfortunate

❝getting your customers' cash flowing sooner rather than later is the best way to lower your company's burn rate❞

event, hopefully forever. Of course, you already know from Chapter 1 numerous other reasons why, in the early evolution of your venture, it's a much better idea to ring the cash register, in Suster's words, than to spend your time trying to raise investor capital. From Chapter 2, you also know that doing so is as much about mind-set—day in, day out—as anything else, along with the behavior that results from that mind-set. Whose behavior? *Your* behavior and that of everyone else in your company, too. You also know from Chapter 2 that your and your people's mind-set also has to include getting good terms from your suppliers so you can "sit on the float."

If you've read one or more of Chapters 3 through 7, you also now have in hand a series of questions that you, if you are an entrepreneur or an executive seeking to start, finance, or grow a customer-funded business, are likely to be asked—and hence should ask yourself!—about whichever of the five customer-funded models you'll put to work in your business. Asking and answering these questions with careful diligence—and evidence, please!—should give you a pretty good idea about whether one of the models might be right for making the cash register ring in your business, at whatever stage of the journey you now find yourself. In other words, Chapters 3 through 7 are largely about *whether* to put to work—either from the start, or as a change of direction in an existing business—any of the five customer-funded models in your particular setting. These five chapters, one for each of the models, also offer a collection of often-inspiring role models, to help you see that *you* can do so, too!

But, as you surely know, the entrepreneurial path is never easy, as we've seen for some of the companies whose captivating but sometimes cautionary tales fill this book. Getting started down the customer-funded path is neither a panacea nor a guarantee of success. Whether setting out from your kitchen table or garage—or setting off on a new direction in an already-established business into new markets or with new products, or even a new business model—there are pitfalls lurking around every corner, as always. So my job is not yet done. In this final chapter, I want to address a handful of critical issues involved in putting the book's ideas to work in your business, to give you—whether you're the one leading the venture, or you're backing it as an angel or other investor—and your customer-funded venture a fighting chance for success:

> **❝there are pitfalls lurking around every corner❞**

- First, this book's lessons, though delivered largely *by* start-ups and their case histories that evolved over time, aren't only *for* startups. So I want to briefly address the "What should I do now?" question to get you on your way. As you might expect, the challenges in "making it happen" differ, depending on where you sit—whether you're an entrepreneur, an investor, or a leader inside an established organization.
- Second, I want to address implementation—without effective implementation, the customer-funded models and mind-set will bear little fruit—and what my research taught

me about three crucial questions relevant to implementing each of the five models:

1. *When* should you use which model? In B2B settings? B2C? C2C? For services, or for products?

2. *How* should you apply the models? What best practices for each model can be gleaned from my research?

3. *What* should you watch out for? Some of the pitfalls are known to those who have applied these models—often learned the hard way, though the "school of hard knocks"—and I want *you* to know them, too.

These lessons, which go well beyond what we've learned in Chapters 3 through 7, are about *how* to apply the five models, not *whether* a particular model makes sense in your setting.

- Third, getting started. Should you simply head out on the entrepreneurial road? Or are there ways or places to find support that can improve your odds?

- Last, *why* do it *now*? Is this *really* the best approach to starting and funding your new venture or initiative? If you can find a sugar daddy or raid the corporate treasury—should the lure of "other people's money" win you over?

❝ *why* do it *now*? ❞

Not Only for Startups: What Should I Do *Now*?

The stories that fill this book have focused largely on startups for a simple reason: because, sad to say, that's where innovation is most likely to be found and to flourish. As Sun Microsystems co-founder and present-day VC investor Bill Joy once noted about innovation in well-established companies, "Big companies almost never innovate. This is unfortunate because innovation is one of the few ways to gain proprietary advantage and stay profitable. It's not that innovation itself is rare—it's occurring everywhere.

Which means, mostly, elsewhere."[2] So, for good reason, the lessons in this book are drawn largely from the experiences of entrepreneurs and the investors who've backed them.

Making Customer Funding Happen If You're an Entrepreneur

If you are an aspiring entrepreneur trying to get a new venture off the ground, or an entrepreneur whose journey is already underway, you are the best placed of the readers of this book to make customer funding work in your business. Why? Because you hold the cards! You don't have to ask anyone if you can do it—other than your customer, of course (and probably some key suppliers, too, in order to get good terms). As the Nike slogan says, "Just do it!" Provided, of course, that one of the five models about which you read in Chapters 3 through 7 appears well suited to the entrepreneurial dream you are pursuing, based on the evidence you've gathered to answer the questions that you're sure to be asked.

> **you are the best placed of the readers of this book to make customer funding work in your business**

Making Customer Funding Happen If You're an Angel Investor

As an angel investor—or someone in an incubator or accelerator who invests your space, your network, your expertise, and perhaps your money in supporting entrepreneurs in *their* efforts to ring *their* cash registers—you might at first glance see this book as a threat to you. "Is Mullins arguing that angels and the like have no role to play in today's entrepreneurial ecosystem?" you may wonder. On the contrary! I argue that the way you can provide the very best support to many of those seeking your capital or other support is to cajole them, push them, or help them (with your contacts if you can) to redirect their focus away from the enticing allure of investors and toward their customers. I want you to help them see that, most of the time, customer-funded models are the best way forward for them, and the best way to get their hands on your money, too, once they've achieved the customer traction that customer-funded models entail. There's a really important role for you to play here, and I hope I've convinced you to give playing it a try.

> **"There's a really important role for you to play here"**

Making Customer Funding Happen If You're in an Established Company

If you're a leader in an established business—whether at or near the most senior levels, or tucked away in a nook or cranny deep in its bowels—who sees an opportunity to make the ideas in this book work in your business, let's be clear from the get-go: It won't be easy. It probably means innovating, changing "the way we do things around here." And, as Bill Joy argues, most big companies don't innovate. Why? For one, it's risky, as most innovations fail. Most people in big companies don't want failure on their resume. Second, as Joy points out, "Innovative people tend to prefer working in smaller organizations that have more focus and less bureaucracy."[3] That means that if you are one of those rare people in a nook or a cranny with a big idea in an existing company and the gumption to pursue it, it's likely to be a solo journey and an uphill climb to get the funding and other support you'll need to pursue your idea. If your established company is a smaller one, or one that has somehow managed to keep its entrepreneurial culture alive as it has grown, your path may be a bit smoother. If you are the gatekeeper to whom others with customer-fundable ideas may come, or you are the person best placed to encourage them to do so, see Sidebar 8.1 for some practical steps Bill Joy suggests for getting innovation, whether customer-funded or otherwise, happening in your company.

Sidebar 8.1: Bill Joy on Innovation in Established Companies

Though real innovation seems to happen mostly outside of established companies, some of them have figured out how to do it. What are their lessons?

- Emulate Google. Hire lots of smart people, organize them into very small groups working in parallel, and keep the bureaucracy (project reviews, milestones, KPIs, and all the rest) at a minimum.
- Create a budget for running small, quirky, controversial projects, which the organization probably wouldn't want to accept, but which might have the potential to grow. "Small" means the projects are carried out by the number of people that would fit around a small table in a local restaurant.
- Don't shoot innovators who fail. As Joy argues, "You can't punish people for attempting great things and sometimes failing."
- Look beyond the borders of the company for companies or technologies that can be bought. Don't build it if you can buy it. This, in essence, has been Cisco's strategy.
- Find a clone of Steve Jobs.

Source: Bill Joy, "Large Problem: How Big Companies Can Innovate," *Fortune*, November 15, 2004, page 214.

Wherever in your organization you are, what if your idea is so good that you can get some customers to fund it, using one of the five models articulated in this book? If that's the case, you won't need to go to the treasurer or investment committee asking for capital. Sure, you may need to convince your boss—or yourself if *you* are the boss—that it's okay to spend some time on it, but selling the potential of your idea to your boss is likely to be far easier than selling it to the wider organization, especially when you explain that you've already got—or will soon get—customer funding.

In fact, we've already seen this practice at work. As we saw in Chapter 6, Jacques-Antoine Granjon and his founding partners were already in the business of liquidating distressed overstock inventory for Parisian fashion designers. With the arrival of the Internet, they simply decided to do so in a different way. Rock Solid's Ángel Pérez (see Chapter 7) already had a nicely growing business doing installations of Microsoft and other vendors' software products, but he saw the possibility of transforming his services business into a more scalable product business, thanks to the cloud. Both Granjon and Pérez were innovators working in already existing businesses that had the potential to be transformed. Are *you*? If so, let's get you rolling!

Implementation: The When, the How, and the Likely Pitfalls of Each of the Five Models

The research that brings forth the lessons of this book didn't stop with unearthing the case histories of the companies about which you've read so far. In fact, that was only a part of my research journey. In addition to studying those companies, I wanted to learn from practitioners—entrepreneurs and investors of various stripes—who had been down the path of actually putting each of the five customer-funded models to work in a variety of settings. A series of in-depth interviews with these experienced players gave me some additional depth and breadth and some additional insights that the case histories alone simply could not provide (See the appendix, "About the Research"). Here they are.

> **❝I wanted to learn from practitioners who had been down the path❞**

Matchmaker Models

These days, it seems like there is no shortage of dot-commers seeking to start one kind of matchmaker business or another—or seeking investment to do so. All the talk of today's "sharing economy" underlies at least part of this trend. If you are among them, what have others learned that might benefit you?

When to apply matchmaker models to build a customer-funded business:

- *Where there is underutilized supply:* Spare bedrooms or under-used vacation homes (Airbnb), cars sitting in one's garage (RelayRides), dog lovers with time on their hands (DogVacay). All these have been targets of matchmaker businesses seeking to monetize underutilized resources and make them available to those who can use them on a temporary basis. The phenomenon is so prevalent that there's now a term for it: the sharing economy. But that doesn't mean that the sharing of just anything can result in a good business. Though underutilized resources are not the only arenas in which to build matchmaker businesses (many travel websites, for example, don't really focus their efforts that way), they do make it easier to build a community of motivated suppliers and potentially reduce the cost of doing so.

- *Where there are actual or perceived differences between what various sellers have to offer.* No two properties at Airbnb are the same, for example. Different airlines schedule their flights at different times. So marketplaces like Airbnb and Expedia that help buyers choose among the not-quite-identical alternatives provide real value, value that would not be there if what was being sold were commodities like books or CDs, where the products offered by different sellers are identical.

- *For goods* and *services:* While Airbnb, DogVacay, and many other matchmaker businesses have focused on services, eBay and Craigslist have thrived selling goods of all kinds. There's no inherent reason not to consider matchmaker models for goods and services alike.

> **There's no inherent reason not to consider matchmaker models for goods and services alike.**

- *For consumers or business buyers?* On this question, the jury is still out. Consumer-focused matchmaker businesses have been far more visible, but that's not to say that business-to-business matchmakers can't work, despite some high-profile failures in the early dot-com years. PivotDesk, for example, matches companies having more office space than they need with companies looking for space on a short-term basis.[4] B2B offerings such as this one may be the next frontier for matchmaker models.

How to apply matchmaker models:

- *Determine the best way to get paid.* Service Magic (now HomeAdvisor.com), one of many matchmakers matching homeowners with home improvement contractors of various kinds, adopted a "lead-fee" approach, whereas most other entrants asked for commissions on the entire job. Service Magic investor Brad Feld explained: "We'd agree to provide only a few leads to any consumer, so the contractor had a decent chance of making the sale. And because the lead fees were very small, not much was lost by those suppliers that didn't get the job."[5] The lead-fee model turned out to be far more attractive to contractors than the possibility of having to pay a commission on what might be a large job. It also mitigates any motivation for contractors to game the system by dealing directly with the customer.

  VRBO.com (Vacation Rental by Owner), a leading matchmaker of homeowners with properties to rent and vacationers who rent them, charges listing fees from its sellers, but takes no commission. There's no incentive for bypassing the system, as there's no commission to pay.

That's a different revenue model than that employed at Airbnb.

How might *you* deter- **❝How might *you*** mine the best way to get **determine the best way to** paid in your setting? Identify **get paid in your** alternative approaches, then **setting?❞** talk to your prospective sellers and find out which approach they prefer. Or, better, run an experiment and see what you can learn. Finding the best way to get paid in *your* business is an important issue. Don't assume there is only one way.

- *Build metrics on both sides:* In a matchmaker business, you'll need to acquire both buyers and sellers, so you'll need to have strategies for, and measure the cost of, acquiring both kinds. Your strategies for acquiring sellers will differ from those for acquiring buyers, will vary across time, and will differ in costs. "You'll need to make your interface with your suppliers just as efficient and easy to use as that for your buyers," says John Erceg, founder of Budget Places, a matchmaker that matches vacationers with low-cost hotels.[6] It's an aspect of matchmaker businesses that is sometimes overlooked.

- *Content is king, so lower your barriers to acquiring it:* The only reason buyers will come to your matchmaker business is the content—the breadth or depth of your sellers—you offer. As Finland's Justinas Katkus, put it, "Content is king."[7] For Erceg, this meant lowering the barriers for his target suppliers—budget hotels in Barcelona, initially, and eventually elsewhere—to sign up. "We gave them the web presence they needed," he recalls, "and it cost them nothing up front other than 30 minutes of their time to load their availability and rates onto our system."[8]

- *Think locally to get started, think locally to grow.* It seems counterintuitive to think that matchmaker businesses should start locally, given the global reach of the Internet. But think about it. DogVacay needed to prove—to itself and to others—that it could build an active marketplace connecting both dog owners and pet sitters in Los Angeles before expanding elsewhere. Adding pet sitters elsewhere would have been largely irrelevant to dog owners there. Similarly, Airbnb started by serving narrowly targeted conferences one conference at a time. As London Business School professor and longtime early-stage investor John Bates notes, "You must get enough buyers *and* sellers. You need to know how large your minimum pool must be, and how much, in time or money, it will cost you to get there."[9]

❝Local issues persist over time❞

Local issues persist over time, too. "There's more roofing to do in the spring in Seattle than there are roofers," the Foundry Group's Brad Feld recalls of Service Magic.[10] If you don't develop an effective plan for getting more roofers to Seattle in the springtime, the roofers there won't need you (they'll have all the business they can handle) and the customers who need roofs will soon conclude that you can't deliver when the need is there. Resolving imbalances like this one, if you can do it inventively, without spending much cash to balance supply and demand, can make yours the go-to source for both sides of the transaction and help your inherently capital-efficient business grow.

- *Put feet on the street to manage seller expectations:* Given the importance of having an adequate supply of whatever you plan to offer your buyers, your content, gaining suppliers is tricky. At the outset, while you build your roster of suppliers to reach critical mass, you'll need to convince them to come on board while letting them know that demand is unlikely to materialize very quickly, until you reach critical mass. This process requires both trust and patience, and is often best built with face-to-face selling, rather than online or telephone appeals. At Budget Places, John Erceg's feet were indeed on the street for his first several months, signing up budget hotels to allow him get bookings for them.

- *Sit on the float:* Venture capital investor and Sussex Place Ventures managing director Richard Gourlay points out a key element of many matchmaker models, those in which the matchmaker handles the cash transaction. As

> **❝A key element of many matchmaker models is sitting on the float. ❞**

we've seen already, the matchmaker can hold onto the buyer's cash for at least some period of time before remitting it to the seller, sitting on the float and using it to finance the acquisition of additional buyers and sellers.[11] For Erceg, who started Budget Places in 2002 in the shadow of the dot-com bust, when no capital was available, sitting on the float was essential. "Our customers would pay us 15 percent of the booking up front," he recalls, "and those were the funds we used to pay our people and buy more Google Adwords, for which we could pay later on 30-day terms."[12]

Of course, not all matchmakers handle the actual transactions, so not all matchmakers have float on which to sit. Thus, deciding whether you will handle the cash or not is an important issue in enabling your business to be customer funded. Airbnb does, thereby benefiting from the float, but at VRBO.com, the cash goes directly from the rental guests to the property owners, never passing through the hands of VRBO. DogVacay offers incentives (free pet insurance and a money-back guarantee) for transacting online, which gives DogVacay the float. These kinds of details matter a great deal!

Matchmaker models: Pitfalls to watch out for:

- *Imbalance.* Feld puts it best: "You're always out of balance, with either not enough sellers for your number of buyers or not enough buyers for your willing sellers."[13] Thus you'll

> **❝You're always out of balance. ❞**

need proactive strategies for attracting *both* buyers *and* sellers, and both strategies will have to be funded—with effort—at the outset, and over the long run, too.

- *Bad actors.* You'll have them, for sure. You'll need a fair and transparent dispute resolution mechanism that is reasonable to both sides.[14]

- *Vanity metrics:* Longtime entrepreneur and investor Randy Komisar of Kleiner Perkins Caufield & Byers observes that builders of matchmaker models sometimes watch the wrong metrics.[15] Mismatches between demand and supply—too much of this and not enough of that—provide better clues about whether the business is really working than membership numbers or sales figures.

Pay-in-Advance Models

Old-fashioned travelers' checks are the classic pay-in-advance business. We gave the bank our money *before* we traveled and they gave us "safe" traveler's checks that we spent later, if ever. And we paid the bank a fee for doing so! In the right settings, pay-in-advance models can build customer-funded businesses as attractive as traveler's checks. If you are on a pay-in-advance path, what lessons from the past should you heed?

When to apply pay-in-advance models to build a customer-funded business:

- *Where there are pockets of truly compelling customer pain:* The more pressing the customer's pain, whether for goods or services, the more likely the customer will be to pay you in advance, even for a solution that is not yet fully developed. John Bates puts it this way: "You've got to find people who can use what you have *now*."[16] As we saw with Via, the Indian travel business in Chapter 4, mom-and-pop travel agents had a genuine need for issuing real-time airline tickets, and for better commissions, too. Addressing these two customer pain points gave Via a healthy start. You can build a better mousetrap later once you start catching mice, as Via did later when it added rail and bus ticketing to its offering. As always, if there isn't any real need for what you hope to sell now, there probably isn't an attractive business there, either.

- *In virtually any B2B setting:* Businesses with genuine problems you can solve are likely to be happy to pay you at least partly in advance for what they see as solutions, whether goods or services. Even in settings where advance payments are insufficient to fully fund your up-front development costs, advance *commitments*—such as letters of intent or, better, purchase orders—may help you raise the funds you need from other sources. So asking prospective B2B customers to pay in advance *always* makes sense. If you find they are not willing to pay you something in advance, maybe that means they won't be willing to pay you at all, ever! You may be on the wrong track.

  > **❝Businesses with genuine problems you can solve are likely to be happy to pay you.❞**

- *In virtually any services business:* Practically forever, those selling services of every kind have been asking their customers to pay for the service, in part or entirely, up front. Customers are willing to pay, too. So if you're planning to start most any kind of services business, there's no reason why you should need investment capital to get started. Just ask for the order, and ask for payment up front, too. As Brad Feld says, "There's no excuse not to!"[17]

- *What about goods?* Building businesses selling tangible goods on a pay-in-advance basis is typically difficult for many reasons. First, there's the cost of product development that must be incurred before the product can be delivered. If you can convince your customer—or even people on a crowdfunding website like Kickstarter—to fund your product development, that's great, at least in theory. But the new product development process is replete with challenges—lack of customer involvement, lack of understanding of the customer's needs, and too-long development cycles among them[18]—that customers are aware of and are typically not willing to fund in advance. So what might you do to build a business selling goods, if you cannot do it with customer funding? You'll probably need a founding team with the skills and available bandwidth to build the product (or at least the first minimally viable version thereof) themselves in their spare time.

Some product businesses require little or no product development, of course. A Suit That Fits sells custom-tailored suits measured locally in London, New York, or dozens of other cities, then cut and sewn in Nepal. Founder Warren Bennett built the business entirely with a customer-funded pay-in-advance model.[19] Threadless, as we saw in Chapter 4, outsourced its product design function to the designer community it served. Who says pay-in-advance models can't work for products? A little bit of ingenuity can go a long way!

> **❛❛Some product businesses require little or no product development. ❜❜**

How to apply pay-in-advance models:

- *Find a category where people are accustomed to paying in advance and waiting for what they buy or consume:* The fast-growing British e-tailer Made.com sells made-to-order designer home furnishings and furniture at affordable prices. How? They assemble orders from consumers, collect payment up front, and then have the goods made to order—with just the right fabric on a new armchair, for example. Everybody knows that for made-to-order merchandise it is reasonable to pay up front and wait for delivery, so they do. And for Made.com, the working capital benefits make all the difference. As the company's founder and 31-year-old CEO, Ning Li, observes, "We have negative working capital because we sell the furniture before we buy it from our manufacturers."[20]

- *What about exclusives?* Your pay-in-advance customer may want exclusive use of your product or service—probably not exactly what you had in mind.

  ❝Your pay-in-advance customer may want exclusive use of your product or service❞

  Ray Johnson, a two-time entrepreneur and now commercialization director at the University of Colorado, suggests that while you shouldn't grant exclusivity that will prevent you from growing your business, you can offer a narrower form of exclusivity, firewalled (as narrowly as possible) to your customer's field of use: They, exclusively, can use it for X, but you can sell it for other uses.[21]

- *Win customers' confidence and trust:* No customer will fork over advance money to a provider they don't trust. In a B2B setting, trust and confidence can be built interpersonally and with references and referrals. For online marketers, it's more difficult to do. Bennett of A Suit that Fits worked hard to generate press clippings, awards, and endorsements on review sites in order to build trust in his early years.[22] Today, social media can carry some of this load.

Pay-in-advance models: Pitfalls to watch out for:

- *The dominant customer:* There's a fine line to walk between meeting your customer's needs and allowing those needs to alter your strategic direction. Though there's learning to be gleaned from such customer involvement, one customer's needs may not be representative of those of the wider market you soon hope to serve.[23]

- *We want it now:* Your pay-in-advance customer will probably have paid because they are so eager to solve their problem that they want the solution *now*. Sometimes, however, as Paul Jerde, who directs the Deming Center for Entrepreneurship at the University of Colorado, notes, "Sometimes you then don't hear from them for months,"[24] which can make it difficult to complete the project and get paid for the rest of the job. Building close customer relationships to set expectations and prevent such problems is essential in pay-in-advance B2B settings.

- *Me first!* As Jerde also points out, if you have multiple pay-in-advance customers, they will all expect you to put their needs at the top of your list. Given that you will likely be underfunded and cannot do everything at once, you'll encounter some difficult choices about which of your customers get served first.[25]

- *Forgetting who you are:* Services businesses often yearn to become product businesses. Why? It's more difficult to scale many services businesses because growing the business means growing (and perhaps training) the service delivery team at a comparable rate. But, as we saw in Chapter 7, service-to-product businesses have their own inherent challenges, and the transition from one to the other is far more difficult than it may appear. Taking your eye off the services ball, in pursuit of a services-to-product transition, is a recipe for potential disaster.

- *Lack of clarity in your vision:* Author, investor, and serial entrepreneur Steve Blank has seen companies drift from one strategic direction to another, as pay-in-advance customers seek to drive their providers' agendas.[26] Saying "No" isn't easy when your customers' money is feeding you, but sometimes it's the right thing to do.

> **Saying 'No' isn't easy when your customers' money is feeding you, but sometimes it's the right thing to do.**

- *Customers wanting equity in your business:* Getting customers to pay up front for what you'll deliver later is a good thing.

Getting or allowing them to take an equity stake often is not. Why? Growth capital investor Hillel Zidel of Kennet Partners puts it simply: "We don't like it."[27] Though you may start your business with a customer-funded pay-in-advance model, you may at some point wish to raise institutional capital to fund further product development or faster growth. Future investors may be deterred, however, if your customers have a seat at the board or shareholder table, as their objectives are likely to diverge from those of the investor.

Ray Johnson concurs. "Any strategic investor *will* be misaligned one day."[28] Thus, having customers in your shareholding structure puts any possible future fundraising prospects at risk. But how can you say "No" if they demand equity? Give them something else: a time-to-market advantage before you sell to anyone else, perhaps; an agreement not to sell (at least for a limited time) to their principal competitor; or an exclusive in their field of use, as suggested above. But be sure to do these things in return for firm purchase commitments, of course![29]

- *Customer A or customer B:* Some customers may not wish to do business with someone already serving their key competitor. You'll need to be careful about taking on a pay-in-advance Customer A if that means foregoing an opportunity to also serve a potentially more attractive Customer B.

Subscription and SaaS Models

If you've read Chapter 5, you'll know that I worry about the recent fascination with subscriptions for seemingly anything and everything. The questions that follow may give you caution, too. On the other hand, with the advent of the cloud, subscription models have become all the rage in the software industry, as SaaS models like that of Salesforce.com have come into widespread use. I suspect there is a wide array of settings where subscription models can potentially be employed in building customer-funded businesses. It's your job to find them. The following lessons may help.

When to apply subscription or SaaS models to build a customer-funded business:

- *When what's bought is perishable or gets consumed predictably:* News is perishable. Fresh flowers are perishable. Disposable diapers are consumed predictably. Fruit and vegetables are perishable *and* consumed predictably. *The Financial Times*, H.Bloom, Diapers.com, and Abel and Cole's weekly deliveries of organic vegetables in the UK all benefit from that reality. As we saw in Chapter 5, subscription models have been deployed across all kinds of merchandise categories that aren't really perishable, but merely get consumed, though not necessarily predictably: men's toiletries from GuyHaus, or videos from Netflix, for example. Whether subscription models make sense—and make profits—in categories like these is largely a function of convenience, cost, and the predictability of usage.

> **Whether subscription models make sense is largely a function of convenience, cost, and the predictability of usage**

  If subscribing is cheaper for the customer or materially more convenient than simply repurchasing when more is needed, and if the usage rate is predictable, then subscription models may work. If one or more of these conditions are not met, beware.

- *Always for software, if you can!* Brad Feld, who has backed numerous SaaS-based software companies, argues that subscription models for software, in which you get paid over time, are *always* preferable to more traditional license models, in which you get paid just once.[30] But he points out that you have choices about *both* payment and delivery, either of which can be up front or spread over time. In Feld's view, getting paid for a renewable subscription (potentially forever) is far better than getting paid just once.

How to apply subscription models:

- *Try before you buy:* Subscription models can materially lower the buyer's risk of purchasing something that's not quite right, by enabling the buyer to try the good or service for a while and see whether it suits his or her needs. Putting in place a low-cost, low-risk, try-before-you-buy program can lower the cost of acquiring customers and provide early metrics, based on renewal rates, to indicate customer satisfaction (or the lack thereof) with the offering.[31]

- *Capture the right metrics:* As TutorVista founder Krishnan Ganesh pointed out in Chapter 5, there are two key metrics that drive the overall economics of subscription businesses: the cost of acquiring a new subscriber, and that customer's lifetime value, as measured by their profit contribution over the period during which they remain your customer.[32] As customer acquisition tactics evolve, of course, the cost to acquire customers changes. And different kinds of customers—those in Market Segment A versus Market Segment B, for example—will have different costs of acquisition, and probably different lifetime values as well. Thus measuring both the costs of acquiring customers and their lifetime value calls for detailed thinking and careful measurement, segment by segment. In addition, tracking such measurements on a cohort-by-cohort basis (e.g., customers acquired in a given month) enables better measurement of the degree to which their contribution to profit, hence their value, decays over time.[33]

- *Measure the payback period:* If you want to build a customer-funded subscription business, the *payback period* of an average new customer is an important metric. You'll need to know

how quickly your investment in acquiring the customer is
paid back with the profit contribution you earn on their first

**❝ the *payback period* of
an average new customer
is an important metric ❞**

purchases. The shorter the payback, the easier it will be to customer-fund your business.

- *"Freemium"/premium models:* In this Internet age, some subscription businesses offer a basic subscription for free (the
  "freemium" version) in the hopes that some users will be
  willing to pay more for a premium version. This works if the
  customer perceives enough additional value to pay for the
  upgrade. I love my free Pandora Radio subscription, which
  lets me listen to music genres I like. The premium version
  promises no ads, but there are rarely any ads on my favorite
  stations anyway, so I have little incentive to upgrade. It's a
  difficult task to know where to draw the line between what's
  good enough to attract the free subscribers without giving
  them so much that there's little incremental value in moving
  up to the paid version.

Subscription models: Pitfalls to watch out for:

- *Churn:* Customers come and customers go. A clear understanding of customer churn rates and what drives them—so
  you can work to reduce them!—is essential.
- *Overestimating customer lifetime value:* It's easy to assume that
  customers will continue to subscribe forever. But they won't.
  Overoptimistic projections of lifetime value (or underesti-
  mating payback period) can lead to overpaying for new

**❝ This is a recipe for
running out of cash
quickly! ❞**

customers who turn out not to be
worth what you paid to acquire
them. This is a recipe for running
out of cash quickly!

- *Failure to understand valuation metrics in your industry:* When
  raising capital or selling your business, many subscription
  businesses are valued based on the lifetime value of

customers. Developing effective strategies to increase customer retention can have a material impact on what your customer-funded subscription business is worth!

- *Freemium freeloaders:* As Institutional Venture Partners' Jules Maltz and Daniel Barney observe, "What entrepreneur doesn't want to see 100K, 1 million, or 100 million people around the world using her product? But if these users don't ever lead to paid customers (directly or indirectly), they can become an expensive burden that slowly bankrupts a company. On average, only 2% to 4% of free users convert to paid."[34] According to Maltz and Barney, there are only two ways out of this trap:

  - When freemium users *become* paid users over time, due to value that increases over time; for example, Dropbox users who need more storage as their initial free Dropbox capacity gets filled up.

  - When freemium users *attract* paid users over time, due to virality. Every survey that SurveyMonkey customers send out—for free!—is an ad that can attract additional SurveyMonkey users. Some of those new users will become future paid users.

- *The absence of perishability or predictable consumption:* Beware the looming bubble of offering practically anything on a subscription basis. How about Tackle Grab (fishing lures), PantyFly (Do women's panties get "used up"?) or Boink Box (X-rated sex toys, for those who don't want to be seen buying them)? As I write in 2013, at least 135 "stuff-in-a-box" startups had launched in the United Sates alone, some prosaic, others outrageously hilarious. Is there a bubble forming here?[35] We'll soon know.

Scarcity and Flash Sales Models

The best scarcity models, like Zara's, are in my eyes beauty incarnate. When implemented well, these models can be among the most difficult to compete against, as is the case for Zara. Sadly, many of the flash sales interpretations of such models haven't

❝ these models can be among the most difficult to compete against ❞

performed nearly as well. They have become far too prevalent for their own good. Faulty implementation may be one of the reasons for their poor performance. If that's so, the following lessons may be of use to you if, despite the risks, you want to head down such a path.

When to apply scarcity or flash sales models to build a customer-funded business:

- *Where there is rapid product or fashion obsolescence:* Women's apparel has rapid fashion cycles: Hemlines rise and fall. Fits get tighter, then looser. Aubergine is the hot new color, then it's not. This rapid change means two things:
  - Manufacturers will always have, at the end of each season, at least some overstock inventory of the fashions that are on the way out, but that some fashionistas will still be eager to wear. This is a problem that merchants like vente-privee or Gilt are able to solve.
  - Fashion-conscious consumers, like Zara's customers, want the latest styles and want to be seen as ahead of, not behind, the fashion curve. They buy frequently in order to stay current, and see their own wardrobe as turning obsolescent, too.

    These factors mean that scarcity models in which customers are encouraged to "Buy now" resonate with fashion customers' needs.
- *In merchandise categories where a fragmented set of vendors faces fragmented market access:* One factor that has probably contributed to Zulily's success was the plethora of small vendors making specialty kids' and moms' products for which there was no good route to market. Many of them were too small

to be able to deal effectively with the likes of Toys "R" Us, and the rest of their potential retail customers were both too fragmented to reach efficiently and too small to provide anything more than local-ized market access. For its vendors, Zulily solved both of these problems.

> **"For its vendors, Zulily solved both of these problems. "**

- *In emerging markets:* In places like India, the retailing infra-structure is far less developed than in more developed coun-tries. This means that, from a customer point of view, there's an inherent scarcity in many merchandise categories outside the big cities. It may be that innovative customer-funded retail strategies using mobile phone technology—in emerging markets the mobile phone is the computer of choice—and scarcity models (order this style today, and you'll have it next week) will be developed that can serve these needs.

How to apply scarcity and flash sales models:

- *Avoid holding inventory in flash sales models:* Blogger and investor Greg Bettinelli says that one of the keys to Zulily's success is that it holds essentially no inventory. "Their non-inventory model has resulted in a negative working capital model which has set them up for long-term success."[36] As British e-commerce veteran Perry Blacher notes, however, the devil is in the details. "You can end up with inventory in spite of your best efforts, from returns or from case-packs that don't fully sell through."[37]
- *Get long vendor terms:* We've already seen that getting good terms from one's vendors is important in building almost any kind of customer-funded business, because the reality is these businesses are vendor funded, too. But long vendor terms are crucial for scarcity models, since the customer, as at Zara, is not always paying far in advance of getting the goods. Getting good terms is getting more difficult in

competitive categories, however. Kennet Partners' Hillel Zidel, an investor in the European flash sales business Buy VIP, says, "Things have changed."[38] Many vendors, with so many flash sales merchants asking for their goods, are now able to require them to commit to quantities of inventory in advance and pay on terms that are more advantageous to the vendor. Thus, in Zidel's view, except in emerging markets, where the underdeveloped retailing infrastructure means scarcity still exists in consumer terms, "It's over."

- *When it's gone, it's gone:* Avoid the temptation to reorder.
When a hot-selling style is gone, that's exactly what you

❝Avoid the temptation to reorder.❞

wanted to happen. Design or order something similar, perhaps, but let that style be gone.

Scarcity and flash sales models: Pitfalls to watch out for:

- *The* absence *of rapid fashion or product obsolescence:* As we saw in Chapter 6, there has been a plethora of startups seeking to build flash sales businesses in all kind of categories where there really isn't the obsolescence to drive purchasing behavior. In such categories, a scarcity model may not be the best way to go, despite the large number of entrepreneurs that still appear to believe in them. Indeed, some such entrants have converted to subscription models—which may not work either, as we saw in Chapter 5!—in efforts to preserve another form of the capital efficiency that drew them to the business in the first place. Even Zara's parent company, Inditex, which now operates retailing businesses in eight formats including Oysho (lingerie) and Zara Home (home decor),[39] has had to adapt parts of its strategy in formats where fashions don't change as quickly. Scarcity has become less central in these formats, and the company's legendary supply chain efficiency has moved to the forefront.

- *Too much competition for too little supply:* The rapid growth of the flash sales phenomenon has meant that in many merchandise categories, including fashion apparel, there is too much demand chasing too little supply. There's only so much overstock available, so manufacturers—always happy to meet buyers' demand—have turned to producing goods specially made for the flash sales merchants.[40] To meet their so-called discount price points, however, they have to cheapen the fabrics or cheapen the "make." The original value proposition for the customer is no longer there. If you cannot find a category where you can fly below the radar and obtain exclusive supply of overstocked inventory, it's likely that, as with most of vente-privee's imitators, sales growth will be much easier to achieve than profitability.

> **"in many merchandise categories, including fashion apparel, there is too much demand chasing too little supply"**

- *Paying too much to acquire customers:* Acquiring customers affordably, in relation to the profit contribution they'll give you over time, is essential. To make matters worse, as Greg Bettinelli observes, the rate at which most e-commerce consumers buy from any given site tends to decline over time, especially in flash sales businesses.[41] This makes it easy to pay more to acquire customers than you should. "All of this requires a deep analytical understanding of how the customer behaves," says Perry Blacher. "The best companies have good analysts, matching inputs to outputs, and are incredibly data-driven."[42]

- *A costly back end:* Operating the business efficiently—from curating and sourcing the right products to producing next week's promotion to quickly fulfilling the customer's order—is a tricky thing to pull off. The wrong products, promoted ineffectively, won't sell. Slow fulfillment means higher likelihood of customer returns. The sometimes modest gross margins with which many scarcity models operate leave little room for error in managing the rest of what it takes to do business. "All of these things are surprisingly un-virtual," says Blacher; rather, they have to do with mundane operational issues like curating the merchandise assortment, dealing with vendors, and managing pick rates and margin-per-foot of shelf space in a distribution center.[43] If your back end operations aren't efficient, you'll have a difficult time building a profitable scarcity-based business.

Service-to-Product Models

Virtually all services businesses, as I noted earlier in this chapter, are potential candidates for building customer-funded pay-in-advance businesses. But what if you

> **Virtually all services businesses are potential candidates for building customer-funded pay-in-advance businesses.**

have a product business in mind that you'd like to fund by starting out as a services business? For starters, all the principles I listed for pay-in-advance businesses—when to apply them, how to apply them, and the pitfalls to watch out for—apply as you get started. But eventually, if a product business is your goal, you'll need to make the not-so-easy transition from a services business to a product business. Here are some lessons to be mindful of when you reach such an inflection point.

When to attempt a service-to-product transition:

- *When technology permits:* Transitions from services to products business are typically technology enabled. CE Info Systems, as we saw in Chapter 1, was able to develop MapmyIndia.com because the Internet made it possible. Rock Solid, as we saw in Chapter 7, was able to make its transition because the cloud made it possible. GoViral was able to make the switch by using technology to automate the distribution of advertisers' video content.

- *When you've got something of value that could be used* without *you:* Just because technology makes your transition possible, that does not mean that buyers—whether your current buyers or new ones—will want the services you now provide delivered on a standalone "productized" basis. Joe Clark, founder and CEO of Prana Business, a consultancy in the throes of a service-to-product transition in search of a business "that can scale," identified an opportunity to make his company's unique approach to strategy execution available to other consultants. But he and his team had to build an online tool, make that tool easy for other consultants to sell and deliver, and get the pricing model right so that both Prana and his new customers' consulting businesses could profit from using the new tools.[44] Prana has made good progress, but getting such details right is usually far more difficult than it looks at first glance.

How to apply service-to-product models at transition time:

- *Iterate, with a target customer on board:* As is the case with nearly all product development efforts, the first version of the product won't be quite right. As Clark recalls, "We had to refine the model." Involving the target customer in your product development is crucial.[45]

- *Explore various pricing models:* Your initial hopes and assumptions about how and how much someone will pay for your *product*—presumably much less than they now pay for your *service*—are probably wrong.[46] You'll need to test some alternatives and see what flies.

> **❝Your initial hopes and assumptions about how and how much someone will pay are probably wrong❞**

Service-to-product models: Pitfalls to watch out for at transition time:

- *Wrong management team:* Services and products businesses require different kinds of skill sets.[47] Do you have the new skills you'll need, or will you need to bring on new kinds of expertise—as GoViral did, in the person of Rene Rechtman, as we saw in Chapter 7—to take full advantage of the potential that lies ahead? Otherwise, you are likely to fall prey to what Brad Feld calls "rookie errors, which are mostly self-inflicted."[48]

- *Wrong relationships:* To make the transition, you may need different kinds of relationships than you have now—with different kinds of suppliers and perhaps a different set of customers, too. Do you have them? Can you build them?

- *Going red to go black:* It's likely that making your transition will entail significant investment. Are you prepared to make and fund that investment if it turns your profitable company into an unprofitable one for a while, in the hopes that you'll return to profitability and faster growth post-transition? Kleiner Perkins' Randy Komisar puts it starkly: "Are you prepared to go red to go black?"[49] And are you willing to do so, with all the pluses and minuses that involves? As I tell my students, "The day you take a dollar or pound or rupee of venture capital is the day you have agreed to sell your business."

  ❝Are you prepared to go red to go black?❞

- *Lack of discipline:* In Steve Blank's view, service-to-product models "require the most discipline."[50] It's easy to lose direction, to have no clear strategy, and despite your best attempts, as Blank puts it, the product business "may never come."[51] Richard Gourlay of Sussex Place Ventures sees the same challenges. "Getting to the right product that meets enough customers' needs is a lot harder than it looks."[52]

- *Diverting your attention from your services business:* As Prana's Joe Clark puts it, "I still need to butter my bread."[53] Taking time away from selling and delivering your services may mean that your services revenue will fall. Are you prepared for that, and can you cushion the fall?

Points of Departure for Your Customer-Funded Journey

Okay, you want to get started on building a customer-funded business. "But how should I begin?" you ask. Fortunately there are a number of great jumping-off points that can provide a helpful platform for getting your journey underway.

- *Find the right incubator or accelerator:* Too many such entrepreneurial hothouses are focused on getting their ventures to a point where they can secure VC funding. That's a noble goal for some entrepreneurs, but not the one we seek here, at least not so early. The best of the incubator or accelerator breed, though, know that what progress is actually about is getting customer traction for something customers really must have. And though many of them don't really say so directly, they love capital efficiency, too. It's no surprise, then, that a vast majority of the startups that TechStars invites into its family fall into three of our five customer-funded categories: companies building matchmaker, pay-in-advance, or subscription models. If you can find an incubator in your geographical area that's on board with the customer-funded mind-set and thinks you meet their tests, you'll probably get lots of good advice there, and good contacts, too.

> **Too many such entrepreneurial hothouses are focused on getting their ventures to a point where they can secure VC funding.**

- *Meet the right business angel:* Some angels "get it," and from the moment they meet you will grill you with questions about customers—instead of ques-

  ❝Some angels 'get it,' others don't❞ tions about your spreadsheets, which are probably little more than a pipe dream, anyway. Others don't. If they—or *you*, if you're an angel—start with the numbers, that's probably a bad sign. Most of them like to "road test" their prospective investees for a considerable period before writing checks, a very good idea, so even though you don't want their money at the outset, you may want it later, once your customer-funded model is proven and ready to grow. Thus, getting to know a few angels—*before* you need money to grow—isn't a bad idea. The fact that you're not seeking a check now, while you prove your concept with customer-funded traction, will probably set you apart from most of the others who are banging down angels' doors. But beware. The skewness curve for business angels' performance—you may recall its harsh lesson from Chapter 1—is probably even more skewed than it is for VCs. So conduct your due diligence on your angel *carefully*.

- *Join a "startup weekend":* It may surprise you to learn that Chapter 3's Rover.com got its start at a startup weekend in Seattle, where the idea was conceived and kicked off.[54] While Rover chose to take capital early, in order to grow quickly from day one, you and the like-minded entrepreneurial types you'll meet at such a weekend can surely focus your efforts on one or more of the customer-funded models as the basis for your work.

So, What Are You Waiting For? Why Not Now?

I began this book by articulating some of the reasons why in many cases raising capital too early is a bad idea, and why, if you are an aspiring entrepreneur, getting your early funding from your customers is a better way to go. It's true, too, for those in established businesses who have read this far. If you're among the business angels—or supporters like them in incubators or accelerators—who are also reading this book, you'll have seen that investing in young companies *later* than most entrepreneurs would like makes a great deal of sense, for them and for you, and is likely to improve your investment returns, too.

So, whichever of these readers you are, you have now seen that building a customer-funded business can actually be done. No, it's not a mirage! You've also seen the inspiring stories of a collection of twenty-first-century and earlier entrepreneurs and their companies who have done just that. Thus, let's close by recapping why you should do it *now*—or, if you're a business angel, why you should stay in touch with or mentor someone who's doing it, with an eye toward backing his or her business later, once customer traction is proven.

So why now, you ask? Why *not* now? Somebody down the street or around the world is

> **why now, you ask? Why *not* now?**

probably working on pretty much the same idea as you are. If he or she is busy chasing investors and you're focused on customers, my bet is on you to win the race. And I'm betting you'll have more fun, too. As serial entrepreneur Erick Mueller recalls of his past entrepreneurial journeys, some of which included external investors and some of which did not, "It's a lot more fun solving customer problems than pandering to investors. I'd *much* rather have customer problems than investor problems."[55] iDoneThis founder Walter Chen concurs. "I noticed that the questions that our customers asked were different. Unlike VC's questions, our customers' questions were less focused on the size of the opportunity and they were more focused on the product and the soul behind it, and that's how we got to know each other better."[56]

At the end of the day, as Harvard Business School's entrepreneurial finance guru Bill Sahlman reaffirms, "The best money comes from customers, not investors . . . Selling a product or service early in the life of a company provides great feedback *and* the cash needed to refine the idea."[57] So, to say it one more time before I sign off, if you can, get your initial money from

> **The best money comes from customers, not investors.**

your customers, not from investors. When the time is right, then raise investor money, if that's the right thing to do in your situation. And when will that be the right thing to do? Steve Blank, the godfather of the lean startup movement and an active angel investor and mentor, puts it simply. "When it's repeatable and scalable, then raise money."[58] So choose your model—there's a menu of five to choose from—and get on with your journey. I wish you bon voyage!

Acknowledgments

L ike almost anything else meaningful that I've ever been involved with, this book has been a team effort from the very start. It began with my students, whose remarkable efforts to conceive of and start a wide array of sometimes extraordinary entrepreneurial ventures, have been an inspiration to me and to others. But one of these students, Nell Derick-Debevoise, stands out.

After earning her MBA at Columbia and London Business Schools and while getting her own entrepreneurial venture, Inspiring Capital (see www.inspiringcapital.ly) underway, Nell was kind enough to share a portion of her time to assist me on the research project that has evolved into this book. Her dogged identification and examination of dozens of companies, and her ability to organize what we learned about those companies—and the entrepreneurs who founded and grew them—into a series of coherent and accessible case histories, were crucial. Her work made possible the insights that led to the typology of customer-funded models, and it brought forth the stories that bring them to life. Thank you, Nell. Without your work—not to mention your good humor and patience with me!—this book would not exist.

Thanks go, too, to those who so kindly consented to lengthy and detailed interviews that Nell and I conducted, especially those whose stories are profiled in several of the book's case histories: MapmyIndia's Rakesh and Rashmi Verma, and Rohan Verma, too; Rud Browne of Ryzex; Petals for the People's Sam Pollaro and H.Bloom's Bryan Burkhart; Jimmy Maymann and Claus Moseholm of GoViral; and Rock Solid's Ángel Pérez.

Whether sourced from interviews like these or from secondary data, the case histories that bring each of the chapters to life are only the tip of the iceberg. My more difficult research task was to seek insights from entrepreneurs and investors who have had the experience of actually putting customer-funded models to work. Their names are too numerous to acknowledge here, but are found alongside the lessons they provide in Chapter 8, and occasionally elsewhere. Most of whatever useful ideas and best practices found in this book are probably theirs. Any errors in interpretation are mine alone.

Conducting any extensive research project and interpreting the results takes people, of course, but it takes the right setting, too. I extend my wholehearted thanks to London Business School and my LBS colleagues for providing a fertile research setting, as well as generous research funding, with which I was able to get on with the work.

In the later stages of the work, as I began to bring an initial and very rough draft into coherent shape, the wisdom of my Wiley editor, Richard Narramore, shone though. Thanks, Richard, for your confidence in this project and for helping to sharpen the messages and to make them more accessible than they would otherwise have been. James Fraleigh then did a superb job in polishing the prose to make it clearer and more readable. Hats off to you, James! My thanks go, too, to Wiley's Tiffany Colón, who cheerfully kept all of us on track.

Finally, I thank my mother, Alice Mullins, and my late father, Jack Mullins, for somehow imparting into the active and energetic boy I was in my youth that reading and writing were as much fun as playing backyard football or schoolyard basketball. Mom, all those nights working on and helping me refine school essays have eventually brought me great joy! My thanks also go to Donna, my wonderful wife of more than 40 years, who somehow tolerated seeing more of "the back of my head" than she would have liked when I changed careers via a PhD at midlife. She got to see more of that side of me, too, during the summer of 2013, when the majority of this book was written. Doubtless she'd have preferred us to be hiking or traveling. Though she'd probably like me to slow down just a bit, Donna has been my gracious and supportive companion every step of the way. As she's come to know, "slow" and "stop" simply aren't in my lexicon. But somehow, she loves and supports me anyway.

I'll close by giving my heartfelt thanks to the hundreds of millions of entrepreneurs—including those hidden in nooks and crannies of large companies, in big cities, or in remote villages in places like India and Africa—who by their creativity and ingenuity make the world go 'round. It is my view that the rest of the business world has much to learn from them, as the stories in this book attest. Without the livelihoods they create, both directly and indirectly, and without their innovations that are changing our world at an ever-increasing pace, our lives would be far less interesting and satisfying, for sure. Thanks to you all!

John Mullins
London and Colorado
March 2014
http://faculty.london.edu/jmullins
www.thecustomerfundedbusiness.com
www.johnwmullins.com

Notes

Why This Book?

1. David S. Rose, comment on "How Many Start-ups in the US Get Seed/VC Funding per Year?" *Quora*, April 21, 2012, www.quora.com/Venture-Capital/How-many-start-ups-in-the-US-get-seed-VC-funding-per-year; Gust website, accessed February 8, 2014, www.gust.com.
2. Laura Montini, "Startups Saw More Seed Funding Deals in 2013," *Inc.*, March 13, 2014, www.inc.com/laura-montini/startups-are-finding-seed-funding-easier-to-come-by.html?cid=em01011week09day28c.
3. Fred Wilson, "Maximizing Runway Can Minimize Success," *A VC* (blog), September 18, 2018, www.avc.com/a_vc/2013/09/maximizing-runway-can-minimize-success.html.
4. Mark Suster, "Why You Need to Ring the Freaking Cash Register," *Both Sides of the Table* (blog), July 16, 2013, www.bothsidesofthetable.com/2013/07/16/ring-the-freaking-cash-register/.
5. Bill Joy, "Large Problem: How Big Companies Can Innovate," *Fortune*, November 15, 2004, 214.
6. John Mullins, *The New Business Road Test: What Entrepreneurs and Executives Should Do before Launching a Lean Start-up*, 1st ed. (London: Pearson/FT Publishing, 2003) and 4th ed. (London: Pearson/FT Publishing, 2013).
7. John Mullins and Randy Komisar, *Getting to Plan B: Breaking Through to a Better Business Model* (Boston: Harvard Business Review Press, 2009).

Chapter 1   Craving Crowdfunding? Pandering to VCs? Groveling to Your CFO?: The Magic of Traction and the Customer-Funded Revolution

1. The Vermas' case history is based on an interview with Rakesh, Rashmi, and Rohan Verma in New Delhi, June 24, 2012.

2. Peter Drucker, *Innovation and Entrepreneurship*, reprint edition (New York: HarperBusiness, 2006).

3. Rud Browne, interview with the author, December 2, 2013.

4. Erika Brown Ekiel, "The Entrepreneur Questionnaire: Brian Chesky, Co-founder of Airbnb," Greylock Partners, April 8, 2011, http://greylockvc .com/post/47569079798/the-entrepreneur-questionnaire-brian-chesky.

5. Figures as of December 2013. Source: Airbnb.com.

6. TFW Bureau, "Travelling to New Heights," *Franchise India*, March 22, 2011, www.franchiseindia.com/magazine/2011/top-franchise/debutant/ via_120/.

7. Prashant K. Nanda, "Pearson Acquires Whole of TutorVista," *LiveMint*, February 24, 2013, www.livemint.com/Companies/LkipTPnsANIBwtrL BJOnHJ/Pearson-acquires-whole-of-TutorVista.html.

8. "Vente-privee.com," *Wikipedia*, last modified January 22, 2014, http://en .wikipedia.org/wiki/Vente-privee.com.

9. Mike Butcher, "AOL Europe Acquires Branded Video Distribution Network Goviral for 96.7 Million," *TechCrunch* (blog), January 31, 2011, http://techcrunch.com/2011/01/31/aol-europe-acquires-branded-video-distribution-network-goviral-for-96-7-million/.

10. The best of breed in this category, in my view, are Greg Gianforte's *Bootstrapping Your Business* (Avon, MA: Adams Media, 2005) and portions of David Cohen and Brad Feld's *Do More Faster* (Hoboken, NJ: John Wiley & Sons, 2010).

11. See Javier Rojas, "Bootstrapping Your Business for Success: Knowing When & How to Approach VC Firms" (white paper, Kennet Partners, 2008), www.kennet.com/ideas-resources/whitepaper-bootstrap-your-business-for-success/.

12. Harry McCracken, "The Kickstarter Economy," *Time*, October 1, 2012, www.time.com/time/magazine/article/0,9171,2125023,00.html.

13. Ethan Mollick, "The Dynamics of Crowdfunding: An Exploratory Study," *Journal of Business Venturing* 29, no. 1 (January 2014): 1–16; Abigail Tracy, "Kickstarter's Nine-Figure Milestone," *Inc.* March 3, 2014, www.inc.com/ abigail-tracy/kickstarter-raises-over-one-billion-in-pledges.html?cid= em01011week10day03d.

14. Chase Hoffberger, "'Inocente': A Big Oscars Win for Kickstarter," *Daily Dot*, February 25, 2013, www.dailydot.com/entertainment/inocente-kickstarter-oscars-win-documentary/.

15. Tim Bradshaw, "Crowdfunded Start-ups Face Production Challenges," *Financial Times*, May 5, 2013, www.ft.com/intl/cms/s/0/56a05e82-b34f-11e2–95b3–00144feabdc0.html#axzz2ZhK9Pzae.

16. Mollick, "The Dynamics of Crowdfunding."

17. Dan Marom, co-author of *The Crowdfunding Revolution*, interviewed by Gary Dushnitsky, "Crowdfunding," *Business Strategy Review*, March 2014, http://communications.london.edu/go.asp?/bLBS001/mLNTHEAG/uR3NIL/x9AA3FAG.

18. Ibid.

19. Ibid.

20. Bradshaw, "Crowdfunded Start-ups."

21. Ibid.

22. Michael Blanding, "The Problems and Promises of Crowdfunding," *Forbes*, contributed by HBS Working Knowledge, July 1, 2013, www.forbes.com/sites/hbsworkingknowledge/2013/07/01/the-problems-and-promises-of-crowdfunding/.

23. Cohen and Feld, *Do More Faster*, 203–4.

24. Todd Hixon, "Spring in Venture Capital," *Forbes*, September 18, 2013, www.forbes.com/sites/toddhixon/2013/09/18/spring-in-venture-capital/.

25. McCracken, "The Kickstarter Economy."

26. Hixon, "Spring in Venture Capital."

27. Henry Mance, "UK Venture Capital Boom Slows," *Financial Times Tech Hub*, July 21, 2013, www.ft.com/intl/cms/s/0/924b8050-f09a-11e2-929c-00144feabdc0.html?ftcamp=crm/email/2013722/nbe/UKMorning-Headlines/product#axzz2ZhK9Pzae.

28. Hixon, "Spring in Venture Capital."

29. Jon Swartz, "Twitter IPO Kick Starts Tech," *USA Today*, September 13, 2013, 1A–2A.

30. For a systematic approach to assessing entrepreneurial opportunities, there's another great book you might want to read—my first one, from 2003, now in its fourth edition—John Mullins, *The New Business Road Test: What Entrepreneurs and Executives Should Do* before *Launching a Lean Start-up*, 4th ed. (London: Pearson/FT Publishing, 2013). Pursuing a fundamentally flawed opportunity is a sure-fire path to disaster. From a societal perspective, it's even worse, as it's a waste of entrepreneurial time and talent. Whose? Hopefully not yours!

31. Quoted in "Venture Capital Has Gone from One Unreality to Another," *Knowledge @ Wharton*, January 16, 2002, http://knowledge.wharton.upenn.edu/article/venture-capital-has-gone-from-one-unreality-to-another/.

32. Alistair Barr and Clare Baldwin, "Groupon's IPO Biggest by US Web Company Since Google," *Reuters*, November 4, 2011, www.reuters.com/article/2011/11/04/us-groupon-idUSTRE7A352020111104.

33. Jonathan Weil, "Groupon IPO Scandal Is the Sleaze That's Legal," *Bloomberg Opinion*, April 4, 2012, www.bloomberg.com/news/2012–04–04/groupon-ipo-scandal-is-the-sleaze-that-s-legal.html.

34. Jonathan Weil, "Groupon IPO Scandal Is the Sleaze That's Legal," *Bloomberg Opinion*, April 4, 2012, www.bloomberg.com/news/2012–04–04/groupon-ipo-scandal-is-the-sleaze-that-s-legal.html; and Michael J. de la Merced, "Groupon's Shares Fall on Revision," *DealBook*, March 30, 2012, http://dealbook.nytimes.com/2012/03/30/restating-earnings-groupon-discloses-accounting-issues/.

35. Ibid., de la Merced.

36. M.G., "Discounted Out," *Schumpeter* (blog), *The Economist*, March 1, 2013, www.economist.com/blogs/schumpeter/2013/03/groupon-fires-its-boss.

37. See Groupon's two-year stock price history, http://finance.yahoo.com/echarts?s=GRPN+Interactive#symbol=grpn;range=2y;compare=;indicator=volume;charttype=area;crosshair=on;ohlcvalues=0;logscale=off;source=undefined;.

38. The Vermas' case history is based on an interview with Rakesh, Rashmi, and Rohan Verma in New Delhi, June 24, 2012.

Chapter 2 Customer-Funded Models: Mirage or Mind-Set? Old or New?

1. Except where noted, the story of Christopher Columbus and Queen Isabella is sourced from Infocordoba, "Columbus, Queen Isabella and King Ferdinand in Cordoba: The Real Connections," accessed February 8, 2014, www.infocordoba.com/spain/andalusia/cordoba/articles/christopher_columbus_isabella_ferdinand.htm.

2. Melanie Filiziani and Lynn Isaacs, "Queen Isabella I of Spain," *Prof. Pavlac's Women's History Site*, last modified May 31, 2008, http://departments.kings.edu/womens_history/isabel.html.

3. Steven N. Kaplan and Josh Lerner, "It Ain't Broke: The Past, Present, and Future of Venture Capital," *Journal of Applied Corporate Finance* 22, no. 2 (Spring 2010), 36–47.

4. Brent Lundell Sr., "History of Venture Capital," *Gain Stream Group* (blog), July 8, 2013, www.gainstreamgroup.com/2013/07/08/history-of-venture-capital/.

5. See, for example, SeedCamp (www.seedcamp.com), Y Combinator (www.ycombinator.com) and TechStars (www.techstars.com).

6. Except where otherwise noted, the Dell case history is drawn from "Dell Inc. History," *Funding Universe*, accessed February 8, 2014, www .fundinguniverse.com/company-histories/dell-inc-history/; and Michael Dell with Catherine Fredman, *Direct from Dell: Strategies That Revolutionized an Industry* (New York: HarperBusiness, 1999).

7. Dell and Fredman, *Direct from Dell*, 9.

8. Ibid.

9. Except where otherwise noted, the Banana Republic case history is taken from Mel Ziegler and Patricia Ziegler, *Wild Company: The Untold Story of Banana Republic* (New York: Simon & Schuster, 2012); Mel Ziegler and Patricia Ziegler, "Coup Lands Banana Republic in The Gap," *Bloomberg News*, September 20, 2012, www.bloomberg.com/news/2012–09–20/coup-lands-banana-republic-in-the-gap.html; Dan Schwabel, "The True Story behind the Banana Republic Brand," *Forbes*, October 2, 2012, www.forbes .com/sites/danschawbel/2012/10/02/the-true-story-behind-the-banana-republic-brand/; and Mel Ziegler and Patricia Ziegler, "An Empire Built on Short-Armed Shirts," *Bloomberg News*, September 18, 2012, www .bloomberg.com/news/2012–09–18/an-empire-built-on-short-armed-shirts.html.

10. Ziegler and Ziegler, *Wild Company*, page 6.

11. Ibid., page 8.

12. Ibid., page 10.

13. Ibid., page 14.

14. Ibid., page 15.

15. Ibid., page 18.

16. Ibid.

17. Ibid., 19.

18. Ibid., 20.

19. Ibid., 21.

20. Ibid., 44.

21. Ibid., 73.

22. Ibid., 77.

23. Ibid., 80.

24. Ibid., 81.

25. Ibid., 89–90.

26. Ibid., 90.

27. Dinah Eng, "Turning Khaki Into Gold," *Fortune*, February 28, 2013, 10.

28. Ibid.

29. Dell and Fredman, *Direct from Dell*, 18.

30. Ziegler and Ziegler, *Wild Company*, 94.

31. Ibid.

32. Ibid., 20.

33. Dell and Fredman, *Direct from Dell*, 17.

Chapter 3   Buyers and Sellers, but Not *Your* Goods: Matchmaker Models

1. Ekiel, "The Entrepreneur Questionnaire: Brian Chesky."

2. Brian Chesky video at www.airbnbcom/story. Accessed December 15, 2012.

3. Jessi Hempel, "Airbnb: More Than a Place to Crash," *CNN Money*, May 3, 2012, http://tech.fortune.cnn.com/2012/05/03/airbnb-apartments-social-media/.

4. Fred Wilson, "Airbnb," *A VC* (blog), March 16, 2011, www.avc.com/a_vc/2011/03/airbnb.html.

5. grantgrant, "Founder Story: Airbnb's 11 Steps to Success," *GuoTime* (blog), April 4, 2012, www.guotime.com/2012/04/7-steps-idea-main-stream-adoptions-airbnb/.

6. Wilson, "Airbnb."

7. Om Malik, "What Every Startup Can Learn from Airbnb," *Om Says* (blog), *GigaOM*, February 22, 2011, http://gigaom.com/2011/02/22/airbnb/.

8. grantgrant, "Founder Story."

9. "Airbnb," *CrunchBase*, last modified February 6, 2014, www.crunchbase.com/company/airbnb.

10. Hempel, "Airbnb."

11. Paul Graham, "Subject: Airbnb," *Paulgraham.com*, March 17, 2011, Accessed December 8, 2013, www.paulgraham.com/airbnb.html.

12. Figures as of December 2013. Source: Airbnb.com.

13. grantgrant, "Founder Story."

14. Benjamin F. Kuo, "Interview with Aaron Hirschhorn, DogVacay.com," Socaltech.com, March 5, 2012, www.socaltech.com/interview_with_aaron_hirschhorn_dogvacay_com/s-0041300.html.

15. Nicky George, "Thoughts on Being an Entrepreneur with Aaron Hirschhorn—Founder of DogVacay," NG, May 20, 2012, www.nickygeorge.com/aaron-hirschhorn-founder-of-dogvacay-com/.

16. Jeff Gelles, "Tech Life: Sending Your Pooch on a DogVacay," *Philly.com*, May 18, 2012, http://articles.philly.com/2012–05–18/business/31750014_1_aaron-hirschhorn-dog-owners-three-dogs.

17. Wendy W., "DogVacay" review posted May 17, 2010, retrieved from *Yelp*, September 28, 2012, www.yelp.com/biz/dogvacay-santa-monica?sort_by=date_desc.

18. Kuo, "Interview with Aaron Hirschhorn."

19. Tomio Geron, "Dog Sitter Site DogVacay Expands Nationwide As Kennel Alternative," *Forbes*, July 2, 2012, www.forbes.com/sites/tomiogeron/2012/07/02/dog-sitter-site-dogvacay-expands-nationwide-as-kennel-alternative/.

20. George, "Thoughts on Being an Entrepreneur."

21. Ibid.

22. Leena Rao, "The Art of Science," *TechCrunch* (blog), February 2, 2013, http://techcrunch.com/2013/02/02/the-art-of-science/#.

23. Kuo, "Interview with Aaron Hirschhorn."

24. Amy Sacks, "Doggie B&B Service Places Pets in Homey Spots during Vacations," *New York Daily News*, April 14, 2012, www.nydailynews.com/life-style/doggie-b-b-service-places-pets-homey-spots-vacations-article-1.1061644.

25. Kuo, "Interview with Aaron Hirschhorn."

26. Tomio Geron, "How People Make Cash in the Share Economy," *Forbes*, January 23, 2013, www.forbes.com/sites/tomiogeron/2013/01/23/how-people-make-cash-in-the-share-economy/.

27. Leena Rao, "The Airbnb for Pets, DogVacay, Raises $6M," *TechCrunch* (blog), November 13, 2012, http://techcrunch.com/2012/11/13/the-airbnb-for-pets-dogvacay-raises-6m-from-benchmark/.

28. Geena Urango, "Year One: DogVacay Barks Its Way up the Ladder," *LA Tech Rise* (blog), February 26, 2013, http://latechrise.com/2013/02/26/year-one-dogvacay-barks-its-way-up-the-ladder/.

29. Colleen Taylor, "Pet Boarding Marketplace DogVacay Fetches $15 Million Series B Led by Foundation Capital," *TechCrunch* (blog), October 10, 2013, http://techcrunch.com/2013/10/10/pet-boarding-marketplace-dogvacay-fetches-15-million-series-b-led-by-foundation-capital/.

30. Kuo, "Interview with Aaron Hirschhorn."

31. "About Us," DogVacay, accessed February 8, 2014, http://dogvacay.com/about.

32. Tiffany Swift, "ProFounder Delivers for Entrepreneurs, and the Communities That Believe in Them," *Sheepless*, March 30, 2011, www.sheepless.org/magazine/features/profounder-delivers-entrepreneurs-and-communities-believe-them.

33. "ProFounder: About" (archive), accessed February 8, 2014, https://web .archive.org/web/20120707182807/http://www.profounder.com/about.

34. Leena Rao, "ProFounder Launches to Help Small Businesses Crowdsource Fundraising," *TechCrunch* (blog), November 30, 2010, http://techcrunch.com/2010/11/30/profounder-launches-to-help-small-businesses-crowdsource-fundraising/.

35. Leena Rao, "Crowdsourced Fundraising Platform ProFounder Now Offers Equity-Based Investment Tools, *TechCrunch* (blog), May 3, 2011, http:// techcrunch.com/2011/05/03/crowdsourced-fundraising-platform-profounder-now-offers-equity-based-investment-tools/.

36. Tom Cheshire, "ProFounder: Putting Investors Wheels in Motion," *Wired UK*, August 22, 2011, www.wired.co.uk/magazine/archive/2011/ 09/start/investors-wheels-in-motion.

37. Tiffany Swift, "Profounder Delivers."

38. Cheshire, "ProFounder: Putting Investors Wheels in Motion."

39. Leena Rao, "Crowdsourced Fundraising Platform ProFounder."

40. "Profounder Shutting Down," *Profounder, the blog* (archive), February 17, 2012, accessed February 8, 2014, http://web.archive.org/web/ 20130115172605/http://blog.profounder.com/2012/02/17/profounder-shutting-down/.

41. Simon Rothman, "How to Structure a Marketplace," *TechCrunch* (blog), August 19, 2012, http://techcrunch.com/2012/08/19/how-to-structure-a-marketplace/.

42. Ibid.

43. PRWeb, "Dog Vacay Raises $1 Million in Seed Funding Lead by First Round Capital to Fuel Nationwide Expansion," news release, March 19, 2012, www.prweb.com/releases/2012/3/prweb9299700.htm.

44. Michael Arrington, "The Moment of Truth for Airbnb As User's Home Is Utterly Trashed," *TechCrunch* (blog), July 27, 2011, http://techcrunch. com/2011/07/27/the-moment-of-truth-for-airbnb-as-users-home-is-utterly-trashed/.

45. Mike Butcher, "Police Bust Prostitutes Using Airbnb Apartment in Stockholm," *TechCrunch* (blog), August 14, 2012, http://techcrunch .com/2012/08/14/police-bust-prostitutes-using-airbnb-apartment-in-stockhom/.

46. PRWeb, "DogVacay.com Launches Superior Alternative to Caged Kennels with a Community of Loving and Trusted Home-Based Dog Boarders," March 1, 2012, www.prweb.com/releases/2012/3/prweb9243962.htm.

47. David Hsu, conversation with the author, July 13, 2013.

Chapter 4   Ask for the Cash: Pay-in-Advance Models

1. Membership fees as of July 2013, www.costco.com and www.costco.co.uk.
2. The Costco business model is discussed in considerable detail in Chapter 6 of John Mullins and Randy Komisar, *Getting to Plan B: Breaking Through to a Better Business Model* (Boston: Harvard Business Review Press, 2009).
3. Costco Wholesale Corp. information page, *BloombergBusinessweek*, accessed February 10, 2013, http://investing.businessweek.com/research/stocks/financials/financials.asp?ticker=COST.
4. Max Chafkin, "The Customer is the Company," *Inc.*, June 1, 2008, www.inc.com/magazine/20080601/the-customer-is-the-company_pagen_2.html.
5. Except where otherwise noted, the Threadless case history is sourced from Jake Nickell, *Threadless: Ten Years of T-shirts from the World's Most Inspiring Online Community* (New York: Abrams Image, 2010).
6. Nickell, *Threadless*, 12.
7. Marcia Froelke Coburn, "How Jake Nickell Built His Threadless Empire," *Chicago Magazine*, June 20, 2012, www.chicagomag.com/Chicago-Magazine/July-2012/How-Jake-Nickell-Built-His-Threadless-Empire/.
8. Nickell, *Threadless*, 12.
9. Ben Lang, "An Interview with Jake Nickell: Founder of Threadless," *EpicLaunch*, November 16, 2011, http://epiclaunch.com/an-interview-with-jake-nickell-founder-of-threadless/.
10. "Jake Nickell, Co-founder of Threadless, on Innovation," video chat, *Inc.*, May 24, 2010, www.inc.com/inctv/2010/05/inc-live-jake-nickell.html.
11. Chris Lake, "Threadless Founder Jake Nickell on Community and Crowdsourcing," *eConsultancy* (blog), September 22, 2010, http://econsultancy.com/us/blog/6627-threadless-founder-jake-nickell-on-community-and-crowdsourcing.
12. Coburn, "How Jake Nickell Built His Threadless Empire."
13. Nickell, *Threadless*, 15.
14. Ibid., 50–51.
15. Ibid., 76.
16. Ibid., 67.
17. Coburn, "How Jake Nickell Built His Threadless Empire."
18. Nickell, *Threadless*, 78.
19. Don Peppers, "Why Not Pay Customers for Their Good Ideas?" *LinkedIn*, Jul 30, 2013, www.linkedin.com/today/post/article/20130730121107-17102372-why-not-pay-customers-for-their-good-ideas.
20. Coburn, "How Jake Nickell Built His Threadless Empire."

21. Ibid.

22. Lake, "Threadless Founder Jake Nickell."

23. Ibid.

24. Bhisham Mansukhani, "FlightRaja Involves Agents in Unprecedented E-commerce Venture," *Express Travel World*, November 2006, www.expresstravelworld.com/200611/market02.shtml.

25. Regina Anthony, "Real Journeys, but It's Still Virtual Profit for Online Travel Firms," *LiveMint*, June 6, 2007, www.livemint.com/Companies/FnhdAkkZbUZtCka5fYpMUN/Real-journeys-but-its-still-virtual-profit-for-online-trav.html.

26. Vani Kola, "Indo US Ventures," video, 2009, London Business School.

27. Vani Kola, NEA Indo US Ventures, conversation with the author, January 2009.

28. Mansukhani, "FlightRaja Involves Agents."

29. Ibid.

30. Praveena Sharma, "Travel Solution Firm Via Books VC Funding," *Daily News and Analysis*, June 5, 2007, www.dnaindia.com/money/report_travel-solution-firm-via-books-vc-funding_1101467.

31. Gayatri Vijaykumar, "Flightraja Now Via, Announces US$ 5 Million VC," *Express Travel World*, July 2007, www.expresstravelworld.com/200707/aviationworld15.shtml.

32. Ibid.

33. Vani Kola, conversation with the author, January 2009.

34. Dennis Schaal, "Sequoia India Boosts Coffers of Online Travel Portal with $10 Million Investment," Tnooz, January 27, 2010, www.tnooz.com/2010/01/27/news/sequoia-india-boosts-coffers-of-online-travel-portal-with-10m-investment/.

35. Deepti Chaudhary, "Travel Company Via to Raise $100 Million," *Wall Street Journal*, March 29, 2011, http://online.wsj.com/article/SB10001424052748704559904576230272614332228.html.

36. Schaal, "Sequoia India Boosts Coffers."

37. TFW Bureau, "Travelling to New Heights," *Franchise India*, March 22, 2011, www.franchiseindia.com/magazine/2011/top-franchise/debutant/via_120/.

38. Vijay C. Roy, "Via to Take over Jalandhar-Based Firm," *Business Standard*, November 12, 2011, www.business-standard.com/india/news/via-to-takeover-jalandhar-based-firm/455248/.

39. Amit Mitra, "Via Bus Bets Big on Domestic Pilgrimage," *The Hindu Business Line*, December 8, 2011, www.thehindubusinessline.com/industry-and-economy/logistics/article2698708.ece?homepage=true&ref=wl_government-and-policy_art.

40. "Via and Tiger Airways Singapore Sign Exclusive Travel Agent Alliance," Via.com, December 5, 2012, http://in.via.com/go/world/press#.

41. Ibid.

42. Namita Bhagat, "Filling the Gap of Indian Travel Biz," *Franchise India*, April 30, 2012, www.franchiseindia.com/interviews/established/Filling-the-gap-of-Indian-travel-biz-454/.

43. Except where otherwise noted, The Loot's story is sourced from and used with the permission of Ambika Patni, Shreedar Munshi, and John Mullins, "The Loot (A)," 2010, London Business School and the National Entrepreneurship Network, www.thecasecentre.org.

44. Ibid., 2.

45. Ibid.

46. Ibid., 4.

47. Ibid., 5.

48. Ibid.

49. Ibid., 6.

50. Ibid., 7.

51. Ibid.

52. Ibid.

53. Ibid., 8.

54. Ambika Patni, Shreedar Munshi, and John Mullins, "The Loot (B)," 2010, London Business School and the National Entrepreneurship Network, page 3.

55. Abhishek Raghunath, "The Robin Hood of Retail," *Forbes India*, July 10, 2010, http://forbesindia.com/article/work-in-progress/the-robin-hood-of-retail/14952/1.

56. Jay Gupta, interview with the author, January 22, 2013.

57. Namita Bhagat, "Filling the Gap."

Chapter 5   Recurring Revenue: Subscription and SaaS Models

1. Kelly Clay, "Will 2012 Be the Year of Subscription-Based Services?" *Locker Gnome*, January 9, 2012, www.lockergnome.com/news/2012/01/09/will-2012-be-the-year-of-subscription-based-services/.

2. Sam Grobart, "Subscribe Forever," *BloombergBusinessweek*, November 18, 2013, 80.

3. Ibid.

4. Roy Furchgott, "Adobe Sends Boxed Software to the Cloud," *New York Times*, May 7, 2013, http://gadgetwise.blogs.nytimes.com/2013/05/07/adobe-sends-boxed-software-to-the-cloud/?ref=adobesystemsinc.

5. Grobart, "Subscribe Forever."

6. See http://topics.nytimes.com/top/news/business/companies/adobe_systems_inc/.

7. Narayan Krishnamurthy, "Log In and Learn: More and More Teachers Are Learning That It Pays to Move into the Virtual Classroom," *Outlook Money*, January 16, 2006, as run on TutorVista's "In News" page, www.tutorvista.com/press/mediacover/outlookmoneyjuly.php.

8. Philip Anderson, "K. Ganesh at TutorVista," *DARE*, January 1, 2008, http://issuu.com/daretostartup/docs/-04—-january-2008.

9. Sameer, "How Krishnan Ganesh Utilized Indian Tutors to Create TutorVista," *Nagpur Entrepreneurs* (blog), February 20, 2012, www.nagpurentrepreneurs.com/entrepreneur-interviews/how-krishnan-ganesh-utilized-indian-tutors-to-create-tutorvista.

10. Michelle Tsai, "TutorVista Gets $2M To Teach American Kids Online," TutorVista, June 2, 2006, as run on TutorVista's "In News" page, www.tutorvista.com/press/mediacover/djjuly.php.

11. Anderson, "K. Ganesh at TutorVista."

12. "After BPO It Is KPO: Indian Teachers Tutor US and UK kids," *Newind Press*, November 1, 2005, as run on TutorVista's "In News" page, www.tutorvista.com/press/mediacover/newindpressjuly.php.

13. Tsai, "TutorVista Gets $2M."

14. Tripat Preet Singh and John Mullins, "Indo US Ventures" case, 2009, London Business School.

15. Anderson, "K. Ganesh at TutorVista."

16. Steven E. F. Brown, "Outsourced Tutoring Company Raises $2M," *San Francisco Business Times*, June 12, 2006, www.bizjournals.com/sanfrancisco/stories/2006/06/12/daily14.html.

17. Adrienne Sanders, "TutorVista: Investor Steps Up after Hints of Rivals Sniffing Around," *San Francisco Business Times*, August 11, 2006, as run on TutorVista's "In News" page, www.tutorvista.com/press/mediacover/orlandobj.php.

18. Vanessa Hua, "One for the Books—Tutoring Gets Outsourced," *San Francisco Chronicle*, October 22, 2006, www.tutorvista.com/press/mediacover/SanFranciscoChronicle.pdf.

19. Ibid.

20. "After BPO It Is KPO."

21. Stephen David, "Teachers in India Help Students in the West Master Maths and Science through Internet Tuitions," *India Today*, July 15, 2006, as run on TutorVista's "In News" page, www.tutorvista.com/press/mediacover/indiatodayjuly.php.

22. B. M. Thanuja, "Sequoia to Put In $3 million in TutorVista," *The Economic Times*, December 20, 2006, http://articles.economictimes.indiatimes.com/2006–12–20/news/27439188_1_sequoia-capital-india-online-coaching-jv-partner.

23. "TutorVista Secures $10.75 Million Second Round Funding Led by Lightspeed Venture Partners," press release, December 20, 2006, as run on TutorVista's "In News" page, www.tutorvista.co.in/press/mediakitpdf/003-Funding%20Release%20Round%20B%20FINAL.pdf.

24. Dilip Thakur, "TutorVista's Big Catch," *Education World*, January 2007, www.educationworldonline.net/index.php/page-article-choice-more-id-794.

25. Thakur, "TutorVista's Big Catch."

26. Anderson, "K. Ganesh at TutorVista."

27. Moinak Mitra, "TutorVista.com gets $18-m PE Funding," *India Times*, July 24, 2008, http://articles.economictimes.indiatimes.com/2008–07–24/news/27710654_1_hybrid-model-online-education-pc-prices.

28. Anderson, "K. Ganesh at TutorVista."

29. Mitra, "TutorVista.com gets $18-m PE Funding."

30. Ibid.

31. Heather Timmons, "Pearson Acquires Stake in 2 Indian Education Companies," *New York Times*, June 24, 2009, www.nytimes.com/2009/06/25/business/global/25rupee.html?_r=1&dbk.

32. "UPDATE 1-Pearson invests $30 mln in 2 Indian education firms," *Reuters*, June 24, 2009, www.reuters.com/article/2009/06/24/pearson-idUSBNG42796820090624.

33. "Pearson Buys Majority Stake in TutorVista," *The Economic Times*, January 19, 2011, http://articles.economictimes.indiatimes.com/2011–01–19/news/28429453_1_tutorvista-pearson-majority-stake.

34. "Pearson Buys Out Remaining 20% of TutorVista," *TechCircle.in*, February 25, 2013, http://techcircle.vccircle.com/2013/02/25/pearson-buys-out-remaining-20-of-tutorvista/.

35. Nanda, "Pearson Acquires Whole of TutorVista."

36. The Pollaros' story is taken from an interview with Sam Pollaro, April 10, 2013.

37. Sam Pollaro, interview with the author, April 10, 2013.

38. "Petal Pusher," *Daily Candy*, July 29, 2009, www.dailycandy.com/washington-dc/article/71187/Petals-for-the-People-Launches.

39. The H.Bloom story, except where noted otherwise, is taken from an interview with Bryan Burkhart, May 6, 2013.

40. Bryan Burkhart, "Introducing Building the Team: Flower Power," *New York Times*, January 16, 2013, http://boss.blogs.nytimes.com/2013/01/16/ introducing-building-the-team-flower-power/.

41. Bryan Burkhart, interview with Nell Derick-Debevoise, May 6, 2013.

42. Burkhart, "Introducing Building the Team: Flower Power."

43. Bryan Burkhart, interview with Nell Derick-Debevoise, May 6, 2013.

44. Ibid.

45. Jessica Bruder, "Starting the 'Netflix of Flowers,'" *New York Times*, September 22, 2011, http://boss.blogs.nytimes.com/2011/09/22/trying-to-start-the-netflix-of-flowers/.

46. Bruder, "Starting the 'Netflix of Flowers.'"

47. Abha Bhattarai, " Subscription Flower Service H.Bloom Says Washington Revenue Has Tripled in the Past Year," *Washington Post*, September 5, 2012, www.washingtonpost.com/business/capitalbusiness/subscription-flower-service-hbloom-says-washington-revenue-has-tripled-in-the-past-year/2012/09/07/fb410966-eba2–11e1-b811–09036bcb182b_story .html.

48. Bryan Burkhart, interview with Nell Derick-Debevoise, May 6, 2013.

49. Evelyn Rusli, "Flower Delivery Service H.Bloom Picks Up 2.2M in Series A Funding," *TechCrunch* (blog), November 4, 2010, http://techcrunch .com/2010/11/04/floral-delivery-service-h-bloom-picks-up-2–2-million-in-series-a-funding/.

50. Bryan Burkhart, "Introducing Building the Team: Flower Power."

51. Sarah Frier, "H.Bloom Cuts Down on Dead Flowers with Software Picking Lilies," *Bloomberg News*, December 2, 2012, www.bloomberg .com/news/2012–12–21/h-bloom-cuts-down-on-dead-flowers-with-software-picking-lilies.html.

52. Ibid.

53. Bruder, "Starting the 'Netflix of Flowers.'"

54. Ibid.

55. Alyson Shontell, "How A Flower Start-up Is Turning a 25-Year-Old into a Revenue-Generating Machine," *Business Insider*, October 5, 2012, www .businessinsider.com/how-hbloom-is-turning-20-somethings-into-revenue-generating-machines-2012–10.

56. Jessica Bruder, "Why H.Bloom Hires Only from Outside Its Industry," *New York Times*, October 16, 2012, http://boss.blogs.nytimes.com/2012/ 10/16/why-h-bloom-only-hires-from-outside-its-industry/?src=rechp.

57. Bruder, "Starting the 'Netflix of Flowers.'"

58. Bhattarai, " Subscription Flower Service H.Bloom."

59. Shontell, "How A Flower Start-up."

60. Adrianne Pasquarelli, "A New York Merchant Blooms in Dallas," *Crain's New York Business*, October 5, 2012, www.crainsnewyork.com/article/20121005/RETAIL_APPAREL/121009942#ixzz2JO46THak.

61. Frederic Lardinois, "Flower Subscription Service H.Bloom Raises $10 Million," *TechCrunch* (blog), April 11, 2012, http://techcrunch.com/2012/04/11/flower-subscription-service-h-bloom-raises-10-million/.

62. Alyson Shontell, "H.Bloom's Co-founder Is Allergic to Flowers and Its Top Paying Customers Spend $500,000 Per Year," *Business Insider*, April 13, 2012, http://articles.businessinsider.com/2012–04–13/tech/31335602_1_flowers-subscription-model-markets#ixzz2JNy2iSjA.

63. Benjamin F. Kuo, "Interview with Bryan Burkhart, H.Bloom," Socaltech .com, July 17, 2013, www.socaltech.com/interview_with_bryan_burkhart_h_bloom/s-0050353.html.

64. Ibid.

65. Claire Cain Miller, "Building Start-ups via Stars' Ties to Fans," *New York Times*, November 25, 2012, www.nytimes.com/2012/11/26/technology/building-start-ups-using-stars-ties-to-fans.html?_r=0.

66. "Manpacks," BuzzSpark.org, accessed February 10, 2014, http://buzzsparks.org/manpacks.

67. Miller, "Building Start-ups."

68. Drew Olanoff, "GuyHaus Makes Shopping Simple and 'Magical' for Guys," *The Next Web*, September 23, 2011, http://thenextweb.com/apps/2011/09/23/guyhaus-makes-shopping-simple-and-magical-for-guys/.

69. "Lollihop Snack Boxes Are the Gift That Keeps On Giving," *Diets in Review*, November 8, 2011, www.dietsinreview.com/diet_column/11/lollihop-snack-boxes-are-the-perfect-gift-that-keeps-giving/.

70. Erin Griffith, "Jesse Middleton and the Importance of 100% Focus on Your Best Idea," *Pando Daily*, April 27, 2012, http://pandodaily.com/2012/04/27/jesse-middleton-and-the-importance-of-100-focus-on-your-best-idea/.

71. Lollihop landing page, accessed February 10, 2014, www.lollihop.com.

72. Kola, "Indo US Ventures."

73. Anderson, "K. Ganesh at TutorVista."

74. Ibid.

75. Frier, "H.Bloom Cuts Down."

76. Edmund Lee, "The Year of the Paywall," *BloombergBusinessweek*, November 18, 2013, www.businessweek.com/articles/2013–11–14/2014-outlook-online-publishers-paywall-strategy.

77. Avi Dan, "When It Comes to Billionaires Buying Newspapers, Marketers Should Pay Attention to Warren Buffett, Not Jeff Bezos," *Forbes*, August 11, 2013, www.forbes.com/sites/avidan/2013/08/11/when-it-comes-to-billionaires-buying-newspapers-marketers-should-pay-attention-to-warren-buffett-not-jeff-bezos/.

78. Ibid.

Chapter 6   Sell Less, Earn More: Scarcity and Flash Sales Models

1. Vivienne Walt, "Meet Amancio Ortega: The Third Richest Man in the World," *Fortune*, January 8, 2013, http://management.fortune.cnn.com/2013/01/08/zara-amancio-ortega/.

2. "Vente-Privee: Management," vente-privee, accessed February 10, 2014, http://pressroom.vente-privee.com/Management/Jacques-Antoine_Granjon.aspx.

3. Ben Rooney, "Vente Privee: The Art of Trading Discounted High-End Goods," *Wall Street Journal Tech Europe*, September 16, 2011, http://blogs.wsj.com/tech-europe/2011/09/16/vente-privee-the-art-of-trading-discounted-high-end-goods/.

4. Ibid.

5. Jennifer L. Schenker, "Vente-privee.com Refashions Closeouts," *BloombergBusinessWeek*, January 11, 2008, www.businessweek.com/stories/2008-01-11/vente-privee-dot-com-refashions-closeoutsbusinessweek-business-news-stock-market-and-financial-advice.

6. Rooney, "Vente Privee."

7. Schenker, "Vente-privee.com Refashions Closeouts."

8. Rooney, "Vente Privee."

9. Pascal-Emmanuel Gobry, "Vente Privée Founder Explains How He Will Squash His American Copycats (EXCLUSIVE INTERVIEW)," *Business Insider*, May 12, 2011, http://articles.businessinsider.com/2011-05-12/tech/30007776_1_e-commerce-flash-sales-long-term.

10. Douglas MacMillan, "French E-tailer Vente-privee Designs an Expansion," *Bloomberg Businessweek*, May 24, 2010, www.businessweek.com/technology/content/may2010/tc20100524_876704.htm.

11. Schenker, "Vente-privee.com Refashions Closeouts."

12. Lauren Indvik, "Flash Sales Powerhouse Vente-privee Launches in the US," *Mashable*, November 9, 2011, http://mashable.com/2011/11/09/vente-privee-us-launch/.

13. MacMillan, "French E-tailer Vente-privee."
14. Schenker, "Vente-privee.com Refashions Closeouts."
15. Riley McDermid, "Spanish Shopping Club Privalia Aims for Latin America with $95M Score," *New York Times*, October 4, 2010, www.nytimes .com/external/venturebeat/2010/10/04/04venturebeat-spanish-shopping-club-privalia-aims-for-lati-15434.html.
16. MacMillan, "French E-tailer Vente-privee."
17. Gobry, "Vente Privée Founder Explains."
18. Ibid.
19. "Why Flash Sale Site Vente-Privée Is Not a Flash in the Pan," *Fashionista*, August 21, 2012, http://fashionista.com/2012/08/why-flash-sale-site-vente-privee-is-not-a-flash-in-the-pan/.
20. "Vente Privée: Management."
21. "Vente Privée," Summit Partners Case Studies, accessed December 10, 2014, www.summitpartners.com/investments/vente-privee-case-study .aspx.
22. Jason Del Rey, "Vente-Privee's Granjon, Flash Sales Pioneer, on Competing in the U.S.," July 1, 2013, *All Things D*, http://allthingsd .com/20130701/vente-privees-granjon-flash-sales-pioneer-on-competing-in-the-u-s/.
23. Ibid.
24. Andrew Rice, "What's a Dress Worth?" *New York Magazine*, February 14, 2010, http://nymag.com/fashion/10/spring/63807/.
25. Colleen Debaise, "Launching Gilt Groupe, A Fashionable Enterprise," *Wall Street Journal*, October 19, 2010, http://online.wsj.com/article/ SB10001424052748703792704575366842447271892.html.
26. Molly Cain, "Insider Secrets of Gilt Groupe's Alexandra Wison," *Forbes*, August 29, 2012, www.forbes.com/sites/glassheel/2012/08/29/insider-secrets-of-gilt-groupes-alexandra-wilson/3/.
27. Matthew Carroll, "The Rise of Gilt Groupe: Gilt's Strategy to Combat Full Frontal Assault by Competitors [Part 3]," *Forbes*, January 5, 2012, www.forbes.com/sites/matthewcarroll/2012/01/05/the-rise-of-gilt-groupe-part-3/.
28. Ibid.
29. Jessica Wohl, "Amazon's Site Best Satisfies Shoppers," *Denver Post*, December 12, 2012.
30. Spencer E. Ante and Dana Mattioli, "Gilt's Flash Hunt: New Chief for IPO," *Wall Street Journal*, November 8, 2012, http://online.wsj.com/ article/SB10001424127887323894704578107303377319238.html.

31. Teresa Novellino, "As new Gilt CEO, Pressure's on Peluso," *Upstart Business Journal*, December 7, 2012, http://upstart.bizjournals.com/ entrepreneurs/hot-shots/2012/12/07/pressure-is-on-for-new-gilt-groupe-ceo.html?page=all.

32. Ibid.

33. Sarah Frier, "Gilt Groupe Stakes IPO Future on Bringing Back Flash," *BloombergBusinessweek*, August 1, 2013, www.businessweek.com/news/ 2013–07–31/gilt-groupe-stakes-ipo-future-on-bringing-back-the-flash-tech.

34. Ibid.

35. Tom Taulli, "Could Gilt Groupe Pull Off an IPO?" *InvestorPlace*, August 1, 2013, http://investorplace.com/ipo-playbook/could-gilt-groupe-pull-off-an-ipo/.

36. Ari Levy and Leslie Picker, *Bloomberg*, "Gilt Groupe Said to Choose Goldman to Manage IPO," February 12, 2014, www.bloomberg.com/ news/2014–02–10/gilt-groupe-said-to-choose-goldman-to-manage-web-retailer-s-ipo.html.

37. Robin Wauters, "Totsy Lands $5 Million in Funding for Flash Sales Site for Children Products," *TechCrunch* (blog), http://techcrunch.com/2010/ 11/30/totsy-lands-5-million-in-funding-for-flash-sales-site-for-children-products/.

38. Rip Empson, "Flash Deals Site Totsy Lands $18.5M to Take On Zulily in the Battle for Shopping Moms," *TechCrunch* (blog), July 17, 2012, http:// techcrunch.com/2012/07/17/totsy-series-b/.

39. Adrianne Pasquarelli, "Flash-Sale Site Totsy Is Toppling," *Crain's New York Business*, May 17, 2013, www.crainsnewyork.com/article/20130517/ RETAIL_APPAREL/130519886.

40. Ibid.

41. John Cook, "Daily Deal Site Zulily Raises $43 million at Huge Valuation of More Than $700 million," *GeekWire*, August 10, 2011, www.geekwire .com/2011/daily-deal-site-zulily-raises-43-million-huge-valuation-700-million/.

42. Empson, "Flash Deals Site Totsy."

43. Erin Griffith, "Totsy Burns through $34 million, Lays Off Its 83 Employees, Selling Assets," *PandoDaily*, May 22, 2013, http://pan dodaily.com/2013/05/22/totsy-burns-through-34-million-lays-off-its-83-employees-selling-assets/.

44. Leena Rao, "Flash Sales Site For Moms, Zulily Raises $85M from Andreessen Horowitz; Valued at $1B," *TechCrunch* (blog), November 15, 2012, http://techcrunch.com/2012/11/15/flash-sales-site-for-moms-zulily-raises-85m-from-andreessen-horowitz-valued-at-1b/.

45. Cook, "Daily Deal Site Zulily."

46. Scott Martin, "Zulily IPO Zooms 87.5% on First Day of Trading," *USA Today*, November 15, 2013, www.usatoday.com/story/tech/2013/11/15/zulily-ipo-rockets-84-in-trading/3582295/.

47. Daniel Wolfman and Chris Beier, "How a Disaster on Everest Inspired an Entrepreneur," video interview with Philip James, *Inc.com*, June 14, 2012, www.inc.com/chris-beier-and-daniel-wolfman/entrepreneur-lessons-how-a-disaster-on-everest-inspired-lot18-founder-philip-james.html.

48. Alyson Shontell, "Lot18 Closes a Whopping $30 Million Series C Round from Accel Partners," *Business Insider*, November 4, 2011, www.businessinsider.com/lot18–30-million-series-c-accel-partners-2011–11#ixzz2bnLG2XMT.

49. Adrienne Jeffries, "Layoffs at Lot18: 15 Percent of Employees Were Just Let Go from Fast-Growing Luxury Discount Site," *Betabeat*, January 19, 2012, www.betabeat.com/2012/01/19/layoffs-at-lot18-philip-james/.

50. Alyson Shontell, "Turnover at Wine Startup Lot18: 4 Senior Executives Gone in The Last Month," *Business Insider*, May 17, 2012, www.businessinsider.com/lot18-lost-4-senior-executives-in-the-last-month-2012–5.

51. Ibid.

52. Alyson Shontell, "Lot18 Continues To Crumble, Lays Off 11 More People," *Business Insider*, May 13, 2013, www.businessinsider.com/exclusive-lot18-lays-off-11-employees-2013–5.

53. Shontell, "Turnover."

54. Colleen Taylor, "Wine Site Lot18 Downsizes Again: UK Operations to Shut Down This Week," *TechCrunch* (blog), July 19, 2012, http://techcrunch.com/2012/07/19/lot18-closes-uk-operations/.

55. Scott Kirsner, "What's Next for Rue La La, Fast-Growing 'Flash Sale' Specialist Based in Boston?" *Boston Globe*, December 22, 2011, www.boston.com/business/technology/innoeco/2011/12/whats_next_for_rue_la_la_fast-.html.

56. Ina Steiner, "Rue La La Lays off Staff and Absorbs SmartBargains Discount Site," *eCommerceBytes*, January 13, 2012, www.ecommercebytes.com/cab/abn/y12/m01/i13/s02.

57. Kirsner, "What's Next for Rue La La."

58. Del Rey, "Vente-Privee's Granjon."

59. Rooney, "Vente Privee."

60. Misty McHenry, owner of Tutu Mania, comment on Empson, "Flash Deals Site Totsy," *TechCrunch* (blog), June 7, 2013, http://techcrunch.com/2012/07/17/totsy-series-b/?fb_comment_id=fbc_10151016464595816_26291425_10151622279875816#f131195cd600c.

61. Manish Sabharwal, CEO TeamLease, "TeamLease" video, London Business School, 2010.

62. Gobry, "Vente Privée Founder Explains."

63. Susan Berfield and Manuel Baigorri, "Knitting a Supply Chain," *BloombergBusinessweek*, November 18, 2013, 90–92.

64. Del Rey, "Vente-Privee's Granjon."

Chapter 7   Build It for One, Then Sell It to All: Service-to-Product Models

1. Bill Gates, *The Road Ahead* (New York: Viking Penguin, 1995), 16–17.

2. Brent Schlender, "Bill Gates & Paul Allen Talk: Check out the Ultimate Buddy Act in Business History," *Fortune*, October 2, 1995, http://money.cnn.com/magazines/fortune/fortune_archive/1995/10/02/206528/index.htm.

3. Ibid.

4. Ibid.

5. Gates, *The Road Ahead*, page 48.

6. Schlender, "Bill Gates and Paul Allen Talk."

7. Gates, *The Road Ahead*, 49.

8. The GoViral story, except where otherwise noted, is drawn from interviews with Claus Moseholm, March 18, 2013, and Jimmy Maymann, March 27, 2013.

9. Claus Moseholm, interview with the author, March 18, 2013.

10. Ibid.

11. Ibid.

12. Ibid.

13. Jimmy Maymann, interview with the author, March 27, 2013.

14. Claus Moseholm, interview with the author, March 18, 2013.

15. Ibid.

16. Jimmy Maymann, interview with the author, March 27, 2013.

17. Ibid.

18. Claus Moseholm, interview with the author, March 18, 2013.

19. Ibid.

20. Butcher, "AOL Europe Acquires Branded Video Distribution Network."

21. The Rock Solid story is drawn from interviews with Ángel Pérez, September 16, 2012 and September 7, 2013.

22. Ángel Pérez, interview with the author, September 16, 2012.

23. Ibid.

24. The QuEST Global Services case history is drawn from Elizabeth Philp and John Mullins, "QuEST Global Services (A)" and "QuEST Global Services (B)," 2012, London Business School.

25. Philp and Mullins, "QuEST Global Services (A)," 9.

26. Ibid., 7.

27. Philp and Mullins, "QuEST Global Services (B)," 3.

28. For a structured way of assessing the attractiveness of new market opportunities such as these, see John Mullins, *The New Business Road Test: What Entrepreneurs and Executives Should Do* before *Launching a Lean Start-up*, 4th ed. (London: Pearson/FT Publishing, 2013).

Chapter 8   Make It Happen: Put a Customer-Funded Model to Work in *Your* Business

1. Suster, "Why You Need to Ring the Freaking Cash Register."

2. Joy, "Large Problem," 214.

3. Ibid.

4. See www.pivotdesk.com.

5. TechStars' and the Foundry Group's Brad Feld, interview with the author, August 21, 2013.

6. Budgetplaces' John Erceg, interview with the author, September 5, 2013.

7. Finnish entrepreneur Justinas Katkus, interview with the author, September 6, 2012.

8. John Erceg, interview with the author, September 5, 2013.

9. Professor John Bates, London Business School, interview with the author, April 23, 2013.

10. Brad Feld, interview with the author, August 21, 2013.

11. Sussex Place Ventures' Richard Gourlay, interview with the author, May 9, 2013.

12. John Erceg, interview with the author, September 5, 2013.

13. Brad Feld, interview with the author, August 21, 2013.

14. Ibid.

15. Randy Komisar, Kleiner Perkins Caufield & Byers, interview with the author, December 3, 2012.

16. Professor John Bates, interview with the author, April 23, 2013.

17. Brad Feld, interview with the author, August 21, 2013.

18. Ibid.

19. A Suit That Fits founder Warren Bennett, interview with the author, July 12, 2013.

20. Jonathan Moules, "Made.com Gleefully Shuns High Street," *Financial Times*, January 31, 2013.

21. Raymond Johnson, University of Colorado, interview with the author, April 8, 2013.

22. Warren Bennett, interview with the author, July 12, 2013.

23. Paul Jerde, University of Colorado, interview with the author, April 3, 2013.

24. Ibid.

25. Ibid.

26. Author, educator, and investor Steve Blank, interview with the author, December 3, 2012.

27. Kennet Partners' Hillel Zidel, interview with the author, April 10, 2012.

28. Raymond Johnson, interview with the author, April 8, 2013.

29. Ibid.

30. Brad Feld, interview with the author, August 21, 2013.

31. Author, educator, and investor Steve Blank, interview with the author, December 3, 2012.

32. Anderson, "K. Ganesh at TutorVista."

33. Perry Blacher, Zulily Europe, interview with the author, December 17, 2013.

34. Jules Maltz and Daniel Barney, "Should Your Startup Go Freemium?" *TechCrunch* (blog), November 4, 2012, http://techcrunch.com/2012/11/04/should-your-startup-go-freemium/.

35. Patrick Clark and John Tozzi, "Unpacking the Box Bubble," *BloombergBusinessweek*, May 20, 2013, 53.

36. Greg Bettinelli, "My Reaction to Zulily's IPO Filing and Flash Sales Explained," *#LongLA* (blog), October 9, 2013, http://gregbettinelli.com/2013/10/09/reaction-to-zulilys-ipo-filing-and-flash-sales-explained/.

37. Perry Blacher, interview with the author, December 17, 2013.

38. Hillel Zidel, interview with the author, April 10, 2012.

39. Lydia Dishman, "The Strategic Retail Genius behind Zara," *Fortune*, March 23, 2012, www.forbes.com/sites/lydiadishman/2012/03/23/the-strategic-retail-genius-behind-zara/.

40. Rice, "What's a Dress Worth?"

41. Bettinelli, "My Reaction to Zulily's IPO Filing."

42. Perry Blacher, interview with the author, December 17, 2013.

43. Ibid.

44. Joe Clark, CEO of Prana Business, interview with the author, April 8, 2013.

45. For guidance on developing new products that your customers will actually want, see Steve Blank, *The Four Steps to the Epiphany* (Café Press, 2013).

46. Joe Clark, interview with the author, April 8, 2013.

47. Randy Komisar, interview with the author, December 3, 2012.

48. Brad Feld, interview with the author, August 21, 2013.

49. Randy Komisar, interview with the author, December 3, 2012.

50. Author, educator, and investor Steve Blank, interview with the author, December 3, 2012.

51. Ibid.

52. Richard Gourlay, interview with the author, May 9, 2013.

53. Joe Clark, interview with the author, April 8, 2013.

54. Brad Feld, interview with the author, August 21, 2013.

55. Eric Mueller, Chairman, Funovation, interview with the author, April 4, 2013.

56. Walter Chen, "Avoid the Series A Crunch by Customerstrapping Your Company," *Pando Daily*, July 26, 2013, http://pandodaily.com/2013/07/26/avoid-the-series-a-crunch-by-customerstrapping-your-company/.

57. Quoted in Gianforte and Gibson, *Bootstrapping Your Business*, i.

58. Author, educator, and investor Steve Blank, interview with the author, December 3, 2012.

About the Research

The research journey of which this book is a part began during my sabbatical in 2000 at London Business School. There, freed to think and study for several months, I sought to identify what I hoped would be a better and more disciplined way to assess entrepreneurial opportunities, in an effort to nudge the needle downward on the entrepreneurial failure rate. Fortunately, that research bore fruit in my "seven domains" framework, developed in *The New Business Road Test*, first published in 2003, with new updated editions published in 2006, 2010, and 2013.

In time, my work applying the seven domains framework with hundreds of entrepreneurs led me to dig deeper into business models, especially those that spurred real breakthroughs in their industries—like Southwest and Ryanair in airlines and Zara in apparel retailing. Once again, a book, *Getting to Plan B*, co-authored with Randy Komisar, was the happy result.

In researching the companies whose stories are told in *Getting to Plan B*, and in my ongoing work with growth-minded entrepreneurs and other business leaders who instinctively understand that cash flow—not profit—lies at the heart of most business breakthroughs, I became further intrigued with companies profiled therein like Dow Jones and Costco, whose working capital models lay at the heart of their continued success. "How might even better working capital models be constructed?" I wondered. "And, if they're constructed well enough, might they enable entrepreneurs to fund their businesses with their customers' cash, at least at the outset, if not forever, rather than having to take time away from their customers to raise the capital required?"

As this latest phase of my research journey got underway in early 2012, my research partner and former student (and an inspiring entrepreneur in her own right), Nell Derick-Debevoise and I began searching for companies who appeared to get their starts with customer funds. We then examined their approaches to learn whether and how they had done so, eventually synthesizing the five types of customer-funded models articulated here. Of the more than 40 candidates we found at the outset, we culled the list to the nearly 20 whose captivating stories are told here.

Concurrently, I began interviewing entrepreneurs and investors—both VCs and business angels—with an eye toward better understanding what matters in the effective implementation of customer-funded models. Planning is important, I learned long ago, but implementation is what really matters in delivering results. "What," I wondered, "were the best settings in which to apply each of the five models? How might they best be implemented? What are the common pitfalls that lurk along the path? And what are the key questions about each of the five models that business angels or other investors should ask?"

The results of my and Nell's research are what you now hold in your hands or see on your screen: the often inspiring stories of some of the world's most inventive and ambitious entrepreneurs and the companies they've built, whether successfully or—in several noteworthy cases—not. The stories, organized around the five different customer-funded models we've identified, are perhaps the most engaging part of the book, as they bring to life lessons not only about customer funding but more generally about life as an entrepreneur. I believe people in all kinds of companies—nascent or long established, large or small—and investors, too, can learn important lessons about how to start, finance, or grow their companies from their entrepreneurial brethren and their stories, as recounted here. Perhaps the most concisely instructive parts of the book, though—for entrepreneurs, other business leaders, and investors alike—are the checklists at the end of the five customer-funded model Chapters (3 to

7), and in the book's second (2) and final Chapter (8), which summarize and impart the key lessons our research journey has uncovered.

As this book is the product of what is called in the academic world "inductive research," based on a very modest sample of entrepreneurs and their companies, I won't argue that the lessons presented here are the only ones to be gleaned, nor that 100 percent of them will stand the test of time forever in our fast-changing world. Any errors in the insights I've drawn are mine and mine alone. And I won't even argue that those insights are necessarily "correct," as the entrepreneurial world is full of courageous and thoughtful people who break the rules. You, the reader, may find that some of the rules herein are made to be broken, too.

But it's my hope that the lessons I've learned and recounted in this book will encourage tomorrow's entrepreneurs, investors, and executives to focus their efforts—first and foremost—on solving their customers' problems and unmet needs, rather than on raising money from investors, at least at the outset. As you'll have seen in many of the compelling stories in this book, get it right with your customers, and the investors—if you need them at all!—will in all likelihood follow.

About the Author

W hen he's not out in the world learning from or working with entrepreneurs and those who invest in them, John Mullins divides his time between London, the most captivating and livable big city in the world, and the much smaller and more intimate town of Golden, Colorado, nestled at the edge of the foothills of the Rocky Mountains. A former entrepreneur and now an award-winning professor at London Business School, John is the author of two best-selling books, as well as dozens of case studies of real-world entrepreneurial companies, plus more than 40 other publications.

Now in its fourth edition, John's first book, *The New Business Road Test: What Entrepreneurs and Executives Should Do* Before *Launching a Lean Start-up,* has become the definitive work on assessing entrepreneurial opportunities. His second book, with noted venture capital investor Randy Komisar, the critically acclaimed *Getting to Plan B: Breaking Through to a Better Business Model,* provides a field-tested process and framework for helping entrepreneurs get from their initial "Plan A," which often doesn't work, to a more economically viable "Plan B."

John is a sought-after speaker to audiences around the world on entrepreneurship, on growing one's business, and on starting and financing high-potential ventures. He can be reached at jmullins@london.edu.

Index

NOTE: Page references in *italics* refer to figures.